Ylva Grufstedt
Shaping the Past

Video Games
and the Humanities

Edited by
Nathalie Aghoro, Iro Filippaki, Chris Kempshall,
Esther MacCallum-Stewart, Jeremiah McCall
and Sascha Pöhlmann

Advisory Board
Alenda Y. Chang, UC Santa Barbara
Katherine J Lewis, University of Huddersfield
Dietmar Meinel, University of Duisburg-Essen
Ana Milošević, KU Leuven
Soraya Murray, UC Santa Cruz
Holly Nielsen, University of London
Michael Nitsche, Georgia Tech
Martin Picard, Leipzig University
Melanie Swalwell, Swinburne University
Emma Vossen, University of Waterloo
Mark J.P. Wolf, Concordia University
Esther Wright, Cardiff University

Volume 7

Ylva Grufstedt
Shaping the Past

Counterfactual History and Game Design Practice
in Digital Strategy Games

DE GRUYTER
OLDENBOURG

ISBN 978-3-11-152074-2
e-ISBN (PDF) 978-3-11-069248-8
e-ISBN (EPUB) 978-3-11-069262-4
ISSN 2700-0400

Library of Congress Control Number: 2022933752

Bibliographic information published by the Deutsche Nationalbibliothek
The Deutsche Nationalbibliothek lists this publication in the Deutsche Nationalbibliografie;
detailed bibliographic data are available on the internet at http://dnb.dnb.de.

© 2024 Walter de Gruyter GmbH, Berlin/Boston
This volume is text- and page-identical with the hardback published in 2022.
Cover image: The image portrays a game developer working at their desk against a backdrop
montage based on imagery of Early Modern colonialism and the Second World War,
Illustration by Victor Becker, © Ylva Grufstedt.

www.degruyter.com

Acknowledgements

This book exists thanks to the kind support of the Department of Philosophy, History and Art, and the Digital Humanities initiative at the University of Helsinki, as well as the Oskar Öflund Foundation, who funded this research during my doctoral studies. I also owe thanks to the Ella and Georg Ehrnrooth Foundation whose financial support has contributed to the writing of this book.

My thanks also go out to everyone with whom I have interacted during this process, especially my informants for offering your time and interest in my work, and my editor Dr Jeremiah McCall for your patience and kindness. Thank you also to colleagues and friends at Aalto University and Malmö University for your unwavering willingness to listen and help with this endeavour.

Preface

After acquiring my master's degree in June of 2013, I was still intellectually dissatisfied. I had written a comparative thesis on uses of history in two different kinds of digital games. I concluded that that the methodology and terminology at hand was suitable – but only up to a point. In presenting my findings on the difference between determinism and constructivism in *Call of Duty: World at War* and *Europa Universalis III* respectively, I noted that while digital games can do well in terms of historiographical representation, there was something else at play here too. Something complex about the way factual and counterfactual history coexisted in this context. I just was not sure how to scientifically explain it, or even how to express it. I had this lingering feeling of only having half the answer, and decided that I wanted to pursue it further.

I worked for a couple of years outside of academia, waiting to start in a doctoral program. During this time, I found the perfect opportunity to make use of my proprietary history-but-also-games degree. I took a job in game development. I was struck almost immediately by the practical nature of the trials facing the project. Sustaining a flow of imagination, ambition and innovation was never, ever, the problem. Implementation, however, was. In certain instances, communicating an idea between different teams was a much bigger challenge than changing a string of code. In some cases, it would be the exact opposite due to technical, budgetary or even ideological constraint. Tensions between narrative and mechanics were constantly negotiated within a system composed of hundreds of employees towards a unified vision, although, ultimately, the goal was to create a coherent and viable gameplay experience for the user. Does it matter, then, if we break away from reality just a little?

As a researcher I was intrigued by the complexity of it. Above all, the experience set me on a path to seeing the importance of understanding historical games *as games*, and how not all games are created equal, or created in an equal manner. It made me wonder if developers of historical games could help explain the contradictory nature of history in games, and scratch that nagging feeling of a mystery unsolved.

Furthermore, I have always found that the act of asking what-if questions about the past says more about what and how we know things about things that did happen in history and about ourselves as historically aware beings than it does about causality and contingency in history. In experimenting with, for example, whether Adolf Hitler was – or was not – the singular, scale-tipping element to cause the Second World War and the Holocaust, what we are after, surely, is to deepen and nuance our understanding of the Second

World War and its political and cultural context. Maybe it is even an attempt to remain in control of our present, and sometimes games are reflective of that. This book is the result of a research effort to combine these two premises: the whats, whys and hows of counterfactuals and game-making, and the representations and uses of the past that follow.

Contents

Introduction —— 1

Chapter One: Opening up the Design – *Europa Universalis IV* **and** *Hearts of Iron IV* **Overviews** —— 27

Chapter Two: Shaping the Past: The Surround and Practice of Making Games about the Past —— 66

Chapter Three: Counterfactuals: Uses, Shapes and Problems in *Europa Universalis IV* **and** *Hearts of Iron IV* —— 121

Chapter Four: Approximately History and Ambivalent Desires —— 159

Conclusions —— 193

Appendix 1: DLC and Content Packs Installed and Used for the Study —— 207

Appendix 2: Interviews with Developers and Beta Testers —— 208

Appendix 3: Game Analysis and Technical Reading —— 211

References —— 215

Index —— 226

Introduction

As the title suggests, this book is about counterfactual history, digital strategy games and game design. In the context of historical game studies, these are important concepts used to discuss and explain the nature of history in games. While engaging with all three, the book also focuses on practices of game design and game development. It considers how developers navigate the opportunities and constraints of historical culture, and the pragmatics of design practice. It also explores the understandings and meanings of counterfactual history as uses of history.

As such, this book is an effort to examine the intersection and interplay of game design practice and the representation of the past for two specific purposes. Firstly, game design practices and principles impose themselves on the representation of the past. The details of how this happens is something that we so far know little about, though it deserves to be an integral part of historical game studies, and this book is a partial but optimistic contribution towards that. Secondly, this book proposes a theoretical framework for counterfactual history as a distinct use of history defined above all by its settings, framings and applications.

This book is not about the players or consumers of digital strategy games, other than where developer practices intersect with the perception of player expectations and behaviours. The study itself contains no new player data. Nor is this book about the pedagogical or didactic nature of games, or the logistics of how games teach or transfer knowledge about the past. This book does not cover games of other genres than digital strategy games, although I suspect that the findings are applicable in other contexts, and I would encourage anyone who wishes to explore this further. And when it comes to counterfactuals, this book avoids assessing the actual probability of the designed counterfactual scenarios in the games. It therefore only in passing overlaps with approaches such as game theory and counterfactual conditionals.

The Past in Uses of History and Game Design Practice

In this book, I investigate two specific digital strategy games and their designers. The games in question are *Europa Universalis IV* (2013) and *Hearts of Iron IV* (2016), both developed by Paradox Development Studio. In examining the two games and their makers, I focus on the inherent role of counterfactual history.

https://doi.org/10.1515/9783110692488-003

In general terms, this book is about the intersection of game design practices and representations of the past, and the representation of counterfactual history, in digital strategy games. That is, how the cultural, material and technological underpinnings of making games impose themselves on the representation of the past, and vice versa. I employ a specific perspective of counterfactual history as a theoretical sounding board for exploring how developers rationalise making games about the past and how they do it. The notion of counterfactual history, the possible worlds of paths-not-taken, in this book, drives the analysis and description of digital strategy games as uses of history. That includes investigating why certain parts of our mutual past exist in games, and some do not; or, why some aspects of the past are hardcoded into a game and perpetuated as unavoidable, whereas other scenarios appear to be bendable and playable. Another important aspect is to discuss which counterfactual scenarios are designed and retold more often than others. Simultaneously, this multidisciplinary approach allows me to highlight external as well as internal studio practices and contexts to demystify game design and game making as carriers of historical understandings.

Before I go on and further specify the background and contents of the book, I will briefly clarify some fundamental concepts on which my arguments rely: uses of history and historical culture. The term uses of history (as described by Peter Aronsson and translated from its arguably less bulky Swedish counterpart *historiebruk*) refers to the practice of activating and shaping historical culture for the purpose of communication, signalling, and meaningful application in a given process.[1] Looking for uses of history in general, one will notice that elements of the past are employed in a variety of contexts and for different purposes. In other words, understandings of the past are invoked differently in different settings. Think, for example, of the obvious variations between the function and employment of history in institutions (schools, museums, public monuments), in commodities (memorabilia, heritage tourism, popular culture) or even politics (rhetoric, moral and ideological positioning).[2] Of course, broad categories such as these tend to mix and overlap. Institutions can be political, and the commodification of history interplays with educational purposes at, for example, heritage sites. As discussed by Marianne Sjöland, popular, non-academic uses of history tend to be especially diverse. They might employ represen-

---

[1] Peter Aronsson, *Historiebruk – Att använda det förflutna* (Lund: Studentlitteratur, 2004), 17–19; Peter Aronsson, "Historiekultur, politik och historievetenskap i Norden," *Historisk tidskrift* 122 (2002): 189.
[2] Klas-Göran Karlsson and Ulf Zander (eds.), *Historien är nu – En introduktion till historiedidaktiken* (Lund: Studentlitteratur, 2009), 37–40.

tations of the past primarily for entertainment purposes but in doing so they also make (explicit or implicit) educational, moral and ideological arguments.[3] Following this, as noted by Eugen Pfister, the process of using history is not only instrumental to reproducing understandings about the past, but to shaping and perpetuating them, too.[4]

Historical culture (Sw. historiekultur), here, then, denotes the (amorphous) systems of historical references with contextually attributed meanings.[5] As such, uses of history (the act of employing the past) and historical culture (understandings about the past) interplay. Historical cultures are multifaceted, and spatially and temporally situated. Thus, certain historical cultural elements will likely resonate differently with different individuals as persons of, say, different ages and contexts. An example of historical cultural at work is the aftermath of the removal of Robert E. Lee's statue in Charlottesville, Virginia in 2017. A white supremacist rally followed as a protest to the removal, highlighting the possibility for contention of historical cultural values and artefacts in the public space.[6] Questions of what history, by who and for whom rightfully arise. Popular cultural products such as books and games can, and do, similarly rely on historical culture partly in that they expect consumers to be aware of – more or less – communal historical references and ideals. Historical games (games about the past), then, can be understood as artefacts of historical culture to be used for, among other things, entertainment purposes.

---

3 Marianne Sjöland, *Historia från tidskriftsredaktionen – En komparativ studie av* Populär Historias *och* History Todays *historieskrivning* (PhD diss., Lund University, 2017).
4 Eugen Pfister, "Why History in Digital Games Matters – Historical Authenticity as a Language for Ideological Myths," *History in Games – Contingencies of an Authentic Past*, ed. Martin Lorber and Felix Zimmermann (Bielefeld: transcript, 2020), 48.
5 Aronsson, *Historiebruk*, 17–19; Aronsson, "Historiekultur, politik och historievetenskap i Norden," 189.
6 Ulf Zander, "Lee, Charlottesville och statystriderna i Södern: Försoning, fortsatt förslavande eller främlingsfientlighet?," *Historielärarnas förenings årsskrift* (Lund: 2018), 39–50. For more studies on historical cultural expression in this vein, see Derek Fewster, *Visions of Past Glory – Nationalism and the Construction of Early Finnish History* (Helsinki: SKS, 2008); Marianne Sjöland, *Historia från tidskriftsredaktionen – En komparativ studie av* Populär historias *och* History todays *historieskrivning* (PhD diss., Lund University, 2016); Marie Bennedahl, *Fall in Line – Genus, kropp och minnena av det amerikanska inbördeskriget* (PhD diss., Linnaeus University, 2020). Uses of history are closely related to fields such as public history studies, studies of memory cultures and collective memory studies. See, for example, Jan Assmann, "Collective memory and cultural identity," *New German Critique* 65 (1995); Eviatar Zerubavel, *Time Maps – Collective Memory and the Social Shape of the Past* (Chicago: University of Chicago Press, 2003); Mauritz Halbawchs, *On Collective Memory* (Chicago: University of Chicago Press, 1992).

Historical understandings may be, and often are, challenged. In an academic setting, such contention may be a perfectly expected debate between two historical experts. Between nations, contested ownership of historical narratives may cause long-running conflicts and, ultimately, tragedy. As such, the setting determines the use of history. In certain settings – generally outside of academia – epistemological consensus (or historical accuracy) becomes an ancillary value.[7] For digital strategy games, the primary function of such uses is to represent history in a way that makes sense in its context. For *Europa Universalis IV* and *Hearts of Iron IV* and their developers this means including counterfactual history – the what-ifs of historical thinking – as possible outcomes of gameplay. Granted, these scenarios do not purport to be factual, but they are inherently linked to baseline verisimilitude, which require historical reference to work.

Thus, counterfactual history in digital strategy games, here understood as representations of alternative historical processes, paths-not-taken and outcomes based on historical reference, is a use of history, especially when there is a clear historical cultural connection. This distinction is largely inspired by Catherine Gallagher who notes that there is a distinction in genre between fictional novels that build on hooks in our familiar world and those that do not. She writes:

> Possible-worlds theorists tend to classify all fictions as counterfactuals, enlarging the latter term beyond usefulness for a study of explicitly counterfactual. The more common practice, to which I adhere, is to use 'fiction' as the more inclusive term, and to apply 'counterfactual' to fictions that really are launched and recognized hypothetical conditionals known to be contrary to fact.[8]

For instance, the counterfactual scenario of a vast Roman Empire that survived as a geographically and politically cohesive entity into Early Modern times clearly engages with understandings about the nature of the actual Roman Empire and, among other things, its demise. Similarly, the frequent counterfactual of a post-Second World War world into which Germany emerged victorious has been reiterated so many times that it constitutes a genre in and of itself.[9] As I

---

7 I do not here include blatantly revisionist practices such as denialisms and conscious erasure of historical actors and groups. For fruitful discussion on the functions, structures and processes that encompass denial cultures of the Holocaust and Armenian genocide, see Maria Karlsson, *Cultures of Denial – Comparing Holocaust and Armenian Genocide Denial* (PhD. diss., Lund University, 2015), and Richard Evans, *Telling lies about Hitler – The Holocaust, History and David Irving trial* (London & New York: Verso, 2002).
8 Catherine Gallagher, "What Would Napoleon Do? Historical, Fictional, and Counterfactual Characters," *New Literary History* 42 (2011): 333–334.
9 Richard Evans, *Altered Pasts – Counterfactuals in History* (Brandeis University Press, 2014), 31.

will discuss in later chapters, and like many have done before me, digital strategy games are particularly suitable for representing counterfactual scenarios. The game designer (and subsequently the player) knowingly bend history out of shape for gameplay purposes, and in doing so repeatedly consider and reconsider aspects of historical causality, continuity and contingency.[10]

Game designers, then, work within several contexts and frameworks that facilitate and constrain the depiction of the past and counterfactuals. On the one hand, there is the ecosystem of the game industry and the interplay of common industry goals such as innovation, dissemination and profitability.[11] On the other hand, historical game designers must simultaneously navigate the delimiting nature of historical culture and game design conventions. These synergies of contexts and imperatives ultimately influence the shape and content of the games and references to the past – and counterfactuals – contained therein. Some factors are particularly important as facilitators of historical representation. Regarding *Europa Universalis IV* and *Hearts of Iron IV*, design legacy and genre convention are two such factors that significantly inform design. Heritage design, i.e. the longevity of game series and the use and reuse of game content and mechanics makes design practices monotonous over time. Not for lack of innovation, but because genre convention and player expectations dictate design practice. Similarly, concerns with profitability and monetisation directly correlate with development processes, which, in turn, influence how game developers implement contents and mechanics. A particularly interesting aspect here is the use of beta testers – players and enthusiasts who volunteer their time to design and test the games. In the case of Paradox Development Studio, beta testers are all but integrated in development and, arguably, essential to content design, research and testing.

Other important factors that inform the presentation of history in these games include developer practices for researching historical content and mechanics. In framing games and historical culture, for example, we must seek a deepened understanding of how and where developers acquire the substance and content for games about the past. Developers with and without scholarly training employ a broad set of sources, including other games, to design and build historical events and processes in the games. Counterfactual scenarios and assets, in turn, are constructed by developers using a mix of the same ma-

---

[10] Niall Ferguson cited in Jerome De Groot, *Consuming History: Historians and Heritage in Contemporary Popular Culture* (London & New York: Routledge, 2009), 142–143.
[11] Casey O'Donnell, *Developer's Dilemma – The Secret World of Videogame Creators* (Cambridge: MIT Press, 2014), 4; Annakaisa Kultima, "Game Design Praxiology" (PhD diss., University of Tampere, 2018), 10, 27.

terials and sources. Notably, developer understandings of temporal distance and periodization are particularly important when it comes to including and omitting of content in *Europa Universalis IV* and *Hearts of Iron IV*. In the case of *Europa Universalis IV*, the further back in time something happened, and the longer the in-game period, the less stringent rules of plausibility and verisimilitude appear to be. Conversely, *Hearts of Iron IV* with its strict focus on military and political efforts during the Second World War has a significant focus on counterfactual scenarios. Furthermore, players often expect even tragic outcomes and atrocities of the past (such as war crimes, genocide and disease) to be represented, but these constitute a particular set of challenges for the developers. Notions of gameplay, entertainment and challenge, here, are central, and tend to be preferred over historical verisimilitude, with a few notable exceptions. Again, as this book will show, gameplay values intersect with historical culture in often subtle and nuanced ways.

The hopeful field of historical game studies is the interdisciplinary exploration of the interplay of history and game studies. Questions about the relationship between games and issues like form, historiography, representation, narrative and epistemology are central.[12] Given all of the above, the present book, with all of its ambition and shortcomings, aims to benefit the larger body of the field. Its contributions towards the study of game design practices, and the study of representation of history in digital strategy games specifically, is twofold. Firstly, there are a lack of studies with developer perspectives on digital strategy games, especially concerning uses of history or similar approaches. Such approaches are of course a necessary puzzle piece to historical game studies when reflecting on the development and origins of games and their content. Secondly, developer studies fruitfully support the analysis of the often complex and contradictory relation between historical verisimilitude and counterfactual outcomes in digital strategy games, as they seem to coexist in this context. Developer studies bring some clarity, and provide much-needed nuance, to previous assumptions and blind-spots about developer biases and intent in this area.

The complexity of strategic play, and the intricate work of the developers and players who interact with the past through games, make an interdisciplinary approach to the topic integral. The study of games is always inherently multidisciplinary in nature since games constitute both cultural representations and dynamic systems.[13] Accordingly, this study approaches digital strategy games and

---

[12] Adam Chapman, Anna Foka and Jonathan Westin, "Introduction: What is Historical Game Studies?," *Rethinking History* 21, no. 3 (2017).
[13] Frans Mäyrä, "Getting Into the Game: Doing Multidisciplinary Game Studies," in *The Video Game Theory Reader 2*, ed. Bernard Perron and Mark J.P. Wolf (New York: Routledge, 2009), 319.

counterfactual history with the interdisciplinary toolbox of historical game studies and looks to both historical scholarship and game studies for complementary insights on how to decipher the ludic impact of digital strategy games on representations of the past, and counterfactuals as uses of history.

Counterfactual History

> Historical counterfactuals are not aids to understanding the boundaries that separate the domains of the factual and the fictional; what they assist is our understanding of the boundaries between the factual and the counterfactual.
> Christopher Prendergast, *Counterfactuals – Paths of the Might Have Been* (London: Bloomsbury, 2019), 9.

Players of both *Europa Universalis IV* and *Hearts of Iron IV* must manage and ensure the survival of a playable country or playable nation in their respective eras. *Europa Universalis IV* takes place in Early Modern times, spanning from 1444–1821. *Hearts of Iron IV* covers the Second World War period of 1936–1948. Both games have a global geographic perspective. At the centre of both games are playable models of societal structural elements such as political power, diplomatic relations, trade, culture, ideology and resource management. The dynamic between these structures dictates the course of the game and, by extension, representations of history as well as counterfactuals. They make up the fundamental rulesets of the games. As soon as the game begins, chance and player interaction force the game into dynamic new paths following the logic of the games' systems and design, allowing counterfactual scenarios to play out. For example, the player might choose to play as Germany in *Hearts of Iron IV* and try to win the Second World War, or they might try to keep Germany democratic in the 1930s and prevent the war from happening. A player in *Europa Universalis IV* can choose to explore the Early Modern era from the perspective of China or the Aztecs and end up colonising Europe. The player is not able to change the fundamental rules of the game as they play – only to act within them.[14]

---

[14] This is not true for players who enjoy modding the game. *Modding* (jargon for "modifying") means, for example, accessing the games' code and changing the rules of the game to better fit their playstyle, perception of the past, or other contents of the game. Modding as a player activity is the focus of several important academic works, including Thomas Apperley, "Modding the Historians' Code: Historical Verisimilitude and the Counterfactual Imagination," in *Playing With the Past: Videogames and the Simulation of History*, ed. Matthew Wilhelm Kapell and Andrew

Thus, multiplicity in historical outcomes in digital strategy games is only as varied as its most open-ended design choices allow. That is, the technical parameters and the created content of the games constitute the limits of historical representation. This notion, if true, requires the consideration of design choice and constraint, also with regards to counterfactual history. From a design perspective, counterfactual history is found as designer-created scenarios and outcomes in player-focused and entertainment-focused contexts. Such counterfactuals, while building on historical references, tell us more about uses of history than they do about historical scholarship. The question is not what digital strategy games do for (academic) historical epistemology, but how counterfactuals in historical representation in digital strategy games can be understood. It is important to note that I do not argue that the two – uses of history and historical scholarship – are ontologically mutually exclusive. I do argue, however, that they make up separate aspects on a diverse scale of possible intent.

To understand the positioning of counterfactuals in games as artefacts of historical culture and examples of uses of history it is important to acknowledge the tension between the scholarly epistemic and other applications of the past. In early academic works on historical games, discussions about counterfactuals tended to reference and be contextualised by epistemological discussion involving historians like E.H. Carr and E.P. Thompson on the one hand (who famously dismissed the notion of counterfactual history as nonsense), and Niall Ferguson on the other (who embrace it).[15] Such debates on the validity and viability of counterfactuals in history span decades between two seemingly irreconcilable stances. Connecting to this debate seems to stem from (a possibly inadvertent) need for (historical) game scholarship to position itself in a debate on counterfactual thinking as a methodology for historical scholarship concerned with objectivity and empirical truths. As is hopefully clear from the discussion so far, I find this binary and polarised understanding of counterfactuals as "the scholar-

---

B.R. Elliott (London: Bloomsbury, 2013); Rhett Loban and Thomas Apperley, "Eurocentric Values at Play: Modding the Colonial from the Indigenous Perspective," in *Video Games and the Global South*, ed. Phillip Penix-Tadsen (Pittsburg: ETC Press, 2019); Souvik Mukherjee, "The Playing fields of Empire: Empire and spatiality in video games," *Journal of Gaming and Virtual Worlds* 7 (2015).

15 See Adam Chapman, *Digital Games as History – How Digital Games Represent the Past and Give Access to Historical Practice* (London: Routledge, 2016); Apperley, "Modding the Historian's Code," 186. For applications of counterfactuals for historical and political sciences see also Philip Tetlock and Aaron Belkin, *Counterfactual Thought Experiments in World Politics – Locigal, Methodological, and Phsychological Perspectives* (Princeton: Princeton University Press, 1997); Philip Tetlock, Richard Ned Lebow and Geoffrey Parker (eds.), *Unmaking the West: "What-if? Scenarios that Rewrite World History* (Ann Arbor: University of Michigan Press, 2006).

ly" versus "the invalid or fictional" unnecessary and, above all, inapplicable to counterfactuals as uses of history, and to digital strategy games. As Christopher Prendergast notes, a polemic standoff between the useful and the (merely) entertaining counterfactual runs the risk of causing epistemological chaos.[16] To mitigate this, I here focus on the duality of counterfactual speculation in the vein of Catherine Gallagher who notes that counterfactuals, unlike fiction, are "hinged onto the actual historical record."[17] In other words, counterfactuals in games rely on historical cultural understandings (whether strictly speaking accurate or not) even when history goes off the rails. Following this relationship between the factual and counterfactual, I propose that the understanding of historical representation in digital strategy games will benefit from incorporating the nature and inherent biases of counterfactuals through the lens of uses of history, as well as game design practice.

Digital strategy games on the topic of history are sometimes called history simulators, as if they attempt to produce objectively realistic representations of historical causality.[18] I find the term simulator useful only as a descriptor for the experimental and generative gameplay style. Instead, I align with Thomas Apperley who asserts that digital strategy games "[demonstrate] that received categories of structuring space are no more 'real' or proper than are the arbitrary lenses that we use to make sense of the past."[19] This book supports this view by showing that the games, and their developers, make no claims to depicting historical accuracy. However, the games rely heavily on historical reference, and developers do use the vocabulary of verisimilitude in, for example, discussing player expectations and to describe their games. As such, there is a clear interplay, if not a contradiction, between notions of the simulated factual and counterfactual that seem to supersede polemic disciplinary tension, and that requires closer investigation.

The underlying principle for this book, then, is that the way developers implement and design counterfactual scenarios in *Europa Universalis IV* and *Hearts of Iron IV* ultimately provides insights about the way developers understand the past and navigate historical culture within the framework of game design practice. Of course, exploring possible causes and outcomes of significant historical events is a natural way for anyone to try to make sense of the past, and present,

---

16 Prendergast, *Counterfactuals*, 9.
17 Gallagher, *Telling it Like it Wasn't*, 2.
18 See for example Josef Köstlbauer, "The Strange Attraction of Simulation: Realism, Authenticity, Virtuality," in *Playing With the Past – Digital Games and the Simulation of History*, ed. Matthew Kapell and Andrew B.R. Elliott (London: Bloomsbury, 2013).
19 Apperley, "Modding the Historian's Code," 191.

both inside and outside of academia. After all, counterfactual histories in varying formats have become so frequent that, as Richard Evans notes, "they need investigating as a genre in themselves."[20] As such, counterfactual history can be understood as another expression of humans as historically aware beings.

Wishful Thinking, Possible Worlds and Future Fictions

In discussing counterfactual history and game design practices in digital strategy games, then, I use an analytical framework that draws on thoughts put forward by Richard Evans in *Altered Pasts* (2013), on how types, or categories, of counterfactual history and counterfactual scenarios can be distinguished based on bias and intent. Not all counterfactuals are made equal but, rather, for different arguments and purposes. The framework uses a terminology after three of Evans's essays as follows: wishful thinking, possible worlds and future fiction. The fourth essay, *Virtual history*, is named after Niall Fergusson's anthology *Virtual History – Alternatives and Counterfactuals* (1997). I here make the argument that virtual history, as a scholarly use of history is rendered partly inapplicable in the context of game design practice. This is developed in more detail in chapter three. In employing the framework analytically, I examine meaning and tension between understandings of factual and counterfactual, past and present, causes and outcomes, within the rules and scope of a given context – in this case, digital strategy games. This conceptualisation is meant as a theoretical tool to facilitate more precise and nuanced discussion on counterfactuals as uses of history. Importantly, these are probably not exhaustive, and types of counterfactuals may overlap in a single scenario. Concerning digital strategy games, the motives and questions embodied by the counterfactual histories are specific to the game context, and need to be understood as such.

What would it take to re-establish Austria-Hungary? If only the First World War had never happened!

Wishful thinking counterfactuals centre on nostalgia, hindsight and the notion of continuity – or loss of continuity – between the past and the present. They denote scenarios that encourage looking back, regaining or repairing something lost, remembering and perpetuating aspects of the past. Wishful thinking scenarios are particularly concerned with undoing perceived loss and tragedy or bring-

---

[20] Evans, *Altered Pasts*, 31.

ing back important historical entities. Wishful thinking counterfactuals explicitly juxtapose past scenarios with the present, and highlight such processes that led up to an unwanted or celebrated outcome, with the intent of telling a story of its continued or reinvented existence in the present. In the case of digital strategy games, the present is often represented by the present in in-game time (that is, the fifteenth century for *Europa Universalis IV* and the 1930s for *Hearts of Iron IV*). Wishful thinking scenarios are thus represented by challenges to, for example, reconstitute the glory-days of a former empire within the context of the in-game present. A typical example of this in *Europa Universalis IV* is preventing the demise of the Byzantine Empire in the 1450s and securing the (counterfactual) longevity of the Roman Empire.

What elements were crucial for the inception of the First World War?

Possible world counterfactuals are mainly concerned with causality and focusing on the evaluation of historical events by disconnecting them from their historical context and provide them, in speculation, with possible, yet realistically unattainable, choices. They constitute tools for interpolating counterfactual scenarios in digital strategy games that side-line historical context in favour of either producing a desired outcome, or evaluating a historical event based on unrealistic premises. In terms of the application of such possible world scenarios, the key is not in their ability to explain why something happened, but how they frame the possibility of something turning out differently than it did. Thus, possible world counterfactuals are about understandings of causality and synergy – the specific ways in which the dynamics of actors and events become clear. In possible world scenarios, a specific element in the context of an event is altered to enable a specific outcome. The main concern is the constitution of synergies – the positioning and importance of one element in relation to another. Questions and problems that are identifiers of possible world-counterfactuals are, for example: What could possibly have enabled the Aztecs to invade and colonize Europe? What tipped the scales against imperialist sentiments in the nineteenth century? Possible world-speculation generally ends after the desired outcome has been achieved and therefore disregards questions framed like "what would the world look like today had the Aztecs invaded and colonized Europe?"

What would the world have looked like if the First World War had never happened?

Future fictions counterfactuals are less interested in discussing how history took a specific turn or what events caused specific outcomes. Instead, they concern what happens after, when the alternative scenario is already in motion. The notion of future fiction helps juxtapose the perceived verisimilitude of counterfactual history in the games and in game design practice. Because of the duality between historical baselines and references, and counterfactual content in digital strategy games, future fictions are inevitable outcomes of gameplay. However, counterfactuals, again, are constrained by design, and the borders of the game help conceptualise the scope of counterfactual history in the games. Thus, future fiction counterfactuals are holistic, focused on consequence and contingency. They focus on the aftermath and order of things after a specific event. They can be thought of as an offset timeline, which advertently distances itself from the historical record and largely disregards it. What would the world look like if Germany won the Second World War? What would be different? What would be the same? Future fictions are not always concerned with what happened at the point of divergence, or why, but focuses on the consequences of major historical events. Exactly the manner in which Hitler won the war may not matter here, but the results do.

To go back to the definitions at the start of this introduction, counterfactual history as uses of history are the meaningful application of historical reference in a given context. As will be discussed (primarily in chapter three), the intimacy and tension between understandings of historical reference and counterfactual scenario design in the games is acute. Furthermore, such tensions highlight developers navigating the line between believable and unbelievable scenarios, the expected and the unexpected, and the intricate design task of getting players where they want to go – often off the rails.

Digital Strategy Games

In digital strategy games of the Paradox variety, the player is typically a sort of proxy for an omnipotent and omniscient ruler. They may use policy, religion, trade, marriage and military force to maintain and expand their playable state, nation or country. Players decide for themselves which state, nation, or country to play as, and what objectives to pursue. Will they play to conquer Asia as the Ottomans, or win the Second World War as Japan? In other words, a crucial characteristic of digital strategy games is that gameplay and agency dictates the sequence and, to a point, outcomes of events. This particular form allows for open-ended sessions, sometimes without a clear beginning, middle or end. Gameplay focus is on strategising and resource management. The rules, mechanics and content that the game developers set up give players the opportunity to choose what they want to do within the system provided. Communication between the player and the game is typically facilitated by interface elements like still and moving images, symbols, texts and hypertext. Backend elements like AI and rulesets determine what effect an action will have.²¹

Digital strategy games are the largest single category of historical games.²² The variety and diversity of digital games has caused the genre of digital strategy games to diverge into several lines based on either mechanics or gameplay experience. As Gilles Roy notes, "The strategy genre has developed, over time, into many identifiable sub-genres: the economic and management simulation, the wargame, the turn-based strategy game, the real-time strategy game, etc. [...] Game systems and mechanics have not been, in themselves, the sole defining features of these genres. Common narrative themes have been key ingredients to the success of computer strategy games, two of the most popular being historical civilization, and space conquest."²³ In the larger world of digital strategy games, Paradox Development Studio games stand out in the way they embody most of the above-mentioned characteristics at once.

The cultural understanding of (digital) strategy games has come to mean games that have a top-down camera angle, include building and managing units, and have competitive gameplay, against either human opponents or AI. In the cultural understanding of games of a certain type, genre becomes a way to explain relationships between past and present game design and game experiences. Game scholar Simon Dor notes that the encyclopaedic definition of a strategy game would encompass games that fall into the tradition of war gaming and include certain gameplay conventions that go beyond superficial description of what we see on screen. "A dictionary definition can define strategy using whichever criteria it needs, but it will not be enough to understand the complexity of the historical and cultural phenomenon that led to complex grand strategy games," he writes.²⁴

---

21 In a game design context, AI (artificial intelligence) is a common term used to talk about how a game imitates player behaviour for non-playable characters (or as the case may be here, non-playable nations), to present a challenging enemy or an interesting or supportive ally.
22 Yannick Rochat, "A Quantitative Study of Historical Videogames (1981–2015)," in *Historia Ludens – The Playing Historian*, ed. Alexander von Lünen et al. (London: Routledge, 2019), 5; 10. Rochat's survey of the genres of digital historical games found that, when sorted by genre, strategy games for PC are in the clear majority out of a sample size of 1783 games released between 1981 and 2016. Concerning periodisation, games that depict the Late Modern era dominate, and games about the Second World War alone make up about 30 per cent of games, according to Rochat's study.
23 Gilles Roy, "Being historical: How Strategy Games are Changing Popular History." *Play the Past*, September 24, 2014, accessed April 18, 2019, http://www.playthepast.org/?p=4952.
24 Simon Dor, "Strategy in Games or Strategy Games: Dictionary and Encyclopaedic Definitions for Game Studies," *Game Studies* 18 (2018).

This book uses the notions of design convention and game culture to contextualise its findings. In the case of Paradox Development Studio games, perhaps especially in *Europa Universalis IV* and *Hearts of Iron IV*, genre convention and war gaming tradition frame and influence the company's identity and values. For example, the first *Europa Universalis* game by Paradox Development Studio was a digital adaptation of a French board game with the same name that, in turn, built heavily on war gaming conventions. Additionally, *Europa Universalis IV* still contains code that dates back to the first game in the series, which, as will be discussed further into this book, partly dictates both opportunity and constraint in game design practice for developers. The studio, to this day, maintains a set of gameplay values (known as the Paradox pillars, discussed in chapter two) whose definitions correlate with the cultural understanding of strategy games as a genre and the expectations that come with them. This sense of convention, i.e. common practices, and large-scale gaming is likely one of the reasons some Paradox Development Studio games maintain the specific genre label grand strategy game in certain contexts.

While digital strategy games tend to lend themselves extraordinarily well to open-ended, sandbox gameplay and counterfactual history, it bears reminding that digital games of other genres also employ counterfactuals. Oftentimes they do so as a world-building tool to establish the logic of, for example, a future fiction while maintaining a story-driven gameplay experience. In other words, here, the story dictates the sequence and outcomes of events instead. Notable linear counterfactual historical games are the *Fallout* and the *Wolfenstein* series, both third- or first–person shooter adventure games that take place in worlds different from ours that still rely heavily on familiar historical reference. The *Fallout* world diverges from ours at some point after the Second World War. In 2077, that for reasons unknown bears an aesthetic semblance to our actual 1950s, a nuclear war took place. After this, the humans of the world spent an unspecified amount of time living in bunkers before emerging into a post-apocalyptic world. In each game in the series, the player then gets to explore this counterfactual scenario at their own leisure and by following quest-lines that expose the world and its history.[25] In contrast, *Wolfenstein*, particularly in later iterations

---

[25] For more on historical representation in the *Fallout* series, see Kathleen McClancy, "The Wasteland of the Real: Nostalgia and Simulacra in *Fallout*," *Game Studies* 18 (2018); Matthias Kemmer, "The Politics of Post-Apocalypse: Interactivity, Narrative Framing and Ethics in *Fallout 3*," in *Politics in Fantasy Media – Essays on Ideology and Gender in Fiction, Film, Television and Games*, ed. Gerold Sedlmayr and Nicole Waller (Jefferson: McFarland, 2014); Derek Fewster, "Fallout, Memory and Values: Uses of History and Time in a Sci-Fi-driven Video Game," in

called *Wolfenstein II: The New Order* and *Wolfenstein: The New Colossus*, the player explores a world in which Germany won the Second World War. The story of the game follows a group of resistance fighters from a European and American perspective and highlights the nature of future fictions by juxtaposing historical actuality with the new post-war reality.[26]

Thus, *Fallout* and *Wolfenstein* are examples of games that depict counterfactuals but unlike *Europa Universalis IV* and *Hearts of Iron IV* they do not integrate them as forking sets of outcomes produced by gameplay. The main difference between story-driven adventure games and strategy games, then, is in the variety and scope of mechanics and content. Moreover, digital strategy games place an emphasis on synergies between mechanics that can cause a near-infinite number of outcomes. In other words, given the scope and complexity of the games, gameplay sessions are likely to be specific and unique. Historical events may or may not occur depending on the player – and random chance. As found by folklore and games scholar Jukka Valho, game systems (simulations in particular) provide the building blocks and logic of a narrative discourse, but it remains incomplete without player participation.[27] *Europa Universalis IV* and *Hearts of Iron IV* also contain goal-setting mechanics (suggested objectives, if you will) that represent over-arching counterfactual scenarios. Thus, while the open-ended nature of digital strategy games is likely to cause sporadic counterfactual outcomes, their form provides the scaffolding for more cohesive representations of history, factual and counterfactual.

Game Design Practice

Early disagreements on the definition and focus of game studies as a discipline have led to disorganized and sometimes competing definitions of game studies, and more importantly for the purpose of this book, definitions of game design.[28]

The Enduring Fantastic – Essays on Imagination and Western Culture, ed. Anna Höglund and Cecilia Trenter (Jefferson: McFarland, 2021).

26 For more on historical representation in the *Wolfenstein* series, see Federico Peñate Domínguez, "'Heute gehört uns die Galaxie:' Music and Historical Credibility in Wolfenstein: The New Order's Nazi Dystopia," *GAME – The Italian Journal of Game Studies* 6 (2017); Hans-Joachim Backe, "A Redneck Head on a Nazi Body. Subversive Ludo-Narrative Strategies inWolfenstein II: The New Colossus," *Arts* 7 (2018).

27 Jukka Vahlo, "In Gameplay – The Invariant Structures and Varieties of the Video Game Gameplay Experience" (PhD diss., University of Turku, 2018), 228–229.

28 Annakaisa Kultima, "Multidisciplinary Game Design Research – Ontologies and Other Remarks," in *Game Design Research*, ed. Petri Lankoski and Jussi Holopainen (ETC Press, 2017),

A general lack of focus on design becomes particularly immediate in narrower sub-fields, which might already be trying to reconcile several epistemic fields, say, history and games. In parallel, a fundamental step towards an understanding of historical representation in games is to properly contextualise games as artefacts. To this end, I employ perspectives from the field of game design praxiology – the study of games as created.[29] I here draw on the work of Annakaisa Kultima who has developed five praxiology theses that denote designer or developer incentives, values and practices. Of particular interest to the present book are her findings on timeliness and particularity, opportunism, and the surrounding ecosystem of the game industry.[30] To the issue of the surrounding game industry, and in opening the discussion about how historical game design happens at Paradox Development Studio, it is necessary to place individual design practices within this broader context. The present study, then, also relies on previous research on the field of game production studies, that deal with issues of monetization, game labour, strides in technological development and more.[31]

Game development, like most things, appears to hinge on trends and paradigms in the temporal context. Paradigms denote what constitutes for example good game design or entertaining gameplay at any given time. Paradox Development Studio are notable in the way they have carved out a niche for themselves within which they adhere to a specific set of monetisation and game-release practices. This niche allows the studio not to react to swift changes in market turns, and as such partly avoid, for example, opportunistic design practices. This is also reflected in how history is represented in the games when, for example, established genre convention permits problematic representations – and omissions – of historical atrocities or contested historical culture. Nevertheless,

---

35–38. For further discussion on the ludology-narratology debate, see Eric Zimmerman, "Narrative, Interactivity, Play, and Games: Four Naughty Concepts in Need of Discipline," in *First Person. New Media as Story, Performance, and Game*, ed. Noah Wardrip-Fruin and Pat Harrigan (Cambridge: The MIT Press, 2004); Gonzalo Frasca, "Ludologists Love Stories, too: Notes From a Debate that Never Took Place," in *Level Up: Digital Games Research Conference Proceedings*, ed. Marinka Copier and Joost Raessens (Utrecht: University of Utrecht, 2003); Jesper Juul, "Games Telling Stories? A Brief Note on Narrative and Games," *Game Studies* 1 (2001).
29 Kultima's definition of the field of game design praxiology builds on Nigel Cross's taxonomy of design areas: design epistemology (designerly ways of knowing), design praxiology (study of the practices and processes of design) and design phenomenology (study of the form and configuration of artefacts). For further discussion on games as created, see Kultima, "Game Design Praxiology," 1–20.
30 Kultima, "Game Design Praxiology," 20–21.
31 For an overview of the field of game production studies, see Olli Sotamaa and Jan Svelch (eds.), *Game Production Studies* (Amsterdam: Amsterdam University Press, 2021).

Paradox Development Studio unsurprisingly must and do adhere to the general workings of the games industry, perhaps notably in making their notoriously intimidatingly complex and – to some degree – hard games feel more accessible to a broader player base in accordance with games becoming more mainstream.[32] In the context of game design practice, I will be discussing the ways *Europa Universalis IV* and *Hearts of Iron IV* attempt to balance complexity and complicatedness while maintaining a rigorous and plausible historical depiction.

The key to my findings is in the details of how such cultural and industry-related contexts and practices influence gameplay and the representation of history and counterfactual history in *Europa Universalis IV* and *Hearts of Iron IV*. Most importantly, the praxiology perspective allows me to highlight particularities, and deviations that relate to a) digital strategy games and b) history and counterfactual history, and their influence on said practices and subsequent game design.[33]

Positioning Developer Studies

This book intends to partly fill a gap in both historical game studies and game design studies. In doing so, it draws on – and connects to – previous findings in both fields, and in game studies as well. So far, the understanding of historical

---

32 Douglas Wilson and Miguel Sicart, "Now It's Personal: On Abusive Game Design," Proceedings of *FuturePlay* 2010 (author version), 2. I here use the term accessible as discussed by Wilson and Sicart to denote games that actively maintain "a desired and positive experience" by challenging the player only within the limits of an implied player model. As will be discussed in chapter 2, until recently, Paradox Interactive also used the term to characterise their games. In 2020, this description changed to "smooth and forgiving," though whether we are to infer that Paradox Interactive intends to signal the term "accessible" as specifically relating to disability (and gaming) is unknown.

33 While this research was not conducted with the explicit intention of being prescriptive to game design practitioners, it would be an unnecessary delimitation to assume that two-way communication between scholarship and game development is not possible, or even potentially fruitful. Kultima writes: "Game research is conducted both within the interdisciplinary academic communities as well as increasingly among established disciplines of academia, further nurturing epistemic communities which have no connection to the practitioners at all" ("Multidisciplinary Game Design Research," 39). Similarly, she argues, game designers have little or no connection to research and "[these] latter non-academic epistemic communities, and the knowledge creation processes of the developers, have not been studied rigorously, if at all" ("Multidisciplinary Game Design Research," 29). It is my hope that the present study can partly bridge this gap, and, ideally, bring forward perspectives on game design practices that include the interplay of uses of history as (game) design.

representation and game design has been paired with some degree of guesswork and baseline assumptions about design, and about developer practices and intent. Explicit developer studies are rare. There are, I find, two reasons for this.

Firstly, an issue of discipline. Over the last 20 years, the field of game studies has become increasingly fragmented and grown into islands of homogenous research within established disciplines. This includes the study of games within historical scholarship. As argued by Jaako Stenros and Annakaisa Kultima, such communities risk reinventing the wheel for failure of taking advantage of the plurality and intellectual strength inherent to multidisciplinary fields.[34]

Historical game studies have seen a similar development. Early works have devoted a significant amount of effort to defining game research within the field of historical studies, and arguing for the usefulness of game research in history from the point of view of legitimising games as objects worthy of study: legitimising both in terms of games as historical representation and, in some cases, in terms of games as historical scholarship in and of themselves.[35] Developer studies, i.e. questions about the meaning of design, authorship and intent, have not had a significant place in this debate. Rather, the search for a disciplinary identity has caused periods of disproportionate focus on ontological questions, such as how games constitute (academic) history. This, subsequently, has left not enough room for game studies to reciprocate and enrich the study of historical games with methodological and theoretical perspectives that frame them as, for example, uses of history.

However, epistemologically, historical games studies is both a subfield to historical studies and game studies simultaneously, and benefits from embracing pluralistic, multidisciplinary approaches rather than trying to reconcile between the past and games within historical scholarship. Of course, expanding our understanding of games will increase our ability to be as specific and as proficient as possible in furthering the field, not for the benefit of historical scholarship, but for historical game scholarship. This includes, among other possible

---

34 Jaakko Stenros and Annakaisa Kultima, "On the Expanding Ludosphere," *Simulation & Gaming* 49 (2018): 342, 350–351. In parallel to the notion of fragmentation, Sebastian Deterding argues that game studies as a discrete discipline is fast becoming one of many such islands, "one narrow cultural studies multidiscipline within the growing and diversifying field of game research and education." Sebastian Deterding, "The Pyrric Victory of Game Studies: Assessing the Past, Present, and Future of Interdisciplinary Game Research," *Games and Culture* 12 (2016): 521–543.
35 For example, Jeremie Clyde, Howard Hopkins and Glenn Wilkinson, "Beyond the 'Historical' Simulation: Using Theories of History to Inform Scholarly Game Design," *Loading. The Journal of the Canadian Game Studies Association* 9 (2012); Dawn Spring, "Gaming history: computer and video games as historical scholarship," *Rethinking History* 19 (2015).

paths, perspectives on game design and designers to create a fuller understanding of the topic. Furthermore, developer perspectives are still so uncommon in game studies in general that any efforts in this area are likely to become important contributions also beyond the scope of historical game studies.[36]

That is not to say that strides in this area that do not already exist or are underway. Notably, in *Digital Games as History*, Adam Chapman lays the groundwork on how to approach historical digital games analytically. The book is a theoretical survey in which the author develops an extensive conceptual framework to be used for formalist game analysis.[37] Chapman, granted, does not discuss notions of design, nor design practices. However, in his taxonomical approach to the game form, he helpfully clarifies some of the convoluted misconceptions and faux contradictions that long clouded the path for historical game scholarship, as previously discussed. While the discussion on the nature of the relationship between historical scholarship and representations of the past in historical games continue, the conceptual anchoring of the game form, in Chapman's and related works, has allowed historical game studies to move on from the frequently-ontological to a wider variety of approaches, a development of which the present study on game design practices is a part.[38]

The second reason why developer studies are not as prevalent in historical game studies yet is practical and has to do with game industry protectionism. The rigid proverbial walls behind which much of the game industry continues to reside likely contribute towards the sustained disconnect between history, game studies and design research.[39] Employees in the gaming industry routinely sign non-disclosure agreements in order to maintain a high level of secrecy, especially concerning unannounced projects. Such agreements often extend to in-

---

36 O'Donnell, "Developer's Dilemma," 4.
37 Chapman, "Digital Games as History," 30–55 and 265–285.
38 This development is exemplified by the many interdisciplinary anthology projects published in recent years, including *The Dark Side of Game Play – Controversial Issues in Playful Environments*, ed. Torill Elvira Mortensen, Jonas Linderoth and Ashley M.L. Brown (London: Routledge, 2015); *Historia Ludens – The Playing Historian*, ed. Alexander von Lünen et al. (London: Routledge, 2019); *War Games: Memory, Militarism and the Subject of Play*, ed. Phil Hammond and Pötzsch (London: Bloomsbury, 2020).
39 See for example Reina Y. Arakji and Karl R. Lang, "Digital Consumer Networks and Producer-Consumer Collaboration: Innovation and Product Development in the Video Game Industry," *Journal of Management Information Systems* 24 (2007): 198–199; O'Donnell, *Developer's Dilemma*, 3; Tara Copplestone, "But that's not accurate: The Differing Perceptions of Accuracy in Cultural-heritage Videogames between Creators, Consumers and Critics," *Rethinking History* 21 (2017); Esther Wright, "On the Promotional Context of Historical Video Games," *Rethinking History* 22 (2018).

clude past projects and events within the company as well. It is therefore worth acknowledging that developers can be generally unavailable for research for reasons of this nature.[40] Nevertheless, game production studies and game industry studies are on the rise. In exploring the various contexts that impose themselves on historical game design as I do here, it is necessary to include questions of game development labour. As intricately discussed by Ergin Bulut in *A Precarious Game* (2020), the game industry can often be observed to struggle with the entanglement of notions of "the dream job" on the one hand and precarious working conditions in the game industry on the other.[41] In taking a critical look at the day-to-day of Paradox developers and beta testers (mainly in chapters one and two), I discuss the subtle interplay of delegation, time-management and practical historical work against important insights such as Bulut's. While this book's contribution to game labour studies overall is relatively small, I make an earnest attempt at illustrating how important the scaffolding of game design practice is for the representation of history in games. Particular attention is paid to the ongoing tradition of engaging beta testers – unpaid player-workers who significantly contribute to design, content creation and testing.

While developer perspectives and game production studies continue to be a comparatively rare occurrence also in historical game studies there are several important exceptions that have significantly informed my understanding of how developers and game industry stake-holders deal with history in games on various levels. Tara Copplestone has shown through interviews how value is assigned to the notion of authenticity among game developers and cultural heritage stake-holders, and for what purposes.[42] Esther Wright explores the image of the past in marketing and para-texts surrounding games, and examines the intersection of games and cinematic reference in promotional materials. Wright's findings strongly indicate that the game business resells a faux image of cinematic realism which builds directly on top of a culturally and socially recognisable image of a specific time and place through intertextuality – not the authentic experience itself.[43] These results in turn rhyme well with Emil Lundedal Hammar's showing a significant relationship between levels of game production

---

[40] O'Donnell, "Developer's Dilemma," 172; Stenros and Kultima, "On the Expanding Ludosphere"; Wright, "Promotional Context of Historical Video Games," 1–2.
[41] Ergin Bulut, *A Precarious Game – The Illusion of Dream Jobs in the Video Game Industry* (New York: Cornell University Press, 2020), 3–7.
[42] Tara Copplestone, "But that's not accurate: The Differing Perceptions of Accuracy in Cultural-heritage Videogames between Creators, Consumers and Critics," *Rethinking History* 21 (2017).
[43] Esther Wright, "Marketing Authenticity: Rockstar Games and the Use of Cinema in Video Game Production," *Kinephanos* 7 (2017): 133.

and homogeneity in historical games.⁴⁴ Chris Kempshall comments on the "bespoke and self-directed" strategies developers employ to educate themselves about the First World War for game-making purposes, and the results have important similarities and differences with my findings on how developers know things about the past.⁴⁵ Insights such as these help frame Paradox Development Studio as participants in an eco-system of history and game making, as well as their trajectory, strategies and views on history as game developers. As historical game studies continues to develop theories on the relationship between design values and design practice and contemporary historical culture and discourse, these strides are all compelling contributions in this direction. The present state of history and developer perspectives emphatically shows the variety in methodology by which scholars can approach developer studies in spite of industry protectionism, and the significant impact of developer perspectives on historical game studies.

Counterfactual history in the context of historical game studies poses its own set of challenges and issues. To those seeking to evaluate facticity in games, counterfactual history, of course, poses an epistemological conundrum. Perhaps due to this contradiction, and the previously discussed question of how to define counterfactuals in various contexts, scholarship in this area (that is, counterfactuals in games) is relatively scarce. Recent studies, for example the work of Thomas Apperley, address this gap by investigating how player communities frame gameplay by negotiating notions of verisimilitude to set counterfactual goals among themselves.⁴⁶ Furthermore, counterfactuals are often discussed in the context of war gaming and simulation, a natural extension of discussions on realism and probability that is, at this point, inherent to studies on digital strategy games as well.⁴⁷ Strategy games are genetic successors to the centuries-long tradition of war games, whose original purpose was to realistically simulate possible outcomes of war and battle.⁴⁸ In the case of Paradox Development Studio, this tradition is evident on many levels that I will discuss throughout the book. A notable example, however, is the name of the in-house game engine,

---

44 Emil Lundedal Hammar, "Producing and Playing Hegemonic Pasts. Historical Digital Games as Memory-Making Media" (PhD diss., The Arctic University of Norway, 2020), 48–73.
45 Chris Kempshall, "War collaborators: documentary and historical sources in First World War computer games," *First World War Studies* 10 (2020): 13.
46 Thomas Apperley, "Counterfactual communities: strategy games, paratexts and the player's experience of history," *Open library of humanities* 41 (2018).
47 Philip Sabin, "Wargaming in higher education: Contributions and challenges," *Arts and Humanities in Higher Education* 14 (2015): 330–331.
48 Köstlbauer, "The Strange Attraction of Simulation," 176.

Clausewitz. Acknowledging the genetic heritage of historical digital strategy games and the influence of this legacy is particularly important for contextualising the role of counterfactuals as uses of history.[49] Advances such as these enable me to connect similarities and differences between design and the subsequent gameplay values they represent, in the present and over time.

Just as counterfactuals have had a complex treatment in historical scholarship, so have games. The cultural understanding of games as frivolous, superficial or trivial has caused a vein of historians and other scholars to wilfully dismiss them, either by claiming that "the public" is, in fact, not at all interested in real history, or by portraying popular culture as detrimental to the public's historical consciousness.[50] Jerome De Groot rightly argues that the public will consume history regardless, perhaps popular history more than anything, and "if the historian seeks to protect the historical consciousness of the public, they must first understand how that group is informed and resourced."[51] Thanks to competent strides in perception studies, informal learning and pedagogical uses of historical games by scholars such as Robert Houghton, Jeremiah McCall and Sian Beavers, we can now rely on scientific findings in this area as well, and we are beginning to see the empirical impact and role games play in disseminating understandings about history.[52] The benefit of converging fields and approaches becomes especially clear here, when we consider how the plurality of focuses does not just demystify the dissemination of the past through

---

[49] War gaming tradition has had implications for game design also outside of the design of strategy games. In "The Wargame Legacy: How Wargames Shaped the Roleplaying Experience from Tabletop to Digital Games," Dimitra Nikolaidou traces and examines the legacy of combat for the roleplaying genre and notes that the arguably disproportionate role of combat in roleplaying can be traced back to this relationship: Dimitra Nikolaidou, "The Wargame Legacy: How Wargames Shaped the Roleplaying Experience from Tabletop to Digital Games," in *War Games: Memory, Militarism and the Subject of Play*, ed. Phil Hammon and Holger Pözsch (London: Bloomsbury, 2020).
[50] Chapman, *Digital Games as History*, 5.
[51] De Groot, *Consuming History*, 5.
[52] Robert Houghton, "Where Did You Learn That? The Self-Perceived Educational Impact of Historical Computer Games on Undergraduates," *gamevironments* 5 (2016); Jeremiah McCall, *Gaming the Past: Using Video Games to Teach Secondary History* (London: Routledge, 2011); Jeremiah McCall, "Navigating the Problem Space: The Medium of Simulation Games in the Teaching of History," *The History Teacher* 46 (2012); Jeremiah McCall, "Video games as Participatory Public History," in *A Companion to Public History*, ed. David Dean (Hoboken: John Wiley & Sons Ltd., 2018); James Gee, *What Video Games Have to Teach Us about Learning and Literacy* (New York: Macmillan, 2003); Sian Beavers, "The Informal Learning of History with Digital Games" (PhD diss., The Open University, 2019).

games, but circles back and informs the understanding of incentives that drive game making about the past in the first place.

Selection of Material and Methodology

Towards filling the gap in developer perspectives in historical game studies, then, the data for this book was collected by going straight to the source. The arguments of the book are built on a synthesis between developer interviews and game analysis. The interviews highlight the day-to-day in game design and detail decision-making regarding, for example, the sourcing and implementation of historical reference and counterfactuals. The game analysis explores the descriptive and scripted content in the games' files, alongside gameplay. In other words, methodologically speaking, this study looks under the hood of the context of game making and the game product. For additional details on the interviews and game analysis, see Appendices 2 and 3.

As of 2021, the collection of Paradox Development Studio developed game series covers ancient Rome and the Roman Empire (*Imperator: Rome*), the Middle Ages (*Crusader Kings*), Early Modern global history (*Europa Universalis*), nineteenth century industrialisation and global history (*Victoria*), the Second World War (*Hearts of Iron*) and an interstellar, distant future (*Stellaris*).[53] Of these, *Europa Universalis IV* and *Hearts of Iron IV* are the two longest-running Paradox Development Studio titles to date and the focus of the book. Both game series began around the turn of the millennia, which makes them interesting examples of game series that have been in more or less continuous development for a considerable period of time. Furthermore, both games' developers explicitly and consciously design counterfactual scenarios as an integral part of the gameplay experience.

As digital strategy games, each game in the Paradox Development Studio portfolio looks visually largely the same. However, as representations of the past they argue on fundamentally different historical periods and emphasise fundamentally different processes. In the words of Greg Koebel, Paradox Development Studio games "present a vision of history as fully compartmentalized

---

53 *Imperator: Rome* 2019; *Crusader Kings* series 2004–; *Europa Universalis* series 2000–; *Victoria* 2003–; *Hearts of Iron* series 2009; *Stellaris* 2016. Arguably, Paradox Interactive also publishes a strategy game covering the American Prohibition Era (1920s) called *Empire of Sin* (2020). However, firstly, the game is developed by Romero Games (not Paradox Development Studio), and secondly, the game does not appear to follow the same design template as the Paradox Development Studio grand strategy games mentioned.

'ages', which require their own code."⁵⁴ As such, *Europa Universalis IV* and *Hearts of Iron IV* have a number of notable differences in terms of design, mechanics, scope and depiction of history that have bearing on the way content and processes are described in the interviews and how counterfactual history is structured and positioned within each game. For example, *Hearts of Iron IV* is less open-ended and railroads historical scenarios to a larger extent than *Europa Universalis IV* does. The latter allows the player to take bigger liberties with the historical development of their chosen country and to change direction over the course of a game, something that is considerably harder to do successfully in *Hearts of Iron IV*. This juxtaposition of designer perspectives on the freedom of gameplay, as well as the consequences for counterfactuals as uses of history, make *Europa Universalis IV* and *Hearts of Iron IV* suitable cases for studying two different but in-depth ways that games and game developers employ the past and, importantly, counterfactuals, in digital strategy games.

Other paradox games are outside the boundaries of this study for various reasons. *Imperator: Rome* mainly because it was released too late to be included. *Crusader Kings I* and *II*, while Paradox Development Studio historical strategy games, build mainly on the social and political dynamics of noble families during the Middle Ages and the mechanics are weighted towards roleplaying, placing it outside of the genre focus of this study. There are, to be sure, important comparisons to be made between conventional digital strategy games, and games that draw heavily on other genres as well. However, because of the vertical nature of this study, I leave such comparisons to future projects. *Stellaris* does not fit the study thematically. In terms of popularity, both *Crusader Kings II* and *Stellaris* have likely sold more copies than *Europa Universalis IV* and *Hearts of Iron IV*, but assessing the number of copies sold for a game can be very hard as digital distribution distorts numbers across platforms, base games and DLCs. Another determining factor is that it can be hard to ascertain the relevance and meaning of sales-figures as the correlation between copies sold, money spent and invested playtime is usually unclear.

Out of the six in-house Paradox Development Studio titles, the *Victoria* series sports the most similarities with *Europa Universalis* and *Hearts of Iron* from a design and gameplay point of view. It also spans the gap between the in-game periods of *Europa Universalis IV* (1444–1821) and *Hearts of Iron IV* (1936–1948). However, the latest game to be released in the *Victoria* series was the *Victoria II* expansion *Heart of Darkness*, released in 2013. The long-awaited *Victoria*

---

54 Koebel, "Simulating the Ages of Man: Periodization in Civilization V and Europa Universalis IV," *Loading… The Journal of the Canadian Game Studies Association* 10 (2018): 68.

3 was announced in May 2021 and development is ongoing at the time of writing. However, the prolonged hiatus of releases in the *Victoria* series means it has had, and continues to have, a different trajectory than *Europa Universalis IV* and *Hearts of Iron IV*. Thus, due to a lack of relevant developers and beta testers to interview, and the different development trajectory, *Victoria* is not included in the study.[55]

Chapter Overview

The chapters of this book correspond to levels of analysis in the sense that the bearing concepts are discussed somewhat separately in the first few chapters. The book then gradually synthesises the overarching thesis of the book in the final two.

Chapter one begins by presenting *Europa Universalis IV* and *Hearts of Iron* IV in some detail. The chapter is of use to readers who are previously unfamiliar with the games and how to play them, although it also includes aspects on the games' release and reception, game features and their role in historical representation, as well as some conceptual groundwork regarding goal setting and the role of scripting and descriptive text in the games.

Chapter two introduces Paradox Development Studio and discusses the rationale, values and pragmatism that frame game design practice. This chapter positions Paradox Development Studio in a larger game industry context: that of publishing company Paradox Interactive. The chapter also explores their niche profile in the greater industry ecosystem. The company's monetisation and distribution models have significant implications for project management and resource management. The implications of such practices for gameplay values, including the whys, whats and hows of counterfactuals as uses of history, are also brought into focus. I summarise by proposing two main theses on

---

[55] It is possible to play through the entire series of Paradox Development Studio titles as a so-called grand campaign. In short, this entails starting a game in *Imperator: Rome* and using the same game files in each of the other games in chronological order, creating one cohesive playthrough. This puts *Victoria II* in a position to potentially connect the timelines of *Europa Universalis IV* and *Hearts of Iron IV*. However, as pointed out by Greg Koebel ("Simulating the Ages of Man," 66–67), titles from Paradox Development Studio have significant differences in terms of mechanics and content and emphasise particularly important characteristics from each era. As such, *Victoria II* and grand campaigns could be interesting future objects of study, coming from, for example, the perspective of player habits or historiographic representation.

how values of player-centrism and entertainment-centrism guide developers in this context.

Chapter three shifts focus to the games themselves. Here, the shape, form and framings of counterfactuals are analysed and discussed in relation to genre and gameplay. The theoretical framework is used on selected examples to show how counterfactuals harbour historical cultural meaning beyond "not being factual." In doing so, the book here focuses on specific design choices and break down the differences between, for example, emergent counterfactuals and ready-made objectives. It also relies in part on developer testimonials to discuss how game design practice, as well as historical culture, influence the design of the games.

Chapter four focuses on the synthesis of the two previous chapters by examining the interplay of design practices and the representation of history, including counterfactual history, in *Europa Universalis IV* and *Hearts of Iron IV*. The chapter discusses the details of how developers negotiate their understandings of the past for the benefit of game design. Notions of design legacy and genre are juxtaposed with gameplay values, both in relation to historical representation, such as the inclusion and omission of historical atrocities, and in relation to design pragmatics such as resource management.

Chapter five provides a summary and further discussion on the conclusions in this book. Importantly, I here discuss what these outcomes mean for our understanding of history in games, now and going forward.

Chapter One
Opening up the Design – *Europa Universalis IV* and *Hearts of Iron IV* Overviews

This book considers games as intentionally designed artefacts, and this first chapter considers the shape and details of said artefacts. *Europa Universalis IV* and *Hearts of Iron IV* are digital strategy games, and the genre itself comes with a series of conventions, such as the look of the map, the birds-eye perspective and the possibility to play as an omnipotent leader of a historical state, nation or country. Conventions, here, denotes common industry practices that dictate a certain level of continuity – or baseline for change – in how games are made. Including counterfactual history is one such convention. That is, players expect to be able to create historical scenarios that are contrary to fact in *Europa Universalis IV* and *Hearts of Iron IV*.

So, what does that look like, in practice, and how does it work? By outlining the anatomy of counterfactual and historical representation in the games, going from the atomistic to the holistic in content and mechanics, this chapter lays the groundwork for subsequent chapters exploring the surrounding ecosystem of game design practice and counterfactuals as uses of history. This chapter uses gameplay and design examples to establish how the games work and what specific elements may relate to the concept of design in the first place. The aim is to demystify parts of the design of history in these games by discussing the scaffolding and role of rules and scripting, and content. We can begin to tie how form conveys function to the surrounding game design practices and, ultimately, counterfactuals and representations of the past.

The nuanced distinction between games being history and games using history becomes extra poignant from this point of view, and helps us break down the implications of specific design choices. The benefit of using formal analysis for framing historical games as games can be understood through the stipulation of Jeremiah McCall: "A functioning game must be a closed working set of formally defined systems needing player input to function."[56] Design-focused conceptualisations such as these are helpful in highlighting inherent advantages as well as pain-points of designed historical systems (*Europa Universalis IV* and *Hearts of Iron IV*) in relation to representation, and to show how design imposes itself

---

[56] Jeremiah McCall, "The Historical Problem Space Framework: Games as a Historical Medium," *Game Studies* 20 (2020), available at http://gamestudies.org/2003/articles/mccall.

https://doi.org/10.1515/9783110692488-004

on the past and vice versa.[57] Performing design reviews and technical readings, including close readings of rules and scripting, opens design up to a deeper understanding of how digital strategy games function as vehicles of historical culture and uses of history. The materials and methods used here are described in some additional detail in appendix 3.

A note on terminology. Both *Europa Universalis IV* and *Hearts of Iron IV* use the terms "state," "nation" and "country" interchangeably to denote geographical and political units in the games. Especially in the case of *Europa Universalis IV*, which focuses on the Early Modern era, this terminology is (intentionally or unintentionally) anachronistic as, for example, the complex notion of national identity only emerges towards the end of the depicted period.[58] I therefore aim to use the term "playable nation" where appropriate throughout this book to distinguish between in-game entities and other uses. Importantly however, haphazard use of terminology in the games overall comes with noteworthy, often Eurocentric, consequences for whose history is being told, and how. Such implications will be discussed in more detail in the following chapters.

In the present chapter, then, each investigation of the games begins with a journal-style entry, based on one of the author's game sessions, describing gameplay briefly to illustrate some of the complexities at hand. Then, the overall reception of the games will be investigated to provide more context and begin the investigation of the games' design trajectory that will be explored further in chapter two.[59] From there, description and discussion focuses on the anatomy of the games, including content and mechanics of each game. Finally, since designers encode the content using scripting and textual tools, we will survey some

---

[57] McCall, "The Historical Problem Space Framework." To this point, McCall offers a design-sensitive analytical framework of historical gameplay, that distinguishes between player agent, goals, resources and tools, and game world, as their moving parts. The framework also considers the way components frame and facilitate choice and behaviour, as well as the meaning of genre conventions in this context. For analytical approaches that focus on how games constitute history, see Chapman, *Digital Games as History*; Vincenzo Idone Cassone and Mattia Thibault, "The HGR Framework: A Semiotic Approach to the Representation of History in Digital Games," *gamevironments* 5 (2016): 156–204.

[58] Bret Devereaux, "Collections: Teaching Paradox, *Europa Universalis IV*, Part I: State of Play," *A Collection of Unmitigated Pedantry*, April 30, 2021, https://acoup.blog/2021/04/30/collections-teaching-paradox-europa-univeralis-iv-part-i-state-of-play/.

[59] For more on reception history, see, for example, Martin A. Wainwright, *Virtual History – How Videogames Portray the Past* (London: Routledge, 2019), 24–25.

relevant aspects to scripted and textual content in the game to underpin further analysis.[60]

Europa Universalis IV – Four Hundred Years in One Interface

Gameplay Journal: Ottomans. March 1462.

Almost twenty years have passed since the game began, and I have been playing rather aggressively. Playing as the Ottomans, my goal was to envelop the Mediterranean Sea. Twenty years in, I am a little discouraged. I calculated I would pave the way to success by claiming the Byzantine provinces Morea and Constantinople early, and regulating all trade to the Black Sea, but I was unlucky and Byzantium is hanging on. The next step was to pick off the Balkan states, and while my military efforts initially met with success, I must have lost track of internal affairs as unrest in Albania is increasing fast and the Albanians challenge my claims to the area. My current ruler has repeatedly emphasised the importance of Islam, but the Christian Albanians are not keen on living under Muslim rule. Albania is small, but they have summoned their Venetian and Hungarian allies to support them. I have delayed fighting both for good reason – they are terribly strong.

Meanwhile, I am also mired in what should have been an easy conquest to the East. I knew I would not be able to tackle the Mamluk Empire until later, but circumstances pushed us to an early conflict. My bold and likely premature conquest of the neighbouring Karaman provinces provoked a backlash from separatist Karaman Knights, who are allied with the Mamluks. It would appear as if Karaman has better allies than the Ottomans do – the French are my allies, but they are not joining my wars. While I understand that France does not have an as poor opinion of my eastern neighbours as the Ottomans, it would definitely have been useful to count on their support. At this point, I am better off accepting a truce with Venice. A truce means giving up most of my western conquests, not to mention a considerable number of ducats. It will set my plans back many years, but will give me a respite to focus on replenishing my decimated army. At least I can focus on rebuilding. Or, I could start over, learning from this round that even the powerful Ottoman

---

60 The description and analysis of the games in this book always refer to game versions 1.28.3 of *Europa Universalis IV* and version 1.6.2 of *Hearts of Iron IV* unless otherwise stated. Furthermore, this design overview of mechanics and gameplay does not purport to be exhaustive. The scope of both games is sizeable, and it would be difficult and potentially counterproductive to attempt that in a book like this. Instead, the aim is to provide helpful examples that explain how design components fit together and how it might matter.

Figure 1: Ottoman game in 1462 in *Europa Universalis IV*. Uncropped screenshot, reproduced with permission.

Empire will crumble in the wrong circumstances and that manipulating religion and diplomacy in my conquered provinces are important means of achieving my goals.

Imagine playing a game of chess, except you have 120 opponents divided into factions. Each faction battles the others, and you are stuck in the middle. This is, in a simplified way, what playing *Europa Universalis IV* can feel like. The rules are more numerous and abstract than in chess, and a game usually takes much longer. Nevertheless, in order to stay in the game, players need to be familiar with the rules governing them. Players also need to know how to work within said rules constructively – in other words, how to play the game well and reach their goals. The Ottoman gameplay description illustrates some of these intricacies. It is wrought with historical references and counterfactual outcomes simultaneously. The game world is recognisable as Early Modern period based on the names of provinces, battles and rulers. The core conflicts are grounded in familiar historical events and yet, none of the agents behave in a, strictly speaking, historical way. The opponents – the AIs' – behaviours are, as I will show in the following chapters, designed based on the behaviours of historical entities, but the AI's objective is also to be a good gameplay opponent. As such, the game is what I would call predictably unpredictable and can take many forms. The nature of this design, then, is dictated by the push and pull between creative and strategic behaviour, and the constraints of a coherent system. As I will argue throughout the book, this coherency is in itself complex, and builds not only on gameplay values, but on design convention, understandings of historical culture, as well as the pragmatic context of the game industry.

Release and Reception of *Europa Universalis IV*

Europa Universalis IV was released in August 2013. According to a press release from the Paradox Interactive website, in its first few months, *Europa Universalis IV* sold approximately 300,000 copies. The user base continued to grow and in June 2017 Paradox announced that the core game had sold over one million copies.[61] The game was generally well received by reviewers and received a Metacritic score of 87/100.[62] Critics in 2013 agreed that *Europa Universalis IV* was the most accessible and rewarding game in the series thus far. To name a few examples, Australian PC gaming magazine *Hyper Magazine* notes, "For all its depth, it is also Paradox's most accessible game to date."[63] Along the same lines, *IGN Italia* writes: "Another great and extremely deep strategy game from Paradox, *Europa Universalis IV* is better than the previous instalment in every single aspect and it's got enough content to go on playing for years."[64] Some critics, however, point out that while *Europa Universalis IV* is easier to learn and play than *Europa Universalis III*, it is still a very detailed and very complex game, and some of the changes appeared to make "no sense" concerning the way history works in the game.[65] Players and reviewers alike noted that the game now harboured inconsistencies and dissonance between gameplay and design. In other words, player actions did not seem to correspond well enough with the expected outcomes.

Upon release, the most notable changes between *Europa Universalis III* and *Europa Universalis IV* were mechanics and UI changes intended to make the rule-

---

61 Paradox Interactive, "Paradox Interactive Announces Grand Success for Grand Strategy Titles." Press release, June 21, 2017. Numbers do not include expansion packs or downloadable content.
62 Metacritic.com is a site that collects and combines reviews and ratings for different kinds of media, including games.
63 Hyper Magazine review, as listed by Metacritic, *Europa Universalis IV*, accessed June 30, 2021, https://www.metacritic.com/game/pc/europa-universalis-iv/critic-reviews.
64 IGN Italia review, as listed by Metacritic, *Europa Universalis IV*.
65 Tobias Garsten, "Europa Universalis IV," *Game Reactor*, August 26, 2013, accessed June 30, 2021, https://www.gamereactor.se/recensioner/120054/Europa+Universalis+IV.

sets more transparent.⁶⁶ The underlying idea was that players needed to be able to decode the logic of the game and the consequences of their actions more easily than in previous games. Consequently, players would learn to manipulate the different game mechanics more effectively. To facilitate this need, Paradox abstracted parts of the design. One example of this is the monarch power system, the design of which I will go into in detail further into this chapter. To players and reviewers, the monarch power and point system was a controversial change from *Europa Universalis III* because some players had a hard time grasping what historical factors, or "currency," the points were supposed to represent. As a user called Taure on the Paradox forums puts it: "To reduce unrest within your nation you don't really have to change anything about the way you behave as a player. You just have to save up [points] and dump them into stability."⁶⁷ In other words, the unrest does not encourage interesting choices. Monarch power quickly gained the nickname mana points,⁶⁸ which in generic game jargon refers to magic fuel and resource management system. Originally inspired by anthropological writings on indigenous Pacific cultures and languages, used in 1960s fantasy novels and made popular through table-top roleplaying game *Dungeons and Dragons*, mana denotes the metaphorical cost of casting spells.⁶⁹ The nickname was intentionally meant to be joking and unflattering, and played off the contrast of *Europa Universalis* games having been broadly considered among the most detailed, literal and historically realistic games on the market. In that light, the reference to mana emphasises that this system seems ahistorical.

On the one hand, voices in the game's community noted that while developers may change and exclude what they perceive to be historical or not as necessary, the games should remain in a certain style: conventional and realistic enough to convey a sense of historical verisimilitude. In turn, developers should avoid venturing into abstract designs that detract from the "real" historical experience. On the other hand, the design move – ultimately a shift towards a more mainstream audience – likely paid off for the studio. It is worth noting that while

---

66 Chris Salt, "The History and Future of Paradox Grand Strategy Interview with Johan Andersson," *Space Sector*, February 7, 2014, accessed July 1, 2021, https://www.spacesector.com/blog/2014/02/the-history-and-future-of-paradox-grand-strategy/.
67 Paradox Plaza, *EU4 without monarch points* by Taure, December 30, 2017, accessed April 16, 2018, https://forum.paradoxplaza.com/forum/index.php?threads/eu4-without-monarch-points.1062864/.
68 Johan Andersson and Martin Anward, *Europa Universalis IV – An alternate history of the game* (video resource, 2019).
69 Alex Golub and Jon Peterson, "How Mana Left the Pacific and Became a Video Game Mechanic," in *New Mana: Transformations of a Classic Concept in Pacific Languages and Cultures*, ed. Matt Tomlinson and Ty P. Kāwika Tengan (Canberra: ANU Press, 2016), 321–331.

Europa Universalis IV and other Paradox games are successful entities, the grand strategy genre is relatively niche, and Paradox Development Studio enjoys a position as one of only a few developers of this type of game in this range of sales. From this point of view, game sales in the seven-figures is a tall feat and considered a success. The release and reception of *Europa Universalis IV* exposes the tension and balancing act between convention and innovation, game culture expectations and exploring new territories. It can be argued that it is a defining feature of many design and marketing decisions made about history in games. This is certainly true at Paradox Development Studio, as it will be a prominent topic throughout this book.

Starting a Game

Your starting point in *Europa Universalis IV* is decided by the following two choices: at which point along the game's timeline do you wish to start, and as which playable state, nation or country? It is possible to start a game at any day, month and year between November 11, 1444 and January 3, 1821, although the game offers a selection of prepared dates and scenarios. As such, the player is presented with a set of curated historical paths quite early on. The scenarios correspond to certain events, or particularly influential processes, such as for example 1453 and The Fall of Byzantium, 1618 and the Thirty Years War, 1776 and the American War of Independence, and 1789 and The French Revolution.[70] Each of these specific scenarios are also connected to a relevant playable nation, though the player can choose to play as any region on the map.

The earliest available starting date is attributed to when the Battle of Varna took place, a battle that effectively ended an ongoing war between the Ottomans and an alliance of Wladyslaw III, Bohemia, Lithuania, Poland, the Teutonic Knights and Hungary.[71] The end date denotes the end of the Napoleonic era. In normal game mode players may continue after the official end date if they so choose, but there is very little by way of designed content (events, missions, technological development and so on) past that point. In Ironman mode, the game ends in 1821 regardless. Ironman mode means that the game only saves a player's current progress, and that the player is able to unlock so-called Achievements. Achievements is an important goal-setting mechanic that will be discussed in more detail in chapter three. In Ironman mode, it is not possible to

---

70 Paradox Wikis, *Europa Universalis IV: Scenarios*.
71 Paradox Wikis, *Europa Universalis IV: Scenarios*.

Figure 2: Starting screen. Highlighted statistics and national ideas for France in 1492. Cropped screenshot reproduced with permission. *Europa Universalis IV.* Patch 1.28.3.

save incrementally, which means the player is prevented from going back to earlier points in the game to, for example, have additional attempts at encounters or choices. As the name perhaps suggests, Ironman mode is generally viewed as considerably more challenging than normal mode.

The *Europa Universalis IV* start menu provides the starting conditions for each playable nation (see Figure 2). This gives the player an idea of the state of affairs in the chosen playable nation, and what some of the most important elements currently influencing the playable nation are. Who is the ruler? Which is its dominating religion? What is the format of the current administration, and the size of its military power? It also gives the player a sample of predominant national ideas in the current time and place. National ideas is a mechanic that represents important ideas, ideologies, technological development, religious movements, etc., that influence the specific nature and character of a playable nation. Numbers that denote progression levels, i.e. the size and advancement of forts, the treasury and the size of the playable nation at any given date, are indicated on the starting screen as well. Experienced players might also take neighbouring countries into consideration – who they are and what their goals might be.

As an example, the game tells us that Castile makes an interesting starting nation in 1492 due to the Europeans' encountering "the New World." Starting here gives the player a chance to build a powerful and rich playable Spain over the coming centuries – provided they follow a path of historical verisimilitude. For a player who is perhaps more interested in inter-European politics and military going into the 1500s, the game lets us know that France is a good choice. Playable France is relatively large, it has a stable ruler and a handy baseline for prodding and poking at diplomatic, military and cultural relationships within Europe. That is, until Castile comes knocking, funded by the spoils of colonial expansion.

Each playable nation has a specific framing in the game and while utilising the emphasised historical characteristics and events of a state, nation or country is often beneficial towards playing a powerful and game-logic appropriate session, *Europa Universalis IV* does not come with specific end-game goals. The game may suggest that you start playing as France but whether the goal is to set up and play through the French Revolution or do something else entirely – that is the player's choice. Thus, setting and defining aims is effectively an aspect of gameplay and largely in the hands of the player. However, the game has at least two mechanics that help guide the player towards rewarding challenges and end games: missions and achievements. Both categories are also heavily comprised of counterfactual scenarios. Firstly, each country has a mission tree that represents a series of specific tasks that players may choose to take on. These can range from building a set of military buildings to exploring and conquering specific provinces.[72] Missions are a form of waypoints that provide the player with tutorial quests as well as more tangible, challenging goals. Missions both help players reproduce actual historical events and can suggest specific counterfactual scenarios that are designed into the game. Fulfilling mission criteria also gives players some reward, such as a better diplomatic reputation or a legitimising claim to ruling a specific region. Secondly, achievements are scenario descriptors that, similarly to missions, come with a set of criteria and win conditions and that players may use as inspiration and goals for their games.[73]

Game World in *Europa Universalis IV*

The *Europa Universalis IV* main view is reminiscent of an old map to invoke a historical feel. The colour scheme is stylised, and the text has the appearance of handwriting. Continents are closer together, and islands like Great Britain

---

[72] See for example *Europa Universalis IV*. Missions. building_alliances. 00_Generic_Missions.txt. v1.28.3.
[73] Paradox Wikis, *Europa Universalis IV: Achievements*.

Figure 3: Terrain map mode, provinces, sea and terra incognita. Cropped screenshot. Reproduced with permission.

or Japan are depicted as slightly larger than in reality. Playable nations consist of a number of provinces outlined with borders and painted in each nation's particular colours. Seas and larger bodies of water are also divided into sections (see Figure 3). Variations in the landscape like forests, steppes and mountains are illustrated on the map, symbolically and disproportional to their actual size. At the beginning of a new game, large portions of the map will be covered in the grey clouds of terra incognita – a way to illustrate an imagined lack of information that the inhabitants of the playable nation possess regarding the rest of the world.

Each province has a designated size and can contain a certain number of buildings that the player is able to construct. The province's status and capacity denote what kind of buildings can be built there, for example marketplaces, places of worship and town halls.[74] As they are built and time passes, the image of the town changes, reflecting the size and importance of that particular place. The illustrations are strictly symbolic and informational – any gameplay relating to construction of buildings or development of provinces take place in their respective interface tabs. As military units are produced, they too are illustrated by avatars resembling the typical soldier of the particular playable nation in the chosen

---

[74] See *Europa Universalis IV*. History. Provinces. v1.28.3.

Figure 4: Military units and town avatar close-ups. Cropped screenshot. *Europa Universalis IV.* Patch 1.28.3. Reproduced with permission.

era, most notably by wearing period clothing and equipment, and carrying that nation's banner. Military units appear differently depending on their role as infantry, cavalry and artillery units. Normally, one figure of each type represents a larger unit of troops of that type as the player divides them into manageable armies. The same principle applies for naval units such as heavy ships and light ships, which all have different appearances so as to easily be distinguishable from one another.

Animation in the game is limited to troops and fleets. Idle units are animated to look like they are standing around waiting for orders. Traveling units appear as if they are walking or riding in place until the next turn when they are teleported to the next point on their route. Whenever the player wants to move units across the map, the game will show the given route using arrows on the map. If the army is moving into enemy territory, the arrow will be painted red. If not, the arrow remains golden. If the army cannot traverse or walk into a province, a red crossed marker will be pictured. While fighting, the avatars are animated to look like they are using their weapons on their opponents, stabbing and shooting (see figure 4).

At its primary level, the user interface frames the screen over the map itself (see Figure 5). From here, the player can access the top bar, the mini-map, the map-modes and the outliner. The outliner is a box of text that summarises the

38 —— Chapter One: Opening up the Design

Figure 5: Uncropped screenshot. Overview of game interface. Reproduced with permission.

game so far. The mini-map is a smaller version of the main map that allows the player to move the game camera focus quickly and more easily to any part of the world. The map-mode bar has four main buttons, which correspond to four different ways to view the world map: a diplomatic layer, a geographic layer, a political layer and an economic layer. Available from the same menu there is a subset of about 40 map-modes that can colour the map according to specific requirements such as culture, dynasty, weather, trade value and more. The top bar contains the most vital buttons and tabs for gameplay. This is where the player can access information about their nation, its relationships, incomes and so on, as well as take action to modify and develop their nation as they see fit. The top bar also provides access to the country interface and shows the player their available resources.

The country interface is where the player goes to make most of their vital decisions in the game. Here, the player can both acquire information and act. For example, the diplomacy tab shows the player which AI-controlled nations are currently friendly or hostile towards them and allows them to appoint political advisors as well as name rivals amongst neighbouring regions to manipulate these relationships. Having rivals grants power projection, which in turn is an important aspect to justify going to war and increasing morale among the people. The economy tab tells the player what the financial state of the playable nation is, how many loans they have and where they might be able to save or redirect funds. Positive numbers are displayed in green, negative numbers in red.

Figure 6: Cropped screenshot from *Europa Universalis IV*, depicting early-game progress, highlighting administrative power. Reproduced with permission.

Additionally, the game has a flagging system so that urgent situations requiring player input are highlighted just below the top bar.

Mechanics and Gameplay Overview

Together, the map and interface make up the main space in which the player plays *Europa Universalis IV*. Notions of progress and decline, short- and long-term goal fulfilment, material and human assets – these are all illustrated and conveyed through a symbolic and abstract design that grants the player the ability to understand and master layers of interacting systems.

The fundamentals of gameplay in *Europa Universalis IV* are internal country management and external relations, economy, war and technology. Internal country management is the largest mechanics category in the game. The player must manage their internal affairs alongside the external ones to be successful. For example, the provinces mechanic makes up the framework for collecting taxes or producing trade power, i.e. generating resources or other benefits (illustrated by Figure 6). To maintain a high standing internally, the player may need to adjust the tax burden to minimise unrest. To obtain more provinces and thus expand the number of resources available, the player needs to engage with related mechanics. For example, the player may go the economic route and spend ducats on the military in order to invade a province. Alternatively, they may go the diplomatic route and spend administration points on a war declaration to gobble up an opponent. The external relations category includes mechanics such as espionage, diplomacy, prestige and subject nations – all things related to the player-nation's position on the map, literally and strategically. It dictates the established political structures in the game (such as the Papacy and Holy Roman Empire), as well as the different types of relations available (such as Personal union or Subject nation). These are used to determine the relation between the player nation and the AI opponents, and dictates behaviour based on compatibility and expected AI behaviour towards different factions.

To simulate power and agency, the game combines material and immaterial resources into a quantifiable category called monarch power. The game progresses when the player spends monarch power in three varieties: diplomatic power, military power and administrative power. The pool of available monarch power is refilled slowly, so the player must spend it wisely. The speed at which monarch power regenerates can be manipulated through strategic gameplay choices. Monarch power cannot purchase military units or refill the country treasury directly, i.e. it is not a fiscal currency. However, monarch points can be used to develop ideas and make decisions, which in turn may lead to rewards and benefits that tie into any of the other game systems such as war and technology. This broad dependency on monarch power is indeed the basis of the "mana" nickname, as discussed in the release and reception segment.

The economy category breaks down into economy, taxation, production, trade, development, colonisation and trade goods mechanics. Economy management in *Europa Universalis IV* is about making strategic decisions on a macro level. The player does no actual bartering in the game. Rather, gameplay consists of managing trade routes (where goods go and where the player profits the most from trading), assigning merchants to trade nodes (representatives on site, trading on your playable nation's behalf), developing markets at home (building marketplaces in one's provinces) and increasing income through colonisation. The playable nation's income is used to pay for upkeep, provincial buildings and production. Production, in turn, is heavily tilted towards military expansion. Most economic investments go towards building an army.

The technology category of mechanics breaks down into technology, National ideas, idea groups and institutions. National ideas, as previously mentioned, are specific attributes that help define each playable nation. Idea groups consist of conceptual tendencies, or predispositions for a player to pursue, such as administration or military. Idea groups are unlocked using monarch power. Ideas give perks such as lowering the costs of production, increased diplomatic power, increased discipline amongst soldiers and so on.[75] Ideas also able to start events. Events as a design feature inform the player of developments in the game, oftentimes requiring some kind of input from the player, therefore framing decision-making and contingency in the game. The use and configuration of event criteria will be discussed in more detail later in this chapter and in chapters 4 and 5 because they helpfully expose the imagined causality required to successfully pursue scenarios.

The war mechanics control and support military actions on a macro as well as micro level in the game, and, as such, they are central to all conquest and national expansion aspects. These mechanics control the size and scope of the military forces, including maritime warfare (for example manpower, army, navy, military leaders and land units -mechanics). They also enforce the limits of diplomacy and what constitutes a *casus belli*, a justification for initiating a war (for example the claim, alliance and power projection mechanics).[76]

To summarise, then, *Europa Universalis IV* offers the player agency as a playable nation in a web of political, diplomatic, mercantile, cultural and religious mechanics to depict the material and immaterial basis for technological development, and acquisition of power in the Early Modern world. For all its complexity however, all these layers of gameplay flow towards the same overarching principle: the survival and expansion of the playable nation. The multitude of choices available to the player exist in support of these goals, which, in turn, are usually components in a host of possible gameplay goals. Whilst present in the game, societal aspects such as culture are less emphasised aspects of gameplay and, ultimately, also tie into the war and expansion machinery. It is technically possible to survive and expand without going to war, for example, by seeking out opportune marriages. However, this is complicated by the fact that beneficial marriages usually require high levels of prestige, which, in turn, is partly gained by going to war. I here suggest that the systemic framing of content in *Europa Universalis IV* is in fact less complex than the multiplicity of content leads us to think at face value. As will be discussed in depth further on, this design has significant implications for what arguments *Europa Universalis IV*, and, to a point, *Hearts of Iron IV*, can make.

---

75 *Europa Universalis IV.* Common. Ideas. v1.28.3. For the idea groups attributed to each nation, see *Europa Universalis IV.* Common. Countries. v1.28.3.
76 *Europa Universalis IV.* Common. cb_types. 00_cb_types.txt. v1.28.3.

Hearts of Iron IV – Camo Greens and Industrial Skylines

Gameplay journal: Germany. August 1939.

The game has been mostly predictable and smooth sailing. Till now. My diplomatic relationships are fast deteriorating. Austria was annexed in 1938 as expected. Since the initial set-up for the War, which has yet to fully develop, I have focused primarily on maintaining military resources. I built industries in most of my provinces, increasing the manpower available. To support them I have traded goods and started to research, develop, and build equipment for the land-troops and the navy. I ordered the continued infrastructure effort, which includes building the Autobahn. And the Autobahn, the game tells me, guarantees respite from acute unemployment and civil unrest in Germany. It clearly also offers political bonuses, and my country's stability is high, reflecting a significant support for the government.

Now clouds are starting to form on the horizon. Sometime soon, the Soviet Union will probably attack. This eastern giant has been rather quiet since the beginning of the game. Just moments ago, however, they rejected my proposal for a digital Molotov-Ribbentrop pact, which means I can no longer count on them sitting by placidly in the East for the next two years. To be honest, I would rather not be in this position, but the game – chance, if you will – had a different idea.

At this point, my goal still is to win the war by achieving the following, somewhat arbitrary victory condition: conquering each of the major Western powers: The United States, Great Britain and mainland Europe, including Romania and Bulgaria. My initial strategy was to build a strong Germany and enter the Ribbentrop-Molotov pact with the Soviet Union. History tells me this should pacify them for a considerable amount of time while they focus on acquiring territory in Eastern Europe. Meanwhile, I would try to boost the fascists' political power in the United States, hoping they would eventually get elected. Utilising this counterfactual scenario would hopefully undermine the importance and threat of anti-fascist Allies and pave the way for conquering each of the world powers in turn. Considering that the Soviet Union has already decided not to trust the German government enough to enter a non-aggression pact with me, I shall have to rethink this plan.

It seems I am doing well in terms of building and maintaining my German army, but I know from experience that an army alone will not win me the game. I will have to make some powerful friends and clever moves to be able to achieve the goals I have set for myself. I notice that Greece and Italy are increasingly restless. While these things should not have an immediate effect on my long-term plan, I worry about the possible effect they might have on world tension, which makes it harder to act for everyone. As I consider making a move on Poland that will effectively throw the game into the Second World War, I wonder if my preparation has been enough to face an aggressive Soviet Union and deal with global unrest at the same time.

If *Europa Universalis IV* is a game of historical scope, multiplicity and breadth, *Hearts of Iron IV* is a focused game about a very specific scenario. The conflict is, of course, the Second World War, and the mechanics of the game tie directly into it. In comparison to *Europa Universalis IV*, the player here has a more granular level of control, but the central conflict is clearly defined, and the player is offered a limited set of paths to explore it. While war and colonial expansion are a near-given in *Europa Universalis IV*, there are only a handful of specific events and outcomes in the game that are guaranteed to happen. In *Hearts of Iron IV*, however, a conflict like the Second World War will happen every time. The player is tasked with navigating the path leading up to it and, as the game progresses, participating in it by anticipating and reacting to ally and rival behaviours along the way. Similarly to *Europa Universalis IV*, many available interactions tie into military and economic factors but are supplemented by obstacles in the political and diplomatic arena.

Release and Reception of *Hearts of Iron IV*

Hearts of Iron IV was released on June 6, 2016, not incidentally the same date as the Normandy landings in 1944. The game was highly anticipated, and pre-sales and early sales made it the most successful Paradox Development Studio game release ever at the time.[77] The game had sold two million copies by October 2019.[78] The first game ever in the series, *Hearts of Iron*, was released in 2002, followed by *Hearts of Iron II* in 2005 and *Hearts of Iron III* in 2009. The gaming public received the game mostly positively. As of August 2019, the game has a Metacritic score of 83.[79] While *Hearts of Iron IV*, like most Paradox Development Studio titles, did receive some criticism on its complexity and steep learning curve, it was still generally considered reasonably easy to pick up and fun to play.[80]

---

[77] Paradox Interactive, "Paradox Interactive Announces Grand Success for Grand Strategy Titles," 2017.
[78] Dan Lind, *Hearts of Iron IV: News From the Front* (video resource, 2019).
[79] Metacritic, *Hearts of Iron IV*, accessed June 30, 2021, https://www.metacritic.com/game/pc/hearts-of-iron-iv/critic-reviews.
[80] Leana Hafer "Hearts of Iron 4 review," *IGN Magazine*, June 6, 2016, accessed October 22, 2018, https://www.ign.com/articles/2016/06/06/1558481; Luke Plunkett, "Hearts of Iron IV: The

Following the general accessibility curve for Paradox Development Studio games in the last ten years – i.e. making games that are lower-threshold and more attractive to new audiences outside of their traditional core demographic – designers specifically developed *Hearts of Iron IV* to have better, more understandable AI and to follow a more coherent logic than *Hearts of Iron III*. For this reason, designers kept the faction mechanic – the option for players to align with one of the ideological factions of the Second World War – and introduced new individual focus trees for each playable nation in an attempt to streamline the gameplay experience.[81] As the *Hearts of Iron IV* game director Dan Lind writes in an early developer diary on Paradox Plaza:

> Our goal for *Hearts of Iron IV* is to do something similar to what we did with *Crusader King II* [sic] and *Europa Universalis IV* – keep the flavour and complexity of the game intact while making the game much more streamlined and easier to learn, with much improved interfaces. We also aim for a fresh playing experience so there will be changes from the previous game.[82]

Initial game reviews confirmed that efforts had been made to encourage more players of different player backgrounds to play *Hearts of Iron IV*, although the game was still challenging in typical Paradox fashion. In a mostly positive review, Charlie Hall of gaming journal *Paragon* elaborated on history itself as an aspect of the game's difficulty level, saying: "*Hearts of Iron 4* has challenged what I know about history, about military strategy and about mid-twentieth-century geopolitics. With *Hearts of Iron 4*, Paradox has dared to allow players to feel stupid. It's a gamble that pays off."[83] According to the review, Hall's biggest takeaway from the game is the flexibility and counterfactual playing field that *Hearts of Iron IV* offers the player. He says that the complexity of the game and the amount of detail seems almost inconceivable and argues that the way to fully understand what goes on was trial and error and to become a student of historical fact – knowledge he anticipates will be applicable to future gameplay.[84]

Kotaku Review," *Kotaku*, June 6, 2016, accessed December 2, 2018, https://kotaku.com/hearts-of-iron-iv-the-kotaku-review-1780258434.

81 Dan Lind, *PDXCON 2017: Hearts of Iron: Making a World War Even Bigger* (video resource, 2017).

82 Paradox Plaza. *Our Vision* by podcat. *Hearts of Iron IV* Developer Diary, February 7, 2014, accessed June 12, 2019, https://forum.paradoxplaza.com/forum/index.php?threads/hearts-of-iron-iv-development-diary-1-our-vision.754427/.

83 Charlie Hall, "Hearts of Iron IV Review," *Polygon*, July 19, 2016, accessed December 2, 2018, https://www.polygon.com/2016/7/19/12215976/hearts-of-iron-4-review.

84 Charlie Hall, "Hearts of Iron IV Review."

Another perspective on the discussion about *Hearts of Iron IV* leaning into complexity and counterfactuals came from reviewer and game writer Matthew Hung at gaming journal *Gamespew*, who considered the flexibility in gameplay and counterfactual focus problematic. In his review, Hung expressed concern about what he perceived to be a lack of impact of his actions. He noted that the amount of control the player has over their internal affairs and army building translates poorly into an interesting role to play in the grander conflict of the Second World War.[85] In other words, he felt there were not enough interesting consequences to his actions, a notable similarity to the reception of *Europa Universalis IV*. Hung especially commented on the role and functionality of the AI, which also received criticism from the player community. His complaints were mainly about the AI's occasional inability to play out actions in sync with what he as a player was doing and saw its actions as often illogical and incomprehensible. The AI was described as making detrimental decisions both as an in-game entity and as an ally to the human player.[86]

While some lamented the unpredictability of the game, it seems it was intentional. In early development, Lind explained that "one of the core ideas in *Hearts of Iron IV* is that historical hindsight should be less of an advantage compared to *Hearts of Iron III*."[87] As described by one of the Paradox beta testers, the shift away from hindsight in design focus made gameplay easier for new players since the game now relied more heavily on creating their own battle plans regardless of previous historical knowledge. Simultaneously, this put experienced players in a frustrating position where they would lose control of an otherwise historically thought-out session, due to the AI acting in what felt like an unpredictable, or un-historical, way.

In line with Paradox Interactive's model for long-term development of their grand strategy titles (see chapter three), four major expansions have been released between the original game's release in 2016 and the time of this study: *Together For Victory* (2016), *Death or Dishonor* (2017), *Waking the Tiger* (2018) and *Man the Guns* (2019).[88] Each expansion and DLC focuses on historically sig-

---

85 Richard Hung, "Hearts of Iron Review," *Gamespew*, June 7, 2016, accessed May 26, 2019, https://www.gamespew.com/2016/06/hearts-iron-iv-review/.
86 Jack Trumbull, "Hearts of Iron IV is better than ever but its remaining flaws are becoming more obvious," *Wargamer*, March 7, 2019, accessed July 20, 2019, https://www.wargamer.com/articles/hearts-of-iron-4-1-6-ironclad-ww2/.
87 Andrei Dumitrescu, "Exclusive Hearts of Iron IV Interview with Project Lead Dan Lind," *Softpedia*, March 3, 2014, accessed July 20, 2019, https://news.softpedia.com/news/Exclusive-Hearts-of-Iron-IV-Interview-with-Project-Lead-Dan-Lind-430287.shtml.
88 A fifth expansion called *La Résistance* was released on February 25, 2020.

nificant and eventful regions (Great Britain, Eastern Europe, China and the United States, respectively). They also come with new national focus trees, mechanics and updates, including balance and AI tweaks and bug fixes.

In considering the development of *Hearts of Iron IV* over time, then, we note that the game struggled with finding its balance initially. Where *Europa Universalis IV* had attempted to simplify the user interface and certain mechanics to make the game more accessible, *Hearts of Iron IV* had gone a similar route but by diverging from the perceived robust accuracy in previous games. By embracing counterfactual history as a design method to engage players in creative and imaginative gameplay, *Hearts of Iron VI*, in part, challenged the core demographic by straying from its previously strict historical focus. However, by continuing development (a notable feature of Paradox Development Studio as will be discussed in-depth in chapter three) the game attempts to reconcile between complexity on the one hand and flexibility in gameplay on the other. As an example, three years and four expansions after the game's original release, Jack Trumbull, writer for *Wargamer.co*m, while still critical of the game's historical depth, comments on some improvements in *Hearts of Iron IV*. With the expansions and updates to the original game, he writes "the AI, while not quite at the level of being a master strategist, is leaps and bounds ahead of where it was at launch."[89]

Starting a New Game

Hearts of Iron IV starts from one of two possible scenarios about the road to the Second World War; one beginning in 1936 and one in 1939. The first scenario allows the player to prepare and manipulate international relationships for a longer period, while the second promptly starts the war with almost no build-up. After this the player is prompted to pick a country to lead in the chosen scenario. Each selectable country comes with a brief history and an overview, which states the current leader, ideology and government type; when the next expected election is meant to happen; and which ruling party is currently steering the country. At the top of the screen is a flag denoting the selected country and a calendar showing the chosen date.

---

[89] Jack Trumbull, "Hearts of Iron IV is better than ever but its remaining flaws are becoming more obvious," *Wargamer.com*, March 7, 2019 (updated May 6, 2021), accessed July 6, 2021, https://legacy.wargamer.com/hearts-of-iron-4-1-6-ironclad-ww2/.

Figure 7: Starting screen of *Hearts of Iron IV*. Uncropped screenshot. Reproduced with permission.

At the bottom right, the player may edit the difficulty of the game: whether they want to play in Ironman mode or not and whether the AI shall use historical focuses or not. Again, Ironman mode means that the game only saves current progress, and the player is unable to return to previous points in their game.

Historical focus trees look and function similarly to mission trees in *Europa Universalis IV*. The focus trees have a number of branches with objectives corresponding to certain goals, accomplishments or developments that come with bonuses or new opportunities. If a playable nation does not have its own, designed national focus tree, the generic one is used. In the generic tree, for example, the army effort branch gives bonuses to army research and development. The political effort branch allows the player to take their nation down one of the four ideological paths: democratic, fascist, communist or liberal. Each ideology has a series of sub-ideologies, which come with their own modifiers and traits. For example, communist countries have a trait that allows them to impose their ideology on other countries after occupying them. Fascist countries, on the other hand, have a trait that will prevent them from doing the same. The ideology feature has overarching ramifications for other aspects of the game, including

- what technologies a player is able to research (and thus what weapons they are able to produce),

- what alliances they are able to join (and who they are able to rely on for help),
- what trade deals they are able to make (what resources are made available to them), and
- which conscription laws they can pass (only communist and fascist countries are able to pass the mobilisation laws "Extensive conscription" and "Service by requirement"[90]).[91]

The AI is set to utilise the historical focus trees to determine how they play. As a default, the AI will not be bound to use historical focuses but instead rely on scripted probability when picking objectives and focuses. "Historical mode" is the term used to describe the game mode in which the AI picks focuses from the national focus tree in what is described by developers as "an as close to historically accurate path as possible."[92] In other words, the AI will make its choices to represent the actors and events of the past, mostly disregarding alternate paths and counterfactuals. For example, the German national focus tree has a branch called "Oppose Hitler" that tends towards dethroning Adolf Hitler and allows for Germany to become democratic. An AI using historical focuses will leave Hitler in power every time. A default AI with counterfactual options will, instead rely on a set of scripted options available to it, and pick them based on scripted probability and in response to the choices other playable nations are making at the same time.

At the start screen, the player is also able to manually adjust the strength of each major opposing nation. The player can choose to play as any country on the map, but some countries, such as the primary belligerent nations, enjoy a more elaborate design and unique personality, expressed most notably by the specificity and detail offered in the national focus trees.[93] After setting the starting pa-

---

90 *Hearts of Iron IV.* Ideas: mobilization_laws. _manpower.txt. v1.6.2.
91 Paradox Wikis, *Hearts of Iron: Ideology.*
92 Developer informant Daryl (June 26, 2017).
93 Paradox Wiki, *Hearts of Iron IV: National Focus.* For the original release of *Hearts of Iron IV* the following playable nations received a national focus tree: France, Germany, Italy, Japan, Poland, Soviet Union, United Kingdom, United States. At the time of writing, the following playable nations have received trees available in one of the available DLCs: *Together for Victory:* generic tree (for all other nations), Australia, British Raj, Canada, New Zealand, South Africa; *Death or Dishonor:* Czechoslovakia, Hungary, Romania, Yugoslavia; *Waking the Tiger:* China, Communist China, Manchukuo, Chinese Warlords; *Man the Guns:* Mexico, Netherlands. For an in-depth look at national focus trees in *Hearts of Iron IV* and the way they disseminate partial understandings of the origin of the Second World War, see Michael John Pennington, "Authentic-Lite Rhetoric:

Figure 8: *Hearts of Iron IV* political view on the left. Centre screen: note the map design, including outlined provinces and their terrain textures (forest, plains, etc.). Screenshot reproduced with permission.

rameters of the game, the player presses the "Start" button at the bottom right to begin playing.

The overarching task of the player is to manage the playable nation's path through the years 1936–1948 or 1939–1948 depending on the chosen scenario. The game world is mirrored in the user interface through tables and clickable buttons that correspond to acts of resource management, and political, diplomatic and ideological strategizing. The year 1948 is advertised as the game's end date because there is only a limited amount of content that a player will encounter after this date. If all major wars are resolved, a score screen is displayed ranking player and AI nations based on their performance in the game. However, just like with *Europa Universalis IV*, "end date" is slightly misleading because the player can opt to continue the game past the score screen and go on playing for as long as they can or want to, although there will be significantly less content triggering after 1948. There are a few exceptions, like for example the Improved Jet Fighter air unit that becomes available in 1950 (or earlier, depending on modifiers).[94]

The Curation of Partial Historical Interpretations in *Hearts of Iron IV*" (PhD. Diss., Bath Spa University, 2021).
94 *Hearts of Iron IV*. Common. Units. Equipment. single_enginge_airframe.txt. *jet_fighter_equipment_2.* v1.6.2.

At the top left of the main screen, the player finds their nation's flag, which reveals the Government tab (more on this further into the chapter). To the right of the flag, the top bar contains counters for the metaphorical resources that must be acquired and spent to produce and maintain the war machine in the game. These resources are known as political power, stability, war support, manpower, factories, fuel, convoys and command power. The top bar also has counters for the experience army, navy and air units have obtained so far in the game. Gained experience in each category translates to points which can be spent to upgrade any type of unit in each category. Experience can also be spent on doctrines – technological research focuses which allow military forces to specialise their traits, for example in terms of mobility. On the top right of the screen is a globe with a percentage meter under it that indicates world tension. World tension is a measurement of how volatile the global situation is at any given moment and functions as a trigger bar for aggressive events and actions. In turn, the world tension level is affected by events and actions.

The buttons underneath the status and resource counters open menus for categories of actions related to running the chosen playable nation. They are government, decision, research, diplomacy, trade, construction, production, army planner and logistics. Opening any of these tabs will reveal a subset of tables and buttons, which the player may manipulate to make changes to their game. Throughout the game, the player will need to interact with these sets of actions to steer the session strategically in the desired direction.

Positioned at mid-bottom of the screen is a box that represents an army group. By dragging and dropping military units to this box, players create and manage their armies into personalised, manageable sizes and formats. This is also where players can assign leaders to their military structures. At the bottom right, the user interface contains a shortcut menu that allows the player to choose between map designs based on what data they would like portrayed on screen. Unlike *Europa Universalis IV*, *Hearts of Iron IV* does not have an actual mini-map. Instead, there are three highlighted strategic map modes, one for each type of military unit – ground-based, naval and air.

Game World and Mechanics in *Hearts of Iron IV*

The map itself is a dynamic illustration of the world and contains a lot of information about the geographical and meteorological conditions as well as the local time for each province. Like in *Europa Universalis IV*, each playable nation consists of a number of provinces, which are outlined, highlighted and painted according to whom they belong (friend or enemy), what their main terrain is and if there are any significant buildings in them.

Terrain and weather are important aspects to gameplay because of the way they affect the speed and efficacy with which military units and supplies are able to move across the map. Weather and terrain are illustrated and lightly animated on the map. The weather changes by the hour. The map will also visually reflect whether it is daytime or night-time. This function can be toggled to allow the game to run more smoothly in which case time of day is not visualised but only reflected in the rules such as unit land speed or air superiority modifiers.

The map also has several animated features that aid and conceptualise aspects of gameplay, such as moving units across the map. Like in *Europa Universalis IV*, transferring units is aided by UI features on the map that highlights the direction of the path and potential obstructions along the way. Alongside this, *Hearts of Iron IV* has an offensive lines and front feature that allows the player to establish the position of the frontline at which they would like their army to fight. The frontline feature enables the player to establish the location of frontline war in greater detail and is visible on the map in the form of blue, barbed lines.

The setting of *Hearts of Iron IV* is the Second World War. Unlike *Europa Universalis IV*, which more wholly embodies the notion of open-ended sandbox gameplay, the parameters of the Second World War scenarios in *Hearts of Iron IV* are narrower and already in place. The game is set up so that the likelihood of a world war breaking out is very high. The question is how exactly this scenario is going to play out and how well the player is going to employ the various mechanics in order to survive and win.

In *Hearts of Iron IV* gameplay centres on a logic that always gravitates towards the war machine. The five main categories of mechanics represent the playable nation's material and immaterial power elements. Together these determine how powerful the player army is going to be on the battlefield. In the words of gaming journalist Rob Zacny: "The joy of *Hearts of Iron* is making those high-level compromises between the army you want, the army you have, and the army you can produce."[95] Most actions in the game are steppingstones towards building a strong army. In some cases, like the one Zacny refers to, it is a question of enabling the most beneficial production line to develop optimal equipment manufacturing. In others, the challenge is to join the most advantageous ideological faction, which potentially gives the player some powerful allies. Eventually, it all

---

[95] Rob Zacny, "Hearts of Iron IV Review," June 9, 2016, accessed December 10, 2018, https://www.pcgamer.com/hearts-of-iron-4-review/.

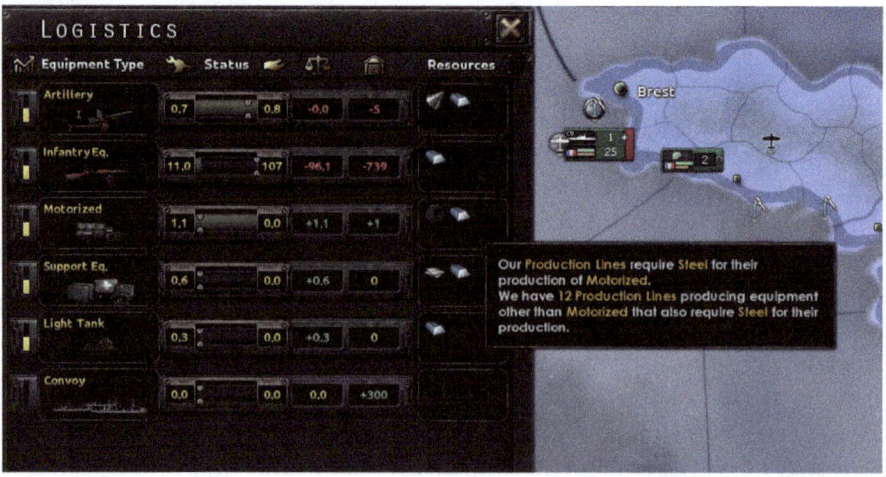

Figure 9: Early game Logistics tab. Tooltip details what materials are currently in demand and how they are distributed between equipment types. Cropped screenshot reproduced with permission 2019 – 06 – 02.

translates into creating the optimal scene for world domination, whether through politics, production, research and technology, military and warfare, or events.

One of the first things a player is likely to do in a game is start production. There are three types: civilian, military and naval production. The interface for civilian factories is where the player manages the production of consumer goods and trade. It is also used for building additional military factories and dockyards, as well as things ranging from infrastructure and fuel silos to nuclear reactors.

By pressing the production button, a player may also begin manufacturing military equipment such as weapons in so-called "production lines." The production tab will then display how many of a certain type of equipment is currently in production, how many of the available factories are devoted to a particular production line and when assembly is likely to be finished. Military equipment production may be sped up by assigning additional factories to a production line. In contrast, naval units like ships and submarines are built one at a time, using dockyards in their construction.

Resources used in production vary over the course of the game. At the beginning of the game, limited amounts of material types are needed. For example, as illustrated by figure 9, most equipment types require steel. Artillery and motorized vehicles also require tungsten and rubber, respectively. As the game progresses, additional resources must be obtained in larger quantities to continue producing army equipment. The player must balance the trade of resources against the cost of production. As their armies grow, the need for continuous support and supply increases. Production is also influenced by production efficiency, which increases over time when producing the same equipment, and is modified by other aspects of gameplay, such as conducting research and political decision-making.

Political power, like monarch power in *Europa Universalis IV*, is a metaphorical resource that indicates the amount of influence the player has over their nation. The player spends political power on actions including law-making, diplomacy, decision-making and hiring commanders to lead armies. For example, if the player wishes to change the conscription law, which heavily influences the amount of available manpower, they would need to spend 150 political power.[96] Political power generates over time, with a baseline of two points per day. The generation speed depends on how powerful the current leader is. For example, playing as Germany, having Adolf Hitler as the country's leader will generate 25 % more political power per day than normal. There are also a number of modifiers to be gained from national statuses such as stability. The greatest amount of political power a player can have at any one time is 2,000 points.[97]

To facilitate technological progress, the player needs to make investments in research and technology. The AI is poised to improve its weapons, vehicles, planes and tanks over time, and the player must do the same to avoid getting overrun. Research is usually a prerequisite for technology – that is, the player must invest time into researching technological advancement before a new and better unit can be produced. The amount of time it takes to research a new technology increases proportionally to how powerful it is. For example, the baseline for researching first tier weapons is 150 days, whereas nuclear technology takes 500 days. The time cost can be decreased by using resources such as political power to invest in research theorists. Or, it can be increased if the player performs an anachronistic act. The latter is known as the "Ahead of time penalty" and is applied when the player tries to develop a technology or piece of equipment before it existed historically. The Ahead of time penalty is 200 % per year and down-scales progressively as the game date closes in on the historical date of production for the item in question.[98]

Warfare mechanics depend upon the country's production and can be broken down into three main types: land, air and naval. Each type requires specific

---

96 *Hearts of Iron IV*. Common. Ideas. _manpower.txt. mobilization_laws. v1.6.2.
97 *Hearts of Iron IV*. Common. Defines: 00_defines.lua. political_power_cap. v1.6.2.
98 *Hearts of Iron IV*. Defines: base_year_ahead_penalty_factor. 00_defines.lua. v1.6.2.

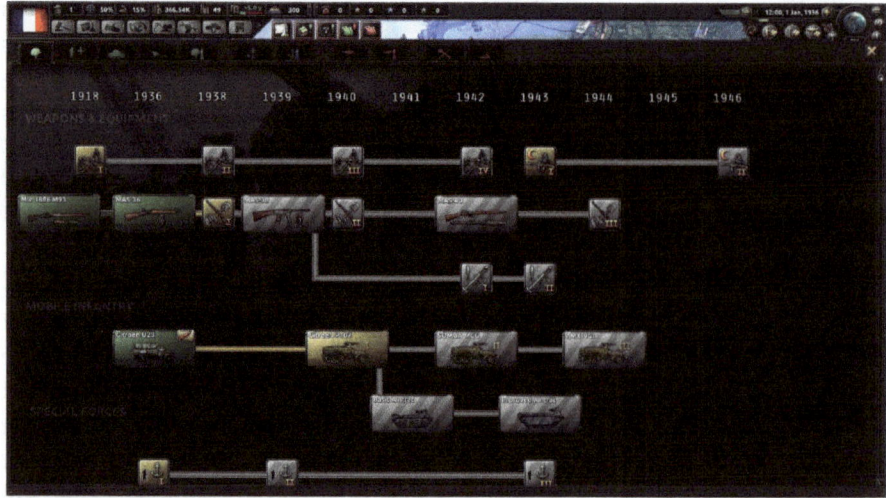

Figure 10: French infantry technology. Options and timeline. Screenshot reproduced with permission 2019 – 06 – 02.

equipment, logistics and skill sets to further advance in the current scenario. Land warfare in *Hearts of Iron IV* is detailed and complex and each unit, army or theatre (larger command groups) will act according to predefined combat tactics, such as attack, shock, ambush, close quarters attack, seize bridge and more.[99] Combat resolves every hour, which gives the player plenty of opportunity to adapt and change tactics depending on how a battle is going. Additionally, the units' ability to perform are influenced by external factors such as weather, terrain, supply, daylight, etc. Air warfare is less detailed, resolves every eight hours and represents air superiority, a statistic which measures how powerful the player's air force is compared to that of the enemy. Air units can perform surveillance, bombings and tactical drops like paratroopers. Finally, naval warfare represents battle at sea. The player builds a fleet, which resides in sea zones that correspond to provinces on land. Fleets can have a variety of tasks like patrolling waters, functioning as strike forces and battling enemy ships when possible or raiding and protecting convoys, depending on their allegiance. Fleets can also support the air force by maintaining aircraft carriers.

---

99 *Hearts of Iron IV.* Localization. tactics_l_english.yml. v1.6.2.

Player Events and AI Events

News and events are, on the one hand, boxes of text with illustrations that present the player with information about what is happening in the world. On the other hand, events are also a mechanic constituting options and progression. Some news and events present the player with choices that will have some effect on the game. For example, events like "The Fall of Leningrad" appear when a player or the AI has taken Leningrad as Germany. The only option given to the player who sees this is to close the window by pressing the button saying "Someone will be shot for this!" and acknowledging the event. The text below is the game's description of the fall of Leningrad, including a description of the event and the button text from the game's localisation files.

> news.103.t:0 "The Fall of Leningrad"
>
> news.103.d:0 "Leningrad, birthplace of the Russian Revolution, has fallen to advancing German forces. \n\nSporadic fighting can still be heard from some suburbs, but a strange calm appears to have settled over the rest of the ruined city.\n\nEarlier today, columns of German soldiers marched past St. Isaac's Cathedral, whose great dome has been painted grey by Red Army engineers to avoid the attention of marauding Luftwaffe bombers. \nDespite their efforts, it is riddled with bullet holes and shrapnel impacts."
>
> news.103.c:0 "Someone will be shot for this!"[100]

Some events force the player to make a decision that can have implications for the continuation of the game, like the example below where AI-controlled France asks player-controlled Britain if France may join the Allies. The player can respond yes or no.

> britain.13.t:0 "France wants to join Allies"
>
> britain.13.d:0 "The world is growing increasingly unsafe. Britain and France remain bastions of democracy and liberty in Europe and France now propose that they join the Allies.\nHow should we reply?"
>
> britain.13.a:0 "Yes"
>
> britain.13.b:0 "No"[101]

These are the kinds of junctions where the game allows overt examination of the moving parts of the war; the interaction between playable nations, as well as the

---

[100] *Hearts of Iron IV*. Localisation. events_l_english.txt. v1.6.2.
[101] *Hearts of Iron IV*. Localisation. events_l_english.txt. v1.6.2.

internal management of the player nation, become tangible whether they are political (as in the example above), economic, or something else entirely. Regardless of the specific mechanic, these interplays are what causes all the contingent events in a gameplay session. Furthermore, designers have allowed for at least one mechanic – the national focus trees – that illustrates the option of more-or-less railroaded counterfactual scenarios. The relationship between generic junctions (emergent stories) and counterfactual history and designed scenarios will be discussed at length in chapter three.

Events present differently depending on whether they happen on the player side or on the AI side of things. For example, news events normally trigger when the player needs to know something has happened but can do nothing about it. News events may trigger as a reaction to something that happens internally in the player nations, but also to notify the player of the actions of AI countries. For example, the Hungarian event chain *Trianon Rapprochement* is triggered by the Hungarian focus "Rapprochement with Little Entente." If the player is playing as either France, Romania, Yugoslavia or Czechoslovakia, they will be presented with the option of accepting or denying the AI Hungary's request for rearmament.[102] Playing as any other nation, for example Spain or China, they will receive a news event noting important incidents related to Hungary's challenge of the Treaty of Trianon as the AI makes its way through the event chain.[103] In these cases, the actions of choice serve as triggers for news events to fire.

The functionality of events and event chains is influenced by how developers and beta testers have chosen to balance historical actuality against counterfactual scenarios in scripting. Playing the default mode (in which the AI can possibly choose counterfactual scenarios, i.e. not historical mode) presents the player with not just the option of going down a counterfactual path themselves, but also responding to the AI doing not-historical things. This is a significant aspect to mastering the game through learning to predict what the AI can do and what its rationale is. Beyond players honing this skill for the sake of strategising, this is where we encounter most of the nuance and details of the available historical and counterfactual paths.

---

102 *Hearts of Iron IV.* Events. DOD_Hungary.txt. *DOD_hungary.30.* v1.6.2.
103 *Hearts of Iron IV.* Localisation. dod_events_l_english.txt. *DOD_hungary.140.* v1.6.2.

Game Scripting and Text – The Rules and Flavour of History

As discussed in the introduction to this book, a typical digital strategy game is inherently, and by-design, suited to presenting a multiplicity of historical processes through gameplay, more so perhaps than presenting singular narratives.[104] In other words, a crucial characteristic of digital strategy games is that gameplay and agency dictate the sequence and, to a point, outcomes of events. This particular design, sometimes called sandbox style, allows for open-ended sessions, sometimes without a clear beginning, middle or end. Gameplay focus is on strategising and resource management. Up to a point, the rules, mechanics and content allow players the opportunity to choose what they want to do within the system provided. Developers as well as game scholars sometimes use the term "emergent stories" to denote this principle of individual story-making and sense-making that happens through play.[105]

However, it is important to note that terms like "sandbox" and "open-endedness" come with their own sets of constraints. A common analogy for this problem is the comparison of having a bucket of randomly assorted LEGO pieces versus one of the pre-planned box sets of LEGO (say, the Police Boat set, or the Medieval Castle). The box set is more likely to produce similar, if not identical, outcomes every time one plays with the LEGO, whist the bucket is more likely to create unique experiences and outcomes. Nevertheless, as argued by philosopher Mary Beth Willard in *LEGO and Philosophy*, true originality – "to have done something that no one has ever done before, and that no one could have anticipated" – is not necessarily achievable.[106] In terms of digital strategy games that rely heavily on historical record, it is not desirable for players to be entirely original or entirely unable to anticipate outcomes of play. There is a balance to be struck between the known and unknown, the predictable and unpredictable. In *Europa Universalis IV* and *Hearts of Iron IV*, this is achieved by providing the player with enough atomistic parts such as contents and mechanics for the player to be creative, but also with enough constraint to make decisions purposeful in the context of the game.

The systemic aspect of this – the causality and outcomes of play – is dictated by programming known as scripting, or scripted content. In other words, histor-

---

104 Chapman, *Digital Games as History*, 127–132.
105 Henrik Fåhraeus, *Emergent Stories in Crusader Kings II* (video resource, 2016); Richard Walsh, "Emergent Narrative in Interactive Media," *Narrative* 19 (2011): 78.
106 Mary Beth Willard, "Constructing Creativity," in *LEGO and Philosophy, Constructing Reality Brick by Brick*, ed. William Irwin, Roy T. Cook and Sondra Bacharach (Hoboken: John Wiley & Sons, 2017), 7–9.

ical development and outcomes in *Europa Universalis IV* and *Hearts of Iron IV* are contingent on design decisions and presented as rules and game logic. The specific likelihood or criteria of a certain outcome is decided within the framework of game design practice, technical as well as historical, as will become clear over the coming chapters.

Furthermore, options, outcomes and consequences are explained and rationalised to players via descriptive text. Textual content such as this is most often presented to the player through events, tooltips and descriptions. This is where contextual details and flavour is provided. "Flavour" is a term used by developers and beta testers to describe content whose function is specifically to dress the gameplay experience in historical tones such as characteristics of cultures, ages or religions, to name a few.

Script language typically looks like the example below. This is from the "Flavor events" file for the playable nation of Portugal in *Europa Universalis IV* and denotes the conditions under which the event "Christopher Columbus" will trigger. The sample below tells us that this is an event that can happen only once under the following criteria: the country (nation tag) must be Portugal and it needs to have at least two exploration ideas running in the game. Columbus must not already have been hired by Portugal. The in-game year must be at least 1470 and North and South America must remain undiscovered by Europeans for the time being. This event will trigger on average one month after the criteria is met.

```
# Christopher Columbus
country_event = {
        id = flavor_por.1
        title = "flavor_por.EVTNAME1"
        desc = "flavor_por.EVTDESC1"
        picture = SHIP_SAILING_eventPicture

        fire_only_once = yes

        trigger = {
                tag = POR
                exploration_ideas = 2
                NOT = { has_global_flag = columbus_happened}
                is_year = 1470
                OR = {
                        NOT = {
                                north_america = {
                                        has_discovered = ROOT
                                }
                        }
```

```
                    NOT = {
                            south_america = {
                                has_discovered = ROOT
                            }
                        }
                    }
                }

            mean_time_to_happen = {
                months = 1¹⁰⁷
```

Analysing scripted content provides the opportunity to study the contingencies for counterfactuals contained therein. In the example above, the causality and contingency of counterfactuals is illustrated through the event options – i.e. choices available to the players (not pictured) – once the "Christopher Columbus" event fires. The options available are "Reject his proposal!" or "Hire Columbus!" The player is free to make either choice whilst playing as Portugal.

However, the script file also denotes the probability factor for each event when Portugal is played by the AI. As per the scripting below, when Portugal is played by the AI and the event fires, the AI has a 75% chance of rejecting Columbus and a 25% chance of hiring him (or a three to one chance).[108]

```
            option = {                   # Reject his proposal
                name = "flavor_por.EVTOPTA1"
                ai_chance = { factor = 75}

            option = {                   # Hire Columbus
                name = "flavor_por.EVTOPTB1"
                ai_chance = { factor = 25}¹⁰⁹
```

Descriptive text is typically formatted as follows and generally accessible in the games' localisation files:

germany.11.t:0 "The Molotov-Ribbentrop Pact"

germany.11.d:0 "The German Foreign Ministry have proposed a non-aggression pact between our two nations. This treaty will greatly increase our mutual trade, and an additional secret protocol suggests the division of Eastern Europe into German and Soviet spheres.\n

---

107 *Europa Universalis IV.* Events. FlavorPOR.txt. *flavor_por.1.* v1.28.3. 2019 – 06 – 05. Note: if Portugal (player or AI) declines the event, i.e. declines to fund Columbus's expedition, the event is passed to Spain.
108 *Europa Universalis IV.* Events. FlavorPOR.txt. *flavor_por.1.* v1.28.3. 2019 – 06 – 05.
109 *Europa Universalis IV.* Events. FlavorPOR.txt. *flavor_por.1.* v1.28.3. 2019 – 06 – 05.

> \nWhile the fascists in Berlin may not be trustworthy, this pact will allow us to deal with Finland, the Baltic States and Romania without fear of outside interference. The eastern territories of Poland will also befall us in the event of a Polish collapse."
>
> germany.11.a:0 "Sign the treaty."
>
> germany.11.a.tt:0 "§RWhile the pact is in effect, the Closed Economy trade policy will be unavailable.\nThe War With Germany focus will be unavailable for two years.§!\n"
>
> germany.11.b:0 "No deals with the fascists!"[110]

The above example is the event text for the Molotov-Ribbentrop Pact in *Hearts of Iron IV*. The identifier, here "germany.11," tells the game what text to display when the event triggers. We then find the name of the event, the contents and the description of what the pact would entail, as well as the choices available to the player ("germany.11" followed by "t" for title, "d" for description, "a" for the first available option, "a.tt" (tt for tool tip) for effect of option a and "b" for the second available option).

Descriptive text illustrates the ongoing game in an explanatory – sometimes prosaic – way and illuminates the historical content in the game files. While the scripting reflects the rules and parameters of actions and events, the descriptive text provides the embellishment, personality and rationale. Through the descriptive text, counterfactual history obtains a voice, a narrative language about what is happening in the game and why. As such, descriptive text does not have convoluted contingencies the way scripted rules do. Nevertheless, the descriptive text can take on several different tones that can be described as fact, narration and roleplay.

For example, a player creating an army in *Europa Universalis IV* must decide which units to build and maintain. In doing so, the player faces descriptions of what the unit options do. According to developers, each unit description has a historical precursor if available.[111] The description reads as follows:

> ottoman_eastern_carabinierDESCR:0 "In essence a mounted foot soldier carrying a short musket or rifle also known as a carbine. Their ability to dismount and fight on foot allowed them great flexibility in the battle."[112]

Here, the Ottoman Eastern Carabinier description is factual in tone; an informative, almost scholarly and to-the-point description of what the unit in question

---

[110] *Hearts of Iron IV*. Localisation. events_l_english.yml. *germany.11*. v1.6.2. 2019–06–05.
[111] Developer informant Devin (June 28, 2017).
[112] *Europa Universalis IV*. Localisation. text_l_english.yml. *Eastern Carabinier*. v1.28.3.

did historically and can do in the game. Notably, the text uses past tense. The tooltip will also include the in-game cost of the unit and the times it takes to train one unit.

Narration lets the player know about goings-on in the game to provide context and guidance to players. In the example below, the game guides the player in strategic decision making by informing them that the advisor they are considering has less skill than the one they currently have employed. The game, i.e. the developers of the game really, alerts the player that advisor A has a different skillset than advisor B.

> ADVISOR_HAVE_LOWER_SKILL_THAN:0 "$ADVISORTYPE$ advisor has lower skill than"[113]

As such, the game informs the player about the consequences of their decision, good or bad. Why one advisor has a specific skillset compared to another may vary. In certain instances, the advisor may even be a fictional character to which the designers assign a generic or even completely random skillset. In most cases, developers give traits and skillsets to historical persons (rulers, advisors, commanders etc.) based on their research. More on this in chapter two.

Developers and beta testers describe playable nations in the game as having personalities. The implications of this will be discussed in more detail in chapters three and four. For now, it is worth noting the traces of personality design that can be found in both scripted code and descriptive text. They contain information on how certain playable nations are juxtaposed to other nations, how designers expect them to act based on their given context and motivations, and how much room they have given them to act contrarily to their given personality. Below is a nation-specific mission for Muscovy in *Europa Universalis IV*, which denotes their attitude towards to Sweden after the consolidation of a number of Russian provinces.

> conquer_finland_desc:0 "Sweden remains a danger to the lands of Holy Mother Russia. To protect Russia once and for all we must conquer Finland to act as a buffer."[114]

This is an example where a playable nation roleplays in a singular voice, discussing a motivation and a historical context that both reads as gameplay incentive and represents historical actuality in the relationship between Sweden and Russia in late Early Modern times, as well as the role of Finland in the same context.

---

[113] *Europa Universalis IV.* Localisation. text_l_english.yml. "Advisor has lower skill than NN." v1.28.3.
[114] *Europa Universalis IV.* Localisation. text_l_english.yml. "Conquer Finland." v1.28.3.

In other cases, most notably events that present the player with a choice to be made, the game contains sets of motivation and context interpretations in order to believably be able to present the player with different personalities for their nation depending on the situation. In other words, both games contain contingency design for every available outcome. To facilitate any potential counterfactual faction construct without having to design for each individual contingency, the games contain a series of generic events. Below is an example from *Hearts of Iron IV* through which any playable nation that fulfils the right criteria can be invited to any faction.

> generic.5.t:0 "[From.GetNameDefCap] invites [Root.GetNameDef] to the [From.GetFactionName]"
>
> generic.5.d.a:0 "With a suspicious eye on recent developments in world politics, [alliance_inviter.GetNameDef] extends us their hand of friendship, offering us their protection and urging us to stand with them in defence of the principles of liberty and democracy. As a member of the [alliance_inviter.GetFactionName], our people's freedom may well be safeguarded."
>
> generic.5.d.b:0 "Recognizing that sometimes even the strong need allies, the [alliance_inviter.GetAdjective] have invited us to join the [alliance_inviter.GetFactionName]. If we choose to accept, this may well provide ample opportunity for us to find our place in the sun."
>
> generic.5.d.c:0 "Our ideological allies in [alliance_inviter.GetNameDef] have made note of our valuable contributions to the workers' cause, and this morning we received an invitation us to join the [alliance_inviter.GetFactionName]. Standing together with other socialist republics, we could spread the revolution with renewed strength."
>
> generic.5.d.e:0 "It appears the [alliance_inviter.GetAdjective] consider us to be of strategic interest to them, and that they deem it more profitable that we work together than that we should let ourselves be divided by our ideological differences. This morning, the [alliance_inviter.GetAdjective] Ambassador delivered an invitation for us to become a member state of the [alliance_inviter.GetFactionName]."
>
> generic.5.a:0 "We will make our stand with them."
>
> generic.5.b:0 "We only need a few thousand dead..."
>
> generic.5.c:0 "We will fight alongside our comrades!"
>
> generic.5.e:0 "It is the profitable choice."[115]

The invitations listed are to join the democratic faction (a), the fascist faction (b), the communist faction (c) and an ideologically "neutral" faction with other mutual interests (e). The description of each contingency contains ideological sig-

---

115 *Hearts of Iron IV.* Localisation. events_l_english.yml. *generic.5.* v1.6.2.

nalling in terms of motivation, context and goals for each faction. In cases like these, the motivation and personality of the playable nation is not railroaded towards a specific goal or to make a specific historical argument (compare to the Muscovy example above), but to provide the player with the opportunity to create their own – possibly counterfactual – context to in turn make new arguments.

Chapter Discussion and Summary

This initial look at the games serves as a steppingstone and facilitator of more complex discussions on the relationship between game design practice and representation of the past in digital strategy games. The following chapters further contextualise the games using the conceptual and empirical underpinnings of the book. They build, in part, on some the insights here. Firstly, the historicising perspective on the games themselves. Understanding the origins and trajectory of digital strategy games allows us to highlight how continuity and change in game design over time frame the content itself. This is here framed as genre convention and design legacy and will be discussed further in chapter two.

Another insight brought forward in the present chapter, that deepens as we go forward, is how scripted and textual content literally shapes counterfactuals. One of the overarching arguments of this book – building on Kultima's praxiology theses – is that game development is timely and particular.[116] In considering the discourse around digital strategy games as facilitators of open-endedness and emergent gameplay, it is worth noting that even the most unlikely counterfactual outcomes are indeed designed. It is through this understanding that a closer investigation of the relationship between the design and content of the games on the one hand and historical culture on the other can be made.

All historical games come with explicit as well as implicit signalling of contemporary understandings of the past and the vehicle and context matters. I here approach the games with an understanding of them as such vehicles, and that games in and of themselves struggle to exhibit historical arguments beyond what is shaped and inserted into this space by designers. Eugen Pfister talks about this principle of uses of history for maintaining the political myth as us always being only able to "verify what we already know."[117] The often-self-fulfilling nature of historical culture, of reproducing what I throughout the book refer

---

[116] Kultima, *Game Design Praxiology*, 51–72.
[117] Pfister, "Why History in Digital Games Matter," 64.

to as familiarity and player expectations as guiding design principles, most certainly relies on intertextual reference, but it also relies on design legacy. The overall design of the games is established to the point where "Paradox style games" almost denotes its own subgenre. I therefore argue that the systemic nature of games, and the "all paths lead to colonial expansion or the Second World War" principles, continue to reinforce dominant historical understandings and are only truly open-ended and multifaceted in selected parts and for specific readings, despite the heavy lifting these concepts do in game marketing (more on this in the following chapter).

Adam Chapman talks about this relationship between game form and historiographical representation as the placement of lexia and framing controls that, in turn, produce story structures, or narratives.[118] As regards digital strategy games, Chapman argues that they afford players the opportunity to compare and "make meaning by allowing multiple narratives that, though bound by the same theoretical model, allow for (and even emphasise) the possibility of difference, rather than offering a conclusive and encompassing account of events."[119] In this, the opportunity for multiplicity in digital strategy games is rightly highlighted and helpfully informs an understanding of digital strategy games as opportune spaces for the critical discussion of dominant, often hegemonic, narratives. Based on the present analysis though, I offer a somewhat contrasting argument by showing that such theoretical models are intrinsic also to counterfactual design in *Europa Universalis IV* and *Hearts of Iron IV*, and thus fosters repetition of established, dominant historical understandings through formality alongside the possibility for critical engagements and multiplicity.

To summarise, then, *Europa Universalis IV* and *Hearts of Iron IV* build on the same template but focus on different areas. They are similar in many ways, especially aesthetically and in gameplay. Upon closer inspection, however, one can also note some significant differences. The strategy genre dictates a certain level of open-endedness and exploratory gameplay. Despite similarities in gameplay design, however, each game sets up goal-setting and counterfactual logic in their own way. In *Europa Universalis IV,* more so than in *Hearts of Iron VI*, players are expected to come up with their own historical challenges and scenarios, lightly guided by the mechanics and content of the games. The game also has a mechanic called missions, which provide the player with waypoints and goals based on historical or counterfactual scenarios. Players can choose to play these as ready-made counterfactual scenarios. *Hearts of Iron IV* exhibits

---

[118] Chapman, *Digital Games as History*, 119–121.
[119] Chapman, *Digital Games as History*, 145.

the same base principle in terms of gameplay, although the constraints are narrower. Due to the setup of national focus trees, and the narrower overall focus of the game, players are more closely tied to the specific scenario of the Second World War, and consequently, content, both historical and counterfactual, is streamlined accordingly.

Compared to previous games in the series, *Europa Universalis III* and *Hearts of Iron III* were harder for players to get into and understand from a gameplay perspective, largely due to design decisions connected to improving mechanics coherency and user interface. According to reviews, *Europa Universalis IV* and *Hearts of Iron IV* both had discernible improvements in this area. Developers appear have made an effort to make the game tutorials clearer and make the games more generally accessible for a broader audience. Both games introduced new, metaphorical mechanics, to replace more literal depictions in previous iterations. For example, for *Europa Universalis IV*, the monarch power system dictates agency by representing power as a form of currency that is used to develop the player nation on varying fronts – technologically, ideologically, culturally, etc. This is represented by political power in *Hearts of Iron IV*. Furthermore, counterfactuals in Paradox Development Studio games have become more emphasised over time. Counterfactual depictions are present in layers, primarily scripted content (rules and outcomes) and descriptive text (tone and flavour). As such, counterfactual history is an inherent aspect to both games. In fact, the mechanics highlight causality and contingency and, ultimately, make counterfactuals unavoidable.

To tie back into the gameplay journals, agency within this system is wrought with counterfactual outcomes, but as noted by Angus Mol, remarking on every player choice as counterfactuals is "akin to pondering why the sky is blue."[120] Giving some control to the players is an ingrained and expected aspect to these games. Therefore, the question as we go forward is not so much what each individual design choice does for historical representation, but how this representation through design relates to the use of history in games.

---

120 Angus Mol, "Toying With History: Counterplay, Counterfactuals, and the Control of the Past," *History in Games – Contingencies of an Authentic Past*, ed. Martin Lorber and Felix Zimmermann (Bielefeld: transcript, 2020), 240.

Chapter Two
Shaping the Past: The Surround and Practice of Making Games about the Past

Outlining Developer Motivation and Tasks

What frameworks and practices are central to making *Europa Universalis IV* and *Hearts of Iron IV*? An important point of this book, as mentioned before, is to illuminate the impact of production and designer needs, motives and production processes on the representation of history and counterfactual history in games. The purpose of this chapter is to lay the empirical foundation for subsequent chapters about how such practices and values ultimately influence, complicate and frame uses of history and counterfactual history in the games.

I will here further contextualise Paradox Development Studio as makers of historical strategy games and present the findings from interviews with developers and beta testers concerning game design practices. It brings forward relevant details to frame the studio's and developers' position in external as well as internal contexts. External contexts include business strategies, publishing and the ecosystem of the game industry. Furthermore, the interviews detail the internal contexts of day-to-day work at Paradox Development Studio, including practical game making issues such as tasks, team composition and technical parameters. The aim here is to highlight the many practical underpinnings of historical representation, such as issues of funding, marketing, sourcing of historical information, engaging beta testers and balancing values and practices pertaining to the design of rules, counterfactuals and gameplay.

Company structure, Monetisation and the Paradox Pillars

At the time of writing, Paradox Development Studio is a subsidiary of Paradox Interactive, a game publishing company originally sprung from role-playing games publisher and developer Target Games in the late 1990s.[121] The studio and the publishing company are based in Stockholm, Sweden.[122] Paradox Inter-

---

[121] Orvar Säfström and Jimmy Wilhelmsson, *Äventyrsspel – Bland mutanter, drakar och demoner* (Malmö: Bokfabriken, 2017), 235.
[122] Johan Andersson, *PDXCON 2017: Europa Universalis – Around the world in 400 years* 2017 (video resource, 2017).

active publishes games by not only Paradox Development Studio, but also external developers and studios. For example, industry veterans Obsidian Entertainment and their role-playing dungeon-crawler *Pillars of Eternity*, Finnish studio Colossal Order's city-builder *Cities Skylines* and Arrowhead Studio's action-adventure game *Magicka*. Additionally, Paradox Interactive publishes table-top role-playing games, including the *World of Darkness* franchise, and board games (including board game versions of Paradox Development Studio games).

Paradox Interactive has published digitally since 2005, primarily on the digital distribution platform *Steam* although other platforms such as those by Epic, Apple and Google are also used.[123] Digital distribution is a fundamental aspect of the business structure of Paradox Interactive and, by extension, Paradox Development Studio. Digital distribution – i.e. uploading the game product to a digital platform for players to purchase, download and install instantly – allows a developer and publisher to disregard certain aspects of release date logistics. When publishing digitally only, the, at this point almost historical, headaches of physical distribution, such as printing and shipping to stores, do not apply. Developers upload the game directly to the distribution platform when it is ready.[124] Subsequently, digital distribution enables players to make instant purchases and downloads of games. Players may also give feedback to the developers via the distribution platform, and game fixes and patches can be delivered to players instantly.[125]

There is a saying in the games industry that successful game-making is not making a hit game, but being able to afford making the next game. This dark-humoured take on the reality of game-making ventures points to the subtle and ever-changing attempts of monetising games in a sustainable way. As the digital games industry has grown and changed, digital distribution affords the opportunity to sustain ongoing development and incrementally ship expansions to existing games. Simultaneously, the plethora of games available in, for example, *Steam*, makes it hard for games to stand out. Paradox Development Studio and Paradox Interactive take advantage of this ecosystem by implementing long-term sale strategies and seamlessly putting revenue from sales of their entire game catalogue back into development of specific games, keeping work on

---

123 Charlie Hall, "Solving Paradox: How the Historical Strategy Game Maker Stayed Alive," *Polygon*, August 7, 2013, accessed October 4, 2020, https://www.polygon.com/features/2013/8/7/4554042/paradox-interactive-history; Paradox Interactive, "Revenue model," accessed July 14, 2021, https://www.paradoxinteractive.com/our-company/our-business/revenue-model.
124 Marco Mereu et al., "Digital Distribution and Games as a Service," *Science and Technology Law Review* 16 (2013): 38.
125 Marco Mereu et al., "Digital Distribution," 40.

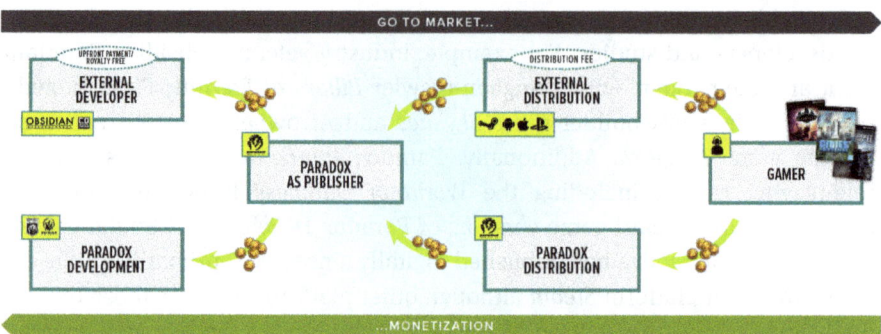

Figure 11: Visualisation of the Paradox Interactive revenue model from https://www.paradoxinteractive.com/en/revenue-model/. Collected on May 21, 2019. Reproduced with permission. In a 2020 revamp of the website, Paradox Interactive removed the visualisation and added a description of their revenue model instead.

new titles and DLCs afloat (see Figure 11). DLC, "downloadable content," denotes such patches, content packs and expansions that are added to the base game and cannot be played as stand-alone games. In an interview in 2013, Paradox Interactive's then-CEO Fredrik Wester noted that during the time when the core game of *Europa Universalis IV* was still in development, sales on *Crusader Kings II* remained steady or increasing. This money thus partly funded the development of *Europa Universalis IV*, even significantly after *Crusader Kings II* was initially released.[126] This revenue-generating principle continues to have important implications for how Paradox Interactive and Paradox Development Studio plan and execute their work.

For Paradox Development Studio, this highly scalable monetisation model, i.e. developing games that take advantage of logistical help from digital distribution and provide a steady flow of revenue, partly frames the role and development of individual games and DLCs. Games developed at the studio tend to follow a similar life cycle: an initial release of a base game (like *Europa Universalis IV* in 2013 and *Hearts of Iron IV* in 2016), after which development continues and downloadable content is released incrementally.[127] That is, they primarily add or tweak new content, mechanics and assets, although they may also change and remove superfluous game elements. Smaller DLCs and content packs tend to be free of charge, but larger expansions to the base games are purchasable items.

---

[126] Charlie Hall, "Solving Paradox."
[127] Marie Carpenter, Nabyla Daidj and Christina Moreno, "Game Console Manufacturers: The End of Sustainable Competitive Advantage?," *Digiworld Economic Journal* 94 (2014): 42–45.

Consequently, players who continue to play *Europa Universalis IV* or *Hearts of Iron IV*, and who wish to stay up to date with the games' development, must make multiple purchases over time. This model is, arguably, a similar strategy to the contentious phenomenon known as microtransactions in games that also strive for maximum possible revenue per user albeit often on a different scale and timeline. Microtransactions on the free-to-play market allow developers to charge players repeatedly to acquire, and sometimes replenish, in-game resources, assets and items, as well as gambling mechanics involving in-game purchases.[128] The Paradox DLC monetisation model generally offers players more substantial content packs for purchase, however, and once those content packs are owned, players do not need to pay for them again. In contrast, other studios and publishers suspend development after a game is released and use the profits to create their next game, in a more traditional value chain.

Given the DLC monetisation model, the scale of content influences how these games represent the past and counterfactual scenarios. As I will discuss further into this chapter, developers reject the idea of reiterating *Europa Universalis* (making a *Europa Universalis V*, that is) unless they come up with a fundamentally different gameplay idea.[129] They would rather continue to add to the *Europa Universalis IV* content for as long as the base game supports it, and continue to explore aspects of the past that are not already in the game. DLCs enable this approach. Perhaps intuitively, and according to the Paradox Interactive website, DLCs are expansions, and so are considerably cheaper to make than new core games.[130] As one example, the 2015 *Women in History* content pack added female characters to the existing stack of rulers in *Europa Universalis IV*.[131] Another example is the *Rule Britannia* DLC, which added new British missions, late-game coal mining and Anglicanism to the game.[132] These are efforts to make the representation of global history in the early modern era more complete. I here call this symbiotic relationship between monetisation and content stacking supplementary design practices. The goal, as per developer testimonies, is to continue to add content to the games for as long as is viable. In other words,

---

[128] Lies van Roessel and Jan Švelch, "Who Creates Microtransactions: The Production Context of Video Game Monetization," *Game Production Studies*, ed. Olli Sotamaa and Jan Švelch (Amsterdam: Amsterdam University Press, 2021), 198; Matthew E. Perks, "Regulating In-Game Monetization: Implications of Regulation on Games Production," in *Game Production Studies*, ed. Olli Sotamaa and Jan Švelch (Amsterdam: Amsterdam University Press, 2021), 217–219.
[129] Developer informant Dale (June 15, 2017).
[130] Paradox Interactive, "Revenue model."
[131] Developer informant Dallas (June 26, 2017).
[132] Paradox Wikis, *Europa Universalis IV: Rule Britannia*.

a fuller description of the past is economically desirable. Notably, this strategy ties into almost every aspect of turning history into games.[133]

To frame what defines a Paradox game, the publisher has defined a set of values and guidelines known as the "Paradox Pillars" (Figure 12). Importantly, developers at Paradox Development Studio state in the interviews that they are aware of the pillars, but that they are not currently being used as a design blueprint. Rather, they say, the pillars are a selection of gameplay experiences that the company are selling, and a list of indicators of what makes, and has made, the company and their games successful.[134] In a 2017 talk, Shams Jorjani, VP Business Developer at Paradox Interactive, describes the pillars as "the concepts of a successful design and marketing strategy."[135] Moreover, Jorjani says that the pillars are the essence of what makes Paradox "unique" and "unwavering" in their approach to be a successful game designer and publisher. Jorjani and Paradox Development Studio developers assert that the company rarely compromises on these points.[136] According to the pillars, a Paradox game can be expected to adhere to the following factors:

Replayability
One does not simply 'finish' a Paradox game. System-driven games with challenging sandbox environments make for unique game sessions each time you play.

Intellectually challenging
Paradox games are played with your mind, not your reflexes. Incredible depth and a balanced learning curve come together to reward players' curiosity.

---

[133] Johan Andersson, *PDXCON 2017: Europa Universalis* (video resource, 2017).
[134] Developer informant Dale (June 15, 2017); Developer informant Devin (June 28, 2017).
[135] Shams Jorjani, *Ideas are Useless! Pitch your game to Paradox!* (video resource, 2017).
[136] Shams Jorjani, *Ideas Are Useless!* (video resource, 2017); Johan Andersson and Martin Anward, *Europa Universalis IV – An alternate history of the game* (video resource, 2019). In 2020, beyond the time frame of this study, Paradox Interactive have rephrased the pillars on their website. The categories have changed but the central vocabulary remains very similar, if not identical, to the version used in the study. The categories as of June 2021 are *Looks Good, Plays Perfect* – "Paradox games never sacrifice function to form, and always prioritize gameplay over everything else," *Gives Agency to the Player* – "Paradox games give players their tools to express their creativity, and make gaming experience their own; from character customization to emergent storytelling, or extensive modding," *Challenges the Mind* – "Paradox games challenge the player's mind more than their reflexes. They reward curiosity, dedication and intelligence," *Offers an Endless Experience* – "Whether through replayability, alternative playthroughs or no end state at all, Paradox games provide content to play for a very long time," and *Invites a Deeper Dive* – "Paradox games provide incredible depth and endless engagement, but strive to onboard players in their worlds and gameplay system in a smooth and forgiving way" (Paradox Interactive, "Revenue model").

Paradox Game Pillars
WHAT MAKES A GAME A **PARADOX** GAME

Replayable
One does not simply "finish" a Paradox game. System-driven games with challenging sandbox environments make for unique game sessions each time you play.

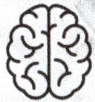
Intellectually Challenging
Paradox games are played with your mind, not your reflexes. Incredible depth and a balanced learning curve come together to reward players' curiosity.

Creativity
We want our players to create and share their own stories from our games - not just the stories we imagined. The game should encourage creativity and experimentation, and should lead to personal, memorable stories.

Form Follows Function
At Paradox we use visuals to complement gameplay, not gameplay to show off visuals. Paradox is function and form in sensible symbiosis.

Accessible
The games take time to master - but each game is still enjoyable. Players don't stop playing our games because they're too intimidating or punishing.

Nerd Out
Regardless of what the game is about, there's always more to discover behind the scenes. The player can always dig deeper into the subject matter of the game even when they're not playing.

Figure 12: Paradox Game Pillars. Source: https://www.paradoxinteractive.com/en/game-pillars/. Collected on May 16, 2017. Reproduced with permission.

Creativity
We want our players to create and share their own stories from our games – not just the stories we imagined. The game should encourage creativity and experimentation, and should lead to personal, memorable stories.

Form follows functionality
At Paradox we use visuals to complement gameplay, not gameplay to show off visuals. Paradox is function and form in sensible symbiosis.

Accessibility
The games take time to master – but each game is still enjoyable. Players don't stop playing our games because they're too intimidating or punishing.

Nerd out
Regardless of what the game is about, there's always more to discover behind the scenes. The player can always dig deeper into the subject matter of the game even when they're not playing.

As discussed in the context of monetisation and returning customers, player retention is at the forefront also in the Paradox pillars when they argue for the benefit of offering creative and complex gameplay experiences, grounded in real-world topics. Replayability is a broadly used term in the gaming world, denoting the ability to sustain and encourage a player to play the same game many times. Players tend to consider replayability an attractive feature in a game because it offers, potentially, infinite hours of entertainment for a finite amount of money.[137] Of course, this hinges on a game's ability to present the player with sufficiently interesting experiences every time to keep them coming back. As noted in 2019 by then-Paradox Interactive CEO Ebba Ljungerud, returning player engagement need to be reciprocated by long-term support from the developer.[138] Paradox accommodates replayability by aiming to create deep and complex games that, in the context of the pillars, have the added value of being "intellectually challenging" and allowing their players to "nerd out," i.e. explore the topics beyond play and beyond the games themselves. Moreover, the pillar of "creativity" specifically denotes the way a Paradox game allows players to experiment completely regardless of the developers. Finally, the "accessibility"

---

137 Timothy Frattesi et al., "Replayability of Video Games," Worchester Polytechnic Insitutute (2011), 20–21, 30–32.
138 Caty McCarthy, "Interview with Paradox CEO Ebba Ljungerud," *US Gamer*, March 19, 2019, accessed May 10, 2019, https://www.usgamer.net/articles/the-paradox-way-paradox-interactive-ceo-strategy-games-interview-dice-summit.

pillar is meant to guarantee that the games are "complex, but not complicated"[139] as noted by Johan Andersson, creative director for *Europa Universalis IV*.

The Paradox pillars serve as heuristic markers of gameplay values. That is, they indicate what players can expect from playing these games. However, the model does not describe design values (how a certain gameplay experience is created or facilitated) nor explain how gameplay values inherently relate to the description and representation of a topic (how gameplay values influence the representation of the past and counterfactuals). Therefore, I argue that the Paradox pillars are a fruitful exposition of the industry setting at hand that helps us to identify certain goals. This in turn helps to determine how external and internal contexts frame decision-making and the representation of the past and counterfactuals in the games.

These gameplay values support notions of historical reference and counterfactual history, simultaneously. The games can be played repeatedly and thus allow the players to engage with stories about the past from the perspective of many different historical nations, cultures, beliefs etc. Players are encouraged to learn about and discuss the Early Modern period and Second World War outside of the games and to change and create their own stories inside the games, and on the same topics.[140] As this and subsequent chapters will illustrate, developers make design decisions partly depending on the game development context and frameworks at hand. Sometimes, such game design practices shape representations of the past, or the way counterfactuals are implemented.

The pillar model ultimately indicates how Paradox Interactive and Paradox Development Studio synthesise notions of structure, monetisation and design into gameplay goals and values. By extension, the pillars also constitute the rationale behind Paradox games as 1) money makers and 2) facilitators of content and gameplay. In other words, they connect notions of historical culture like the commodification of the past with historical culture as a set of values to dictate which history to present and how. Notably, this understanding of the pillars also highlights contradictions and tensions between design goals, pragmatism and creativity. Negotiating the balance between, for example, a complex and intellectually challenging yet at the same time accessible and creative game creates a give-and-take between design objectives and design elements. Again, his-

---

139 Charlie Hall, "Solving Paradox."
140 For example, the Paradox Plaza website hosts and maintains a forum for general discussions of historical topics called the History Forum: https://forum.paradoxplaza.com/forum/forums/history-forum.44/. Similarly, *Crusader Kings II* provides in-game links to Wikipedia articles about many of its characters. I would like to thank Robert Houghton for drawing my attention to these details.

torical reference and counterfactual history co-exist in the game. This comes out in the interviews with specific regards to the representation of the past, and the design of counterfactuals, as I will show below and in the following chapters.

Defining Designer Roles, or are Game Developers Historians?

At the time of the interviews, the *Hearts of Iron IV* and *Europa Universalis IV* teams consisted of ten to 14 persons each, with additional developers who move between several teams as needed.[141] Job titles and, subsequently, the description of each developer role can be meaningful because they frame tasks and aims with a particular game element in focus. Having said that, game design practice is often collaborative in nature, and one should avoid drawing conclusions to research questions from job description alone.[142] Nevertheless, descriptors are necessary for context, and the interview material is comprised of informants in the following categories:

Developers, nine in total, consisting of
– Creative directors, Game directors, Game designers, Content designers, Art directors, and AI programmers for both *Hearts of Iron IV* and *Europa Universalis IV*.

And Beta testers, nine in total, consisting of
– two for both *Hearts of Iron IV* and *Europa Universalis IV*
– four for *Europa Universalis IV*
– three for *Hearts of Iron IV*

Creative directors and game directors' tasks are envisioning and managing the overall design of the game, i.e. the broad strokes of topics, mechanics, settings and functionalities. The main task of content designers is to provide the game with content such as rules, scripting, event design, descriptive text, mission trees, national focuses and more. Content designers also consult on issues related to representing the past with other team members when needed. Artists create visual assets for the game such as maps, flags and buildings, as well as animated assets like military units (barracks, soldiers etc.). Art direction might also involve overseeing the production of visual assets if they are being outsourced to

---

[141] Developer informants Dorian (June 29, 2018); Devin (June 28, 2017); Daryl (June 26, 2017).
[142] Kultima, "Game Design Praxiology," 81–82.

third-party companies or subsidiaries. AI programmers are tasked with programming and maintaining non-player processes in the game. That is, the behind-the-scenes machinery of every other playable nation except the player's in a single-player campaign. Consequently, AI designers also focus on balancing the game as needed, in collaboration with team members from content design and quality assurance.

Beta testers at Paradox Development Studio primarily perform two kinds of tasks: 1) quality assessment, bug hunting and balance and 2) research and content design. Many do both. However, beta testers work with Paradox Development Studio on an unpaid basis. Interestingly, among beta testers who took part in this study, two work as professional game developers independently of Paradox Development Studio – one specialising in writing and localisation, the other in board game development.[143] Outside of beta testing, the remaining beta testers primarily work in professions unrelated to history or game development, although many underline that they have a passion for reading and learning about history, and that they keep game design as a craft and episteme close to their hearts. Some additional details about the developer and beta tester interviews are available in Appendix 2.

As epistemologically complex as they are, the interviews suggest that game design practice builds on an awareness of what constitutes historical actuality – a nebulous idea of the past as it actually happened – while simultaneously adhering to non-scholarly practices and values. In line with the definition of games and counterfactuals as uses of history, and the application of historical knowledge for the benefit of game design and gameplay, *Europa Universalis IV* and *Hearts of Iron IV* rely on the idea of an actual past to create a sense of verisimilitude and provide a real-world framing. This notion is far from controversial. It does, however, come with a series of interesting conceptual problems pertaining to such fickle notions as truth and method, perhaps especially for those versed in historical scholarship, but for game designers as well.

Developers and beta testers all read and draw from historical scholarship and are, to varying degrees, comfortable with evaluating and discussing the usefulness of secondary sources such as academic literature. However, due to the nature of the games and the contexts and frameworks of game design, they all maintain that they ultimately do not make scholarly arguments about the past nor historiography. So, what would be the point in discussing "game history" with "scholarly history" if the comparison, as established in the introduction, is inherently somewhat flawed? Are there any meaningful comparisons to be

---

143 Beta tester Bailey (March 13, 2018); Beta tester Bobbie (February 20, 2018).

made between historical game development and historical scholarship in terms of hands-on practices?

Although there are certain similarities between game design practice and historical scholarship, and indeed some of the Paradox Development Studio developers and beta testers are accomplished readers of history, there are, to be sure, significant differences. Adam Chapman has coined the term developer-historian to describe the particular kind of developer activities and roles that provide historical meaning to digital games.[144] The developer-historian concept is used to denote the agency by which game designers create what Chapman calls the "hi(story)-play-space," the specific structure that affords and constrains the player's agency and subsequent ability to produce historical narratives within a game.[145] The concept highlights the distinction between developers of historical games in particular and others, and the way historical culture frames the designer role. As Chapman astutely notes: "Developers also often use fictional, though *historically typical* [his emphasis], settings and characters within a larger frame of actual historical events."[146] That is to say, while the design of a game inevitably has bearing on historical narratives, the role of the game developer is to construct a play-space, although not a scholarly argument.

Others have framed the developer role from the opposite perspective, and argued for the embrace of games as historical scholarship, and, thus, the possibility of "developer-scholars" (to stay analogous to Chapman's terminology). For example historian and game scholar Dawn Spring notes that: "Similarities exist between the iterative design process used to develop computer and videogames, and the process of researching historical scholarship. In spite of the vastly different outcomes, the process of researching and writing historical scholarship is iterative by nature."[147] Game design methodology is indeed iterative, and while historical scholarship can be iterative at face value, it is worth pointing out, however, that such methodological comparisons do not appear to translate beyond superficial process framing. Historians do revisit sources and understandings but for disparate reasons and, as Spring herself points out, with vastly different outcomes. Developers do rigorous research for the benefit of their games. However, as we will see further into this chapter, the type of research

---

144 Chapman, *Digital Games as History*, 15.
145 Chapman, *Digital Games as History*, 33–34. I opt not to use this term throughout as it risks inadvertently prescribing academic sentiments to development when game design practice is at the forefront.
146 Chapman, *Digital Games as History*, 47.
147 Spring, "Gaming History," 208.

being done at Paradox Development Studio is of a fundamentally different nature than original historical scholarship.

A third aspect on this issue is when scholarly discourse is played for clout. One such example are Rockstar, the makers of historical Americana games *Red Dead Redemption* series and *L.A. Noir*, who are known for diligent historical research as part of their development processes.[148] However, as found by Esther Wright, Rockstar's extravagant research efforts are in part overt marketing strategies, designed to control a discourse of historical authenticity and a discourse of cinematic authenticity. Specifically, by parading their research efforts, Rockstar seek to "preload potential consumers with intertextual reference points, creating a pre-legitimated identity for the games' historical and cultural representations," writes Wright.[149] In other words, the link between historical scholarship and game design, here, appears to have little to do with scholarly methods or doing archival research. Rather, Rockstar's approach underlines the perceived value of signalling – be it historical culture, authenticity or legitimacy. Moreover, concerning the inherent relationship between game making and historical scholarship, to the best of my knowledge, there is currently little to suggest that original historical research – to an academic standard or otherwise – is being conducted within the game development industry, or for the purpose of game design.[150] Note that this argument does not include the employment of historians or cultural heritage professionals to consult as experts on historical game projects. While neither developers nor beta testers confirmed that Paradox Development Studio tend to consult with professional historians as per the interviews, it was later brought to my attention that professional historians have consulted on *Crusader Kinds II* and *Crusader Kings III*. I cannot speak to the implications of that here, but the presence of this phenomenon certainly makes for interesting possible future approaches to the topic.

---

148 See Alexis C Madrigal, "The Hardcore Archival Research Behind 'L.A. Noire'," *The Atlantic*. June 6, 2011, accessed April 14, 2020, https://www.theatlantic.com/technology/archive/2011/06/the-hardcore-archival-research-behind-la-noire/239964/; Rue Liu, "L.A Noir's Rockstar Teams Up with L.A. Times For Interactive 1947 Crime Map," *Slash Gear*, May 5, 2011, accessed April 14, 2020, https://www.slashgear.com/l-a-noires-rockstar-teams-up-with-l-a-times-for-interactive-1947-crime-map-05150481/.
149 Esther Wright, "Rockstar Games and American History" (PhD diss, University of Warwick, 2019), 75.
150 See also Jeremie Clyde, Howard Hopkins and Glenn Wilkinson, "Beyond the 'Historical' Simulation." See also Lisa Traynor and Jonathan Ferguson, "Shooting for Accuracy: Historicity and Video Gaming," in *Historia Ludens – The Playing Historian*, ed. Alexander Von Lünen et al. (London: Routledge, 2020) for points from the historian consultants' perspective.

The present practice – for developers and beta testers to primarily do their own version of research or collaborate internally – appears to be in line with Chris Kempshall's findings. In a study on developers of First World War games *Valiant Hearts: The Great War* and *Battlefield 1*, Kempshall notes that developer practices for doing research are indeed "bespoke and self-directed."[151] While there were instances of historian consultants on those projects, developers in Kempshall's study seem to have yet to engage with consultants or primary sources in a cohesive fashion. Another perspective on this, as noted by Adrienne Shaw, is that consultancy work is not only performed by historians in this context. In her studies, she notes that the production team of *Assassin's Creed III* engaged cultural consultants from a Native tribe of who are depicted in the game. Shaw notes that the kind of constructed realism afforded by consultancy and historical research for *Assassin's Creed* is an aesthetic mean to pre-empt criticism, in the same manner as historians and archives are consulted to construct an air of authenticity around a game.[152] However, at any rate, consultancy work is not prevalent in game design practice at Paradox Development Studio based on the present study.

Thus, going forward, the analysis of the interviews rests on the assumption that the developer informants are first and foremost professional game makers who, in part, engage with historical scholarship in order to produce rulesets, models of historical change and counterfactual history in the two games. As will be discussed again further on, developers work with applied history in a way that hints at an advanced understanding of historical scholarship but that in game design practice can, and will, omit those understandings and employ others where needed.

Technical Parameters and Tools

Arguing on the importance of studying and understanding the material and numerous aspects that can make game development seem like a "jumbled mess," Casey O'Donnell notes that:

> Software/specifications/etc. are made, but they are not made up. We cannot forget that though code is constructed, it is also linked to electrons, silicon, and other elements of

---

[151] Kempshall, "War Collaborators," 13.
[152] Adrienne Shaw, "The Tyranny of Realism: Historical accuracy and politics of representation in *Assassin's Creed III*," *Loading... The journal of Canadian Game Studies Association* 14 (2015): 5; Wright, "Rockstar Games and American History," 75.

the physical world. At this intersection, then, of constructions and their underlying realities, we need ways in which to understand the system of structures that frame the work of developers in the videogame industry.[153]

To better contextualise game design practice, it is indeed helpful to touch on the concrete parameters and tools developers use and have access to in order to identify relevant parts of the community as well as what potential technical constraints appear to have some influence over the decision-making process. In practice, *Europa Universalis IV* and *Hearts of Iron IV* differ in the way they use scripting as discussed in chapter one. The fact that *Hearts of Iron IV* relies so heavily on national focus trees is dependent on technological scaffolding but also supports the game leaning into counterfactuals in a more clear-cut way than *Europa Universalis IV* does. Technological scaffolding cannot alone explain historical and counterfactual representation in games, but this is an effort to draw back the curtain of development practice and provide a fuller picture of what influences history in games.

A few quick points about software usage pertaining to development. Paradox Development Studio works with the in-house game engine *Clausewitz*. Bug tickets and workflow are tracked through the project management software *JIRA*. Beta testers and developers communicate with each other through hidden forums on Paradox Plaza, and *Slack*. No other third-party or in-house proprietary tools were mentioned in the interviews, although from a general game development point of view there are bound to be others.[154]

All developers and beta testers in this study read and use the public Paradox Plaza forums to gain insights on player reception, needs, tensions and ideas, particularly after a new expansion, DLC, content pack or patch release. This is an increasingly common practice in game development practice overall and speaks to another important function of digital distribution. Platforms like *Steam* (and in this case, Paradox Plaza forums) offer players the option to give cohesive feedback on games, providing developers and beta testers with valuable information about what might work or not work about their games. Developers are in turn encouraged to provide updates and engage with their community of players.[155] Beyond *Steam*, The Paradox Plaza forums constitute a long-running and tight-

---

153 O'Donnell, *Developer's Dilemma*, 219–220.
154 See for example Heather Maxwell Chandler, *The Game Production Handbook* (Burlington, MA: Jones & Bartlett Learning, 2014).
155 Xinge Tong, "Positioning Game Review as a Crucial Element of Game User Feedback in the Ongoing Development of Independent Video Games," *Computers in Human Behavior Reports* 3 (2021): 1–4.

knit community of players and fans of these games. For example, one beta tester informant joined the forums as one of the first few hundred users back in 2002. According to the interviews, for most developers keeping track of forum discussions and player comments is a continuous process and part of day-to-day work. Depending on where they are in the workflow, developers are more or less inclined to engage in actual discussion on the forums, but most of them make it clear that they read all of the more extensive threads on both Paradox Plaza and important non-Paradox forums like Reddit.[156] Dorian mentions having interviewed players directly in order to collect information and material regarding player opinion and reception.[157]

The nature of any gameplay experience, particularly with regards to digital games, has traditionally been seen as product of the current level of computer technology available. As established by game scholar Andrew Hutchinson, the distinctive graphics of the game classics *Myst* (1993) and *Doom* (1993) have been attributed not to a certain design path but to the technological framework of the time. The two games do not possess cartoonlike figures, or still images portraying the surroundings, because of a lack of designerly imagination (no matter how iconic they have both become). Rather, "both companies solved the enormous technical limitations of the early 1990s in order to make their virtual worlds manifest as best was possible at the time," Hutchinson writes.[158] The continued development of home computers and video game consoles has allowed game designers greater and greater artistic freedom, as the visual fidelity of the games, and the possibility to store data and manage simultaneous processes, increase. For *Europa Universalis IV* and *Hearts of Iron IV*, this development has primarily meant an increase in visual fidelity, with a steady escalation in the level of map detail, quality of animated assets (such as military avatars and weather simulation) and the speed at which the game operates compared to previous iterations in the series. It also means that *Europa Universalis IV* and *Hearts of Iron IV* can contain a greater number of complex systems and mechanics than their predecessors could, as computers are able to handle more advanced calculations at a higher speed.

At the time of the interviews, and from a design practice perspective, developers at Paradox Development Studio say they are not necessarily affected by technology aging out in developing *Europa Universalis IV* and *Hearts of Iron*

---

156 Developer informant Dorian (June 29, 2018).
157 Developer informant Dorian (June 29, 2018).
158 Andrew Hutchinson, "Making the Water Move: Techno-Historic Limits in the Game Aesthetics of *Myst* and *Doom*," *Game Studies* 8 (2008).

IV.¹⁵⁹ According to Drew, adding, removing or changing elements of the games "[is] not so much about technology, or base-tech, as it is about design."¹⁶⁰ One aspect to the notion that technology is not as delimiting as design itself is run optimisation. Paradox Development Studio games run a significant number of calculations each turn and optimising the use of computer capacity is an important aspect to making and testing for the games to run smoothly.¹⁶¹ The optimisation factor also changes over time as the games grow more complex. One possible indication of this issue is that, at the time of writing, the minimum and recommended requirements for playing *Europa Universalis IV* have increased significantly in comparison to what they were in 2013.¹⁶² In contrast, the requirements to play *Hearts of Iron IV* appear to have not yet changed. This does not speak to whether individual developers and beta testers take or do not take technological issues like this into consideration in designing history, but it does speak to the process of making these kinds of games in this manner, because someone on the team likely will have to address optimisation at one point or another.

Paradox Development Studio games are modular in the sense that the different systems are positioned with varying degrees of integration to core mechanics and the game engine. On the one hand, using an example from *Europa Universalis IV*, combat systems are relatively easy to overhaul without causing a cascade of difficult-to-deal-with consequences for the rest of the game. On the other hand, the monarch points-system ties into almost every other aspect of the game, making it simple to hook into, but difficult to overhaul.¹⁶³

Keeping the Paradox Development Studio monetisation model and incremental development strategy in mind, history in the games thus becomes exposed to modification (not just for players but for developers as well) in an uneven manner, depending on where in this technical structure historical representation is situated for a given scenario. For example, beta tester Blaine notes that the user interfaces for *Europa Universalis IV* and *Hearts of Iron IV*

---

159 Developer informant Dale (June 15, 2017).
160 Developer informant Drew (June 28, 2018).
161 See Paradox Plaza, *CK2 Dev Diary #18: Optimization and modding* by Meneth. *Crusader Kings II* Developer Diary on August 9, 2016, accessed July 29 2021, https://forum.paradoxplaza.com/forum/index.php?threads/hearts-of-iron-iv-development-diary-1-our-vision.754427/; Paradox Plaza, *HOI4 Dev Diary – Patch 1.3.3 Update #2* by podcat. *Hearts of Iron IV* Developer Diary, February 15, 2017, accessed July 29, 2021.
162 Developer informant Devin (follow-up email). Note: It is possible to install older, less demanding versions of the games using Steam's so-called Beta function.
163 Developer informant Drew (June 28, 2018).

are created differently. The *Hearts of Iron IV* UI is scripted, which makes it possible for players to easily mod it, and faster and easier for developers to design and redesign. For *Europa Universalis IV*, the UI is edited via the engine, which makes editing it a more advanced process.[164]

Blaine goes on to note that the *Hearts of Iron IV* principle of using scripting as much as possible in design work and editing appears to be preferred by Paradox Development Studio, because: "[F]rankly, it is much cheaper to hire a content designer that can do [scripting] – build the research, and script and code things in that way, than it is to hire a programmer who has to do all those things in the game engine itself."[165] In instances such as these, the practicality of game making becomes a clear part of the framing of the past itself, particularly in the way the technical parameters and script language influence resource management. The modularity itself, of course, has far-reaching consequences for the representation of the past and counterfactuals, as will be discussed in more detail in chapter four.

Developers Identifying Goals and Expectations

The direction of the games' design – what topics to explore, design and implement, and how to do it – builds on goals and needs identified by the developers. Such goals and expectations inspire, frame and support historical game design, and range from those that make historical games interesting to players (such as familiarity and agency in a historical setting) to monetisation strategies and supplementary design practice (i.e. envisioning a fuller historical description) and to the appeal of counterfactual history.

Asking developers and beta testers why history makes a good theme for games generates mostly the same answer: building on real-world events can elicit an enticing sense of recognition and familiarity in players. Words and phrases like "existing framework," "shorthand," "reflection," "learning from past mistakes" and "backstory" are used to describe this postulate.[166] Developer Dorian compares making games about history to the notion of making licensed franchises – many potential customers are already familiar with, say, the world of Tolkien's *Lord of the Rings*. As a game developer on a project like that, one does not

---

[164] Beta tester informant Blaine (July 4, 2018).
[165] Beta tester informant Blaine (July 4, 2018).
[166] Developer informant Daryl (June 26, 2017), Dylan (June 29, 2018), Dallas (June 26, 2017) and Drew (June 28, 2018), consecutively.

necessarily need to spend hours explaining why this world is interesting, and the task of the player is, if not presupposed, at least more easily explained against the franchise backdrop.[167]

The same principle appears to be true for Paradox Development Studio and their historical games. The past is described as a smorgasbord of premises and content, a wealth of stories to base mechanics and scenarios on that easily tie into players' existing knowledge and interests. Describing the appeal of *Hearts of Iron IV*, in the reductionist albeit to-the-point words of Dorian: "It's the Second World War. Either I play as Germany, or I stop Germany. People understand that goal."[168] As discussed in chapter one, the Second World War plays a unique role in popular history, and digital strategy games are no exception.[169] One developer clarifies that both their grandfathers fought in the Second World War and that this fact has been an important and natural part of their family history.[170] In a similar manner, for *Europa Universalis IV*, the rationale behind making a game about the early modern era appears to be connected to the convenience of not having to engage with fantastical world-building but being able to rely on historical logic for reference.[171] As the developer Dale puts it, "there is so much we don't have to explain to people [...] Even for less famous periods, people are aware there were no mobile phones or railroads in the Middle Ages."[172]

Developers in the interviews underline that the games are not designed to teach those who play any specifics about the past. However, they do say that the games tend to function as a gateway to inspire learning about historical specifics in order to become better at the games. That is, to be able to make informed choices based on a deeper understanding of historical causality. Both developers and beta testers speculate that the dynamic between the players and the games through scripted and textual content is an integral aspect of the interactive experience: players learn about history from the game and understand historical change through play.[173] Conversely, players may read up on their favourite history parts from the game elsewhere. They then go back to playing, expecting that their newfound knowledge can translate into skill and progression in gameplay.[174]

---

167 Developer informant Dorian (June 29, 2018).
168 Developer informant Dorian (June 29, 2018).
169 Rochat, "A Quantitative Study of Historical Videogames," 9–11.
170 Developer informant Drew (June 28, 2018).
171 Developer informant Dylan (June 29, 2018).
172 Developer informant Dale (June 15, 2017).
173 Developer informant Devin (June 28, 2017) and beta tester informant Brett (July 5, 2018).
174 Wainwright, *Virtual History*, 9.

Building on popular presuppositions about the past can be interpreted as an opportunistic design practice. "Opportunistic," here in line with Kultima's findings, indicates the way a design process allows for a certain level of flexibility in order to accommodate influxes of ideas and influences.[175] Regarding *Europa Universalis IV*, *Hearts of Iron IV* and Paradox Development Studio in general, opportunism includes flexibility, for example, in terms of accommodating historical inaccuracies, misconceptions and counterfactuals for the benefit of stringency and gameplay. Similarly, when the games mirror developers' as well as player's historical presuppositions, it generates not only the thrill of recognition, but also the burden of expectation. According to the interviews, utilising historical presupposition to sell copies and draw an interest in the product also entails having to live up to certain expectations regarding gameplay, content and counterfactuals. In some cases, player expectations collide with, or contradict, those of the developers and other players.[176] Developer informants as well as beta testers all recount how they deal with players' varying opinions on what constitutes 1) important eras and events to depict, and 2) what are correct or incorrect depictions of said events. As such, bridging possible divides between verisimilitude and player expectation and presupposition appears to be a part of game design practice.

Interestingly, due to the differences in topics and eras depicted, *Europa Universalis IV* and *Hearts of Iron IV* appear to be subjected to different expectations in terms of content, scale and players' willingness to accept counterfactual outcomes. For example, due to its shorter timeline and faster pace, *Hearts of Iron IV* contains a relatively small number of historical events. *Hearts of Iron IV* developer Dorian notes the reason for this is that *Hearts of Iron IV* often puts the player in a position where historical events risk being a repetitive nuisance rather than flavour.[177] For instance, they say, in a gameplay situation where the player is focused on micro-managing their military, having to engage with historical events as pop-ups at the same time risks taking away from the gameplay experience rather than enhancing it. As a consequence, design emphasis for *Hearts of Iron IV*, especially for beta testers, tends to be on getting the game balance right and adding mechanically sound systems to an already narrow historical window.[178]

---

[175] Kultima, "Game Design Praxiology," 101–102; 156.
[176] Beta tester Brooklyn (October 22, 2018).
[177] Developer informant Dorian (June 29, 2018).
[178] Beta tester informant Blake (August 8, 2018).

Underlining that *Europa Universalis IV* needs more events and descriptive text than *Hearts of Iron IV* to be immersive, the same developer argues that "the longer the historical period you play, the more important historical events become."[179] For *Europa Universalis IV*, while an appropriate number of events and similar content must be balanced against real-time decision-making and gameplay, the notion of supplementary design practice appears to be the guiding star in terms of design goals. *Europa Universalis IV* is tasked with making the 400 years of the Early Modern period come alive with content. Of course, this does not mean that *Europa Universalis IV* does not require balancing, and indeed most DLCs contain some mechanical feature or change, but as expressed by for example the developer Dylan, in the long game, actions in *Europa Universalis IV* are reparable and consequences less immediate.[180] It is, of course, also worth noting that *Europa Universalis IV* was released three years prior to *Hearts of Iron IV*, giving it a head start in terms of supplementary design practice. Nevertheless, developers and beta testers alike assert that events and descriptive texts have different roles in the two games, and that difference affects design practice.

As already discussed, *Heart of Iron IV* builds on the gameplay concept of agency within the framework of the Second World War, agency being an important facilitator of counterfactual history in the game. Its predecessor, *Hearts of Iron III*, has become known for being comparably historically rigid in the sense that it has a limited number of designed contingencies for counterfactual gameplay. As noted by Dorian: "There was no system in place [in *Hears of Iron III*] that dealt with what would happen if 'History' didn't happen."[181] Dorian goes on to say that developers had been wanting to implement more counterfactuals for a long period of time, but had previously hesitated, potentially due to the game's reputation for historical accuracy. Nevertheless, *Hearts of Iron IV*, in comparison to *Hearts of Iron III*, has a continuously increasing number of counterfactual scenarios, the reason for which appears to be a more recent motivation to design for players who want to play the Second World War in *Hearts of Iron IV*, and who are also looking for the possibility to engage with counterfactual scenarios.[182]

To exemplify this, Dorian describes how, upon identifying this appeal and need for counterfactual gameplay, game direction led to the development of national focus trees in *Hearts of Iron IV*.[183] National focus trees work much in the

---

179 Developer informant Dorian (June 29, 2018).
180 Developer informant Dylan (June 29, 2018).
181 Developer informant Dorian (June 29, 2018).
182 Developer informant Dorian (June 29, 2018).
183 Developer informant Dorian (June 29, 2018).

same way as tech trees, a mechanic that has been around in digital strategy games since the original Sid Meyer's *Civilization* in 1991.[184] In *Hearts of Iron IV* they represent development in military, technological and ideological systems for each country. The setting on each tech tree lets the AI decide whether to go with a historical route or a counterfactual one (more on this in chapters 1 and 3). According to Dorian, expanding and increasing design focus on counterfactual history the way Paradox Development Studio has done for *Hearts of Iron IV*, ultimately increasing the share of players who choose to play the counterfactual paths from a few percent to almost half the player base.[185]

Counterfactual history in *Europa Universalis IV* has been a baseline prerequisite since the original board game version. However, in contrast to the more quantitative attitude towards content creation, the design of counterfactual history in *Europa Universalis IV* is more intricately qualitative in nature.[186] Based on the interviews, it appears that the supplementary design practice with regards to counterfactual history consists of 1) goal-setting mechanics such as mission trees and achievements, and 2) art design. Counterfactuals, goal setting, mission trees and achievements will be discussed in detail in chapter four. As previously mentioned, DLCs and content packs tend to focus on a certain theme, often specific regions, and come with a comparably small amount of assets and changes. These assets are often art, for example flags and animated soldiers. Art that illustrates counterfactual history is used as a design tool to illustrate what historical processes comprise a particular historical scenario.

An example is the Prussian soldiers' uniform for the latter half of the game. During this time in historical actuality, Prussia did not exist as a province. However, the player is able to pick Brandenburg as their starting province to create Prussia ahead of time as a counterfactual scenario, for which a uniform, then, has been designed using cultural references from the surrounding German provinces and the Teutonic Knights, a German Catholic order of crusaders.[187] In other words, contingencies for counterfactual gameplay are designed and implemented broadly in the game in order to complement counterfactual scenarios with visual components, as well as objectives and descriptive text.

---

[184] Tuur Ghys, "Technology Trees: Freedom and Determinism in Historical Strategy Games," *Game Studies* 12 (2012).
[185] Developer informant Dorian (June 29, 2018).
[186] Developer informant Dale (June 15, 2017), Devin (June 28, 2017).
[187] Developer informant Delta (June 27, 2017).

Developers' and Beta Testers' Path to History and Games

Among the interviewed developers, a mutual entry-point to games in the strategy genre is via an interest in history and the past, which at some point in their pasts led them to try the games in question.[188] Beta tester Brooklyn expresses the opposite, however, saying that they started playing *Hearts of Iron* ten years prior and from that developed an interest in historical studies[189]: "Once you have started playing, you develop an interest in the epoch and read up on things you find reflected in the game. The more you do [look things up], the more you want to play, and you end up playing even more. [...] There is definitely an intercommunion in how these practices interact and encourage one another."[190]

Some developers harbour a long-standing, personal interest in history. Dale, for example, says they take great pride in their interest in historical study and repeatedly refer to their own collection of books about historical topics. The meaning of this personal home library appears to have a history of its own. When referring to the acquisition of the books, a personalised history of very specific interests and of learning plays out. Dale takes us back to their childhood and references, for example, movies about the Second World War that their father would watch, and muses that this had some influence over the specific historical topics that they later became interested in. This developer has a particular interest in macro perspectives on global history, imperialism in different contexts and military history. Dale mentions that most of the books that they keep and collect are in the vein of *Guns, germs and steel* and *Collapse* by Jared Diamond and that small-scale historical details are of little interest. Their fascination is centred on understanding historical change, and the rise and fall of civilisations.[191]

Developer Dakota was recruited to Paradox through the beta testing community. Their interest in history was initiated by popular culture, games in particular. They work primarily on *Heart of Iron* and state that their interest in military history and the Second World War was partially sparked by playing earlier iterations of the game. Eventually, they started doing volunteer work in the modding community and beta testing and was recruited as a content designer. Apart from

---

[188] Developer informants Drew (June 28, 2018); Dylan (June 29, 2018); Dorian (June 29, 2018).
[189] Beta tester informant Brooklyn (October 22, 2018). Compare with Robert Houghton, "Where Did You Learn That," and Beavers, "The Informal Learning of History with Digital Games."
[190] Beta tester informant Brooklyn (October 22, 2018).
[191] Developer interview Dale (June 15, 2017).

the Second World War, Dakota mentions a particular interest in imperial history and economic history.[192]

As salient as the "history buff" discourse is among developers at Paradox Development Studio, an off-the-clock interest in exploring history is not a prerequisite for working at Paradox Development Studio, even though developers with that interest appear to be in the majority. Daryl, whose role is on the technical side of development and does not require detailed insight into the content of the games, explains their personal interest in history as follows: "I would say it is a passive interest. I am very fascinated when learning new things about [the past], and working here has taught me a lot about various [historical] things, particularly obscure things, details I would not know of otherwise. While learning in school, there are so many broad strokes, while those fun details that are fun to use in games generally tend not to come up."[193] Daryl specifies how working with and thus learning about narrow, micro-historical items has deepened their relationship with history as a subject.

Design Legacy and Contemporary Sensibilities

Game design is timely. Kultima, referencing design scholar Kari Kuutti, notes that artefacts (here, games) are "not built for eternity, but rather for immediate use."[194] This means that concurrent mentalities and game or game-design related paradigms are a part of game development and need to be understood when analysing any game. Developers are both aware of the historical development of the game and its trajectory, and aware that there is a desire to design for state of the art. Similarly, game development also entails tuning in to broader contemporary social and cultural discussions that might have an impact on the development and perception of the games. This segment discusses some contemporary aspects like this in relation to development on *Europa Universalis IV* and *Hearts of Iron IV*.

Design legacy is an impactful element in at least two ways. Firstly, it can be used to discuss whether iteration has generated stagnation or fluctuation in design over time. Secondly, it can be used to discuss how broader genre conventions inform design practice. In other words, what legacy, traditions and expectations stemming from within the game making context impact game

---

192 Developer informant Dakota (June 28, 2017).
193 Developer informant Daryl (June 26, 2017).
194 Kultima, "Game Design Praxiology," 52.

development? With regards to iteration, *Europa Universalis IV* and *Hearts of Iron IV*, as noted in chapter 1, were well received in comparison to their predecessors. In addition to this, one might consider what material such as code and other assets, including ideological heritage such as historical arguments, carry over from one edition of a game to the next – and, of course, what does not. Paradox Development Studio games have longer histories than many other game series and have seen a relatively small change in design over time. As discussed, one observable shift between the present games and ones before is the one towards accessibility and away from steep learning curves and complicated rulesets. This is also reflected in the Paradox pillars. To this end, Paradox Development Studio developers exhibit signs of following the "accessibility turn."[195] That is, they are willing to make design decisions to improve the user experience rather than for the benefit of pursuing a specific design idea.[196] This notion will be explored further into this chapter.

Although game development is certainly influenced by contemporary paradigms and concerns, both games' design fundamentals, ultimately, are slow-to-change and stringent, regardless of paradigm shifts, especially in comparison to the overall change in game design trends over the last decade and a half, in particular the rise of "casual gaming," the normalisation of digital gaming and the inclusion of new user groups.[197] Ergin Bulut studied triple-A game-making (triple-A being the most expensive to make and best-selling games on the market) and concluded that this category is, in part, distinguished by its one-dimensionality. Commercially successful games, Bulut notes, adhere to a technology-driven race to be at the forefront of fidelity and performance, preventing creativity in other aspects of game making, including genre, mechanics and content.[198]

Paradox Development Studio, in contrast, does not constitute a triple-A studio by the same metrics, nor do they aim to have top-of-the-line game tech (see, for example, Paradox pillar "Form follows function"). For Paradox Development

---

[195] Douglas Wilson and Miguel Sicart, "Now It's Personal: On Abusive Game Design," *Proceedings of FuturePlay* (2010): 2.

[196] Wilson and Sicart, "Now It's Personal," 1. Wilson and Sicart argues that games that are made entirely based on player advocacy contain no design elements that provide what they call dialogic relations. Dialogic relation is dialogue through logic; design by which the developer and the player engage in a kind of "conversation that presents itself in the form of a dare." The game system ultimately facilitates a connection between the developer and the players in a way that neither player-centred design nor developer-centred design can do.

[197] See also Kultima, "Game Design Praxiology," 53–63; Annakaisa Kultima, "Casual Game Design Values" in *Proceedings of* MindTrek (2009).

[198] Ergin Bulut, "One-Dimensional Creativity: A Marcusean Critique of Work and Play in the Video Game Industry," *Triple C – Communication, capitalism and critique* 16 (2018): 766–767.

Studio, game design is cohesive over time due to the context provided by the games' genre and the impact of genre convention. This is reflected in Yannick Rochat's quantitative study on historical games. He found that a majority of historical games can in fact be placed in the strategy genre, according to his categorisation. Importantly, Rochat also underlines that the complexity of strategy games has naturally lent itself well to PC gaming, and the requirement to play with keyboard and mouse paraphernalia further constrains – possibly perpetuates – the material conditions under which digital strategy gaming is framed.[199] And, as noted by Jeremiah McCall, these genre conventions impose themselves on historical representation just as much as the historical content shapes the game genre.[200]

A notable example of the impact of design legacy and genre convention with regards to historical representation and the implementation of counterfactuals is that development for *Europa Universalis IV* contains content that was made for previous iterations of the game. There is, in effect, code, scripting and descriptive text in *Europa Universalis IV* that has literally been inherited from earlier versions.[201] Speaking on the relationship between historiography and paradigms in the games, one *Europa Universalis IV* developer, Devin, would like to go through old content for the purpose of looking at it with more "modern eyes," something deemed necessary in some cases, but ultimately difficult due to the large scope of content in the game.[202] That is not to say that *Europa Universalis IV* consists only of ageing or problematic historical paradigms. On the one hand, though, it does show that the legacy practice – i.e. the accumulation and pure scope of content in *Europa Universalis IV* – presents a practical challenge in terms of representing the past. On the other hand, it presents interesting evidence to suggest that game design practice can also be inherently unchanging, a finding that contrasts previous research that underlines the immediacy and timeliness of game design. I here argue that this is also made possible, in part, by genre convention, i.e., what players have come to expect for the specific type of games that Paradox Development Studio make.

Previous research on history and digital games has, as already discussed, focused largely on ideological critique of themes and contents, emphasising their inherent colonialism, eurocentrism and the varying uses of historical atrocities. Digital strategy games often appear in such research, and Paradox Development

---

[199] See Rochat, "A Quantitative Study of Historical Videogames," 10–11.
[200] McCall, "Historical Problem Space Framework."
[201] Developer informant Devin (June 28, 2017).
[202] Developer informant Devin (June 28, 2017).

Studio games are no exception.[203] In light of this historiography, developers and beta testers were asked about what they consider the limits of game design when it comes to historical and counterfactual representation, and what current and/ or historical events and mentalities might influence and help rationalise design decisions in the present.

Answers to this question vary and variations among answers seem to depend partly on which game the interviewee is associated with, and if they are a developer or beta tester. Beta tester Bailey, associated with *Europa Universalis IV*, argues that, for better or worse, colonialism is a core aspect of the games. "There are some game mechanics that give European countries an advantage," they note. However, since *Europa Universalis II*, "developers have tried to provide understandable reasons to any such advantages," suggesting that while the overarching design and message has not changed significantly, the games now provide a more coherent background and context to European powers taking advantage of colonial expansion and the people living there. The increase in content focused on other parts of the world also helps with balancing the Eurocentric perception, according to Bailey.[204]

As another example, Dorian, a developer on *Hearts of Iron IV*, notes that design opportunities as well as limitations are found in both in history and in the contemporary. The framings include current political events and popular discourse, both in regional and local historical culture and in commonly repeated misconceptions, in addition to prejudices.[205] With regards to the latter two, and the importance of tact if you will, developers and beta testers alike mention specifically that it can be difficult as a Westerner to fully comprehend historical developments that led to specific events in, for example, the Middle East. Dorian points specifically to the risk of misunderstanding fundamental aspects of culture and political policy, historical as well as contemporary. "It is not just fact,"[206] Dorian says, underlining the potential moral and emotional consequences to any inadvertent or otherwise misguided faux pas. Along the same lines,

---

203 Souvik Mukherjee, "Playing Subaltern: Video Games and Postcolonialism," in *Games and Culture* 13 (2016); Apperley, "Counterfactual Communities," 4–7. Notably, the discussion continuously extends outside of the academic context into online periodicals and newspapers. See for example Henrik Arnstad, "Får man strunta i Förintelsen," *Svenska Dagbladet*, June 25, 2017, accessed July 14 2021, available at https://www.svd.se/far-man-strunta-i-forintelsen; Luke Winkie, "The struggle over gamers who use mods to create racist alternate histories," Kotaku, June 6, 2018, accessed July 1, 2018, available at https://kotaku.com/the-struggle-over-gamers-who-use-mods-to-create-racist-1826606138.
204 Beta tester informant Bailey (March 13, 2018)
205 Developer informant Dorian (June 29, 2018).
206 Developer informant Dorian (June 29, 2018).

beta tester Brook says that: "The slave trade [had] very little impact on us in Scandinavia, so we don't really think about it all that much, while if you are a player in the U.S., it's probably a lot more sensitive."[207] There are, to be sure, historical as well as contemporary reasons for Scandinavians to be aware of the atrocity of trans-Atlantic slave trade. Nevertheless, the beta tester expresses an awareness of how historical culture and the role of cultural heritage may differ geographically.

While academic research is a major resource for accessing content, and while verisimilitude appears to guide design practice in part, there are cases where designers must go against historical consensus and academic discussion due to contradictory popular belief. One such example is the historical effect of bombing activities in Europe during the Second World War, compared to the same in *Hearts of Iron IV*. According to Dorian, their research shows that the bombings of English cities by the Germans actually had a positive effect on morale. Contrary to intent, as well as popular belief, the bombings made support for the war effort in Britain go up.[208] This is not the case in *Hearts of Iron IV*, however, and there appears to be two reasons for the developers to avoid implementing this mechanic according to their research. The first one is gameplay: "You simply can't implement a mechanic which says 'Bomb the enemy to make them stronger.' It doesn't make sense."[209] The second one is expressed as anchored in a popular hindsight narrative which establishes resilience to discouragement in the face of bombings as a fundamental aspect of the British war effort.[210] Paradox Development Studio's solution to this particular problem is rhetoric. A reverse mechanic has been implemented which lowers the morale of the playable country in question if the player does not defend themselves against the bombings. This solution allows developers to reconcile the tension between what they perceive to be academic consensus (bombings as morality boost) and popular belief (bombings as detrimental to morale), without compromising gameplay.

Another example, this one from *Crusader Kings II*, is described by developer informant Dallas. The game covers the mainly European and Asian Middle Ages and as such could, if it followed a completely historical ideology, potentially contain children marrying and giving birth. However, doing so would, according to the developer, go against PEGI requirements for age-appropriate content and, in-

---

207 Beta tester informant Brook (February 21, 2018).
208 Developer informant Dorian (June 29, 2018).
209 Developer informant Dorian (June 29, 2018).
210 Developer informant Dorian (June 29, 2018).

deed, be deemed immoral. In avoiding this, dates of births and ages of historical persons are modified to fit a contemporary codex and still be recognisable for the players who are familiar with the characters in question.[211]

As such, game design practice at Paradox Development Studio is indeed timely. However, it is not always immediate. Due to the framing of the digital strategy genre and the notion of design legacy, *Europa Universalis IV* and *Hearts of Iron IV* remain cohesive and stringent over time. Simultaneously, developers and beta testers express awareness that, for example, historiography changes over time, and historical culture may differ geographically. Paradox Development Studio navigate the contemporary sensibilities concerning historical culture and historiographical paradigms, especially in terms of understanding what players might expect from the games. Nevertheless, the unchanging systems and content that, for example, continue to define *Europa Universalis IV* as a game about European colonial expansion do come with some severe implications in terms of historical arguments and representation. Developers and beta testers do point these issues out, but addressing them does not seem to be a prioritised task, but rather something that happens at the behest of individual developers and beta testers.

Influences and Sourcing Content

In addition to navigating the complex and abstract fields of external and internal goals and needs, prompts and pressures, in order to make design decisions, how do developers actually research content for the games? How and where is content collected and processed? What other games influence design, and what kind of literature and other material is used?

Games and Play as Research and Influence

As previously mentioned, Paradox Development Studio was founded on the premise of adapting the board game *Europa Universalis* into a digital strategy game, thus aligning with war games that ultimately have their roots in the nineteenth century and explore and imitate historical wars and battles. The focus is usually military history and game elements consist of a map, armies and sup-

---

[211] Developer informant Dallas (June 26, 2017).

plies, and an array of mechanics that denote movement and tactics.²¹² Paradox Development Studio does not draw explicitly or solely from war games, but the trajectory and legacy is present. Furthermore, developers and beta testers all play games as much as they make games.

Playing games is an established way for developers to do research. This is part of the ecosystem of game making and builds partially on creative intertextuality and partially on the notion of player literacy, i.e. the idea that players who are familiar with a variety of different games find new games more easily accessible and progress faster due to having acquired transferable skills in previous sessions.²¹³ Playing other games than that which is currently being developed is also a method used to orient in the fast-moving business of game development where keeping up with trends is valuable for developers in certain roles, if not necessary, in order to stay relevant and sell as many copies as possible. The notion of "game talk" is also, according to Casey O'Donnell, an important skill used between developers. Being able to talk about other games for reference as well as conducting yourself as a "real gamer" are both important aspects to game development's cultural capital.²¹⁴ Furthermore, Olli Sotamaa notes that playing together in the workplace is common practice among developers, and that this has the benefits of teambuilding as well as developers learning from each other.²¹⁵ A notable example of this at Paradox Development Studio are the so called Dev Clashes – regular instalments of developers playing the game together and against each other while streaming.²¹⁶ According to Dylan, to participate in Dev Clashes is not compulsory but somewhat expected, adding that these session are generally scheduled during work hours.²¹⁷

---

212 See for example Stephen J. Patrick, "The History of Wargaming," in *Wargame Design. The History, Production and Use of Conflict Simulation Games, including a New, Completely Updated, Comprehensive Wargame Directory*, ed. Stephen J. Patrick et al. (New York: Hippocrene Books, 1983).
213 See for example Eric Zimmerman, "Gaming Literacy: Game Design as a Model for Literacy in the Twenty-First Century," in *The Video Game Theory Reader 2*, ed. Bernard Perron and Mark J.P. Wolf (London: Routledge, 2008), 23–31.
214 Casey O'Donnell, "The Work/Play of the Interactive New Economy: Video Game Development in the United States and India" (PhD diss., Rensselaer Polytechnic Institute, 2008), 42–44.
215 Sotamaa, "Game Developers Playing Games: Instrumental Play, Game Talk, and Preserving the Joy of Play," in *Game Production Studies*, ed. Olli Sotamaa and Jan Svelch (Amsterdam: Amsterdam University Press, 2021), 111–113.
216 Paradox Wiki, *Dev Clashes*.
217 Developer informant Dylan (June 29, 2018).

At least two of the developer informants play a significant amount of Paradox Development Studio games, also outside of work.[218] Similarly, beta testers like Bobbie and Brett, as gamers, tend to play mostly Paradox Development Studio games – again with some variety; some play only the games they test for, others routinely work their way through the whole catalogue, i.e. *Imperator: Rome*, *Crusader Kings*, *Europa Universalis*, *Victoria*, *Hearts of Iron* and *Stellaris*.[219] Beta testers, when asked about ludic influences, mention games ranging from first person shooters to other strategy games and third-person action games, but decidedly gravitate towards games with a history focus.[220]

Dorian (again, primarily associated with *Hearts of Iron IV*) describes their relationship with games as influence for game design:

> I play solitaire type games, board games for one person against a form of AI. Often management games. Your aim is to manage the German submarine fleet during this or that year, or manage all aspects of the War Pacific. You get this and this much scouting plan, fuel tokens and every time you move, it costs a marker. It is pretty fun [and] pretty old school. It is just a different way to do research in, and one might find [something] which [those games] have made a huge point of and I start to wonder why, and one starts to look into it and if it turns out to be hugely important we might include that in our game.[221]

In a solitaire-style board game, players take turns managing their own moves and the moves of the opponent. The opponent is played through the rules and presents the player with any number of challenges, just like in *Europa Universalis IV* and *Hearts of Iron IV*, although in the digital game the opponent's moves are handled by the AI and engine. It appears as if this developer stays close to the Paradox Development Studio genre in terms of play for research and focuses on getting inspired by content and mechanics that already belong to the genre of historical strategy games.

In some instances, mods to the Paradox Development Studio games in question appear to have been influential to design decision-making because they explore content and mechanics outside the current scope of Paradox Development Studio design and thus may be inspirational on a creative level but also function as a measurement of what players like on an experimental level. Dorian says "I used to look a lot at mods, but we usually have to turn it down a notch. Many of

---

218 Developer informant Dale (June 15, 2017); Developer informant Delta (June 27, 2017).
219 Beta tester informants Bobbie (February 20, 2018), Brett (July 5, 2018).
220 To be clear, it is worth mentioning that the interviews gravitate towards historical topics to the point where it is hard to evaluate whether the questions allow informants to reason outside of this discourse.
221 Developer informant Dorian (June 29, 2018).

them are made to prove a point [and end up] with a very narrow focus."[222] By "making a point", the developer means that certain mods also function as commentary on developer decisions by focusing on a specific topic, mechanic, balance issue etc. In contrast, other informants express a decisive aversion to looking at, and being inspired by, mods in any way. When asked about mods, Dale, a developer primarily associated with *Europa Universalis IV*, says they think the game is perfect without mods. They say they are happy that the modding community is so passionate, as long as they, the developer, do not have to play with mods themself.[223] For some beta testers who are also mod creators, playing is an important aspect of their work, both on the mod and the base game. They use the base game for benchmarking and evaluating how changes will influence their mods and in so doing produce meaningful feedback to developers, primarily on topics regarding stress and optimisation.[224]

In summary, developers and beta testers alike express a consciousness and familiarity with intertextual and contemporary ludic influence on their design. Play that influences design practice at Paradox Development Studio appears focused on games that deal with history. In at least one case, play is in fact limited to war gaming and games that inherently fall within, or very close to, the same genre as *Europa Universalis IV* and *Hearts of Iron IV*. Practices range from staying in touch with current trends in strategy game design to tapping into gaming literacy broadly with regards to both content and mechanics.

Doing Research

I here intend to break down the different research strategies and resources mentioned in the interviews, and how they are adapted in game design practice. A significant distinction that can be made at the outset is that the notion of doing research here encompasses the search, reading and application of literature on historical topics. Academic methods of historical scholarship such as the use and criticism of archives and primary sources, or systematic literature review, are not part of this practice.

Developers and beta testers, regardless of job description, do read and learn about the past by necessity, but they are also driven by a personal interest in history. The degree, origin and impact of said interest vary. Some, such as developer

---

[222] Developer informant Dorian (June 29, 2018).
[223] Developer informant Dale (June 15, 2017).
[224] Beta tester informant Brett (July 5, 2018); beta tester informant Blaine (July 4, 2018).

Daryl, picked up an interest in history when they started working for Paradox Development Studio.[225] Others were recruited by Paradox, or sought out the company as an employer, specifically because they could contribute historical knowledge as beta testers or modders.[226] Furthermore, developers take care to be up to date with historical scholarship on their areas of interest. While several informants appear consciously aware that players in general are not historical experts, and that they sometimes harbour common misconceptions about the past, developers take care to research events and other bits of history from as trustworthy sources as possible.

Most informants mention Wikipedia as the first place they go for information. Developers emphasise being aware that Wikipedia builds on crowd sourcing and can be misleading. For example, Dallas, mainly associated with *Europa Universalis IV*, mentions using Wikipedia as an entry point into a certain topic, but also being in the habit of always checking the listed resources to a given article to make sure they are trustworthy – and that the Wikipedia article has references in the first place.[227] This is put in similar wording by Dorian who says, "it usually starts by digging in Wikipedia. [...] After a while one finds certain details there which we need to dig into in more depth and that is when it gets harder,"[228] noting that research becomes more cumbersome after that, adding: "Sometimes we find theses online, or we simply have to purchase books."[229]

A majority of the interviewed developers and beta testers read and source materials for the purpose of design on their own time. As previously noted, beta testers receive no compensation for their work, and it would appear that developers have a similar attitude to reading up on historical events or other relevant topics that tie into creating the games in question. Dorian again:

> A lot of research, honestly, I do on my own time. I can't sit around reading books at work. That would just be weird. [It is a part of my job] but there is generally no room for it and reading is quite fun so it is just more natural to do it on my own time. I've recently started buying some audio books too. Those fit my schedule better [...] I can listen to them when I commute. There are quite a lot of history-oriented books on Audible these days.[230]

As exemplified by this testimony, doing research is considered a large and important part of game design practices at Paradox Development Studio, but the state-

---

225 Developer informant Daryl (June 26, 2017).
226 Developer informant Devin (June 28, 2017); developer informant Dakota (June 28, 2017).
227 Developer informant Dallas (June 26, 2017).
228 Developer informant Dorian (June 29, 2018).
229 Developer informant Dorian (June 29, 2018).
230 Developer informant Dorian (June 29, 2018).

ment also indicates that there are many other tasks that are considered more important. In fact, those who do spend time researching outside of normal work hours take the opportunity to buy books for themselves and build their own private libraries. The concept of creating "home libraries" is mentioned by several developers and beta testers. If requested, Paradox Development Studio will reimburse costs associated with research for employees but not for beta testers. Among those who mention it, developers prefer to purchase their own reading material for private ownership and use.[231] This is usually in the form of literature, audio books, podcasts (for example *Revolutions Podcast* is specifically mentioned) and TV such as *Discovery Channel*.[232] Some developers and most beta testers claim that academic works are always preferred when possible. Beta tester Brett says they try to always use web-based resources. Purchasing books seems treacherous, they say, after an instance in which they acquired a book about French history that they only later realised was written by someone with a xenophobic agenda.[233] Conversely, Blue mentions usually starting their search on the internet but oftentimes ending by taking time and effort to find information about obscure topics in physical books via for example antique book shops.[234]

On that note, there is little by way of stringency as far as developers' and beta testers' ability or ambition to evaluate literature and sources for research. It is not within the scope of this study to assess their skills in, for example, source criticism, but it is clear from the interviews that strategies vary. Beta tester Bobbie mentions that the beta testing community (that can also include developers) have sometimes-fiery discussions about how to implement certain historical events, and the validity of sources, that are – in their opinion – clearly framed by their individual knowledge and experience as readers of history and as game developers.[235]

For those designers who mention having studied history at university, utilising their academic skills becomes a useful tool in research – primarily in finding and assessing sources but also for being aware of the different ways historical knowledge is produced and communicated within the historians' community and academia in general. Developer Devin describes their personal method for starting to research a topic as follows. It starts with acquiring entry-level histor-

---

231 Developer informant Devin (June 28, 2017); Dorian (June 29, 2018); beta tester informant Blue (August 20, 2018).
232 Developer informant Dorian (June 29, 2018). *Revolutions Podcast*, Duncan 2013.
233 Beta tester informant Brett (July 5, 2018).
234 Beta tester informant Blue (August 20, 2018).
235 Beta tester informant Bobbie (February 20, 2018).

ical works on said topic. After reading the first books, the next step is delving into detailed areas and adapting them to game design, usually event writing and scripting. Knowing which areas are worth exploring further is guided by the goals and needs of the project in question and very often comes down to trusting their own judgment. They underline that trusting one's own judgment is, in their case, supported by their academic background and skills.[236]

Researching history for the development and design of *Europa Universalis IV* and *Hearts of Iron IV* is in many ways similar for both games, with a few notable differences. The extensive research available on the Second World War makes research for *Hearts of Iron IV* easier in the sense that there are more historical details available. As most historians are aware, this comes with the downside of having to sift through a lot of material to find and compile the relevant details. *Europa Universalis IV*-related material, on the other hand, can be hard to locate in the first place due to the scope of the game, both geographically and temporally. Every obscure aspect of disparate spatial and temporal points of interest of the period has not always been studied or made available to, for instance, an English-speaking audience.[237] This is partly mitigated by recruiting beta testers with specific historical insights and knowledge about certain regions and periods. Again, a variety of motivations influence both game design practice and design decisions, and take precedence over historical accuracy where necessary.

Beta Testers: Research, Testing and Brainstorming

In the digital games industry, beta tests are a common way for game developers to test the integrity and playability of games that are not yet released.[238] All game projects go through testing of some kind in order to gauge the quality of their work. Paradox Development Studio, like any comparable studio, have hired game testers to provide in-house quality assessment, and run automated testing

---

236 Developer informant Devin (June 28, 2017).
237 Beta tester informant Brooklyn (October 22, 2018).
238 I have no data on the exact prevalence of beta testing usage in the game development industry. In the digital strategy game genre, there is at least one more example of developers starting their careers as beta testers outside of Paradox Development Studio. In an interview with historical game scholar Jeremiah McCall, Jon Shafer, lead game designer on *Civilization V*, mentions that he started his career in the industry as a beta tester for earlier iterations of *Civilization*. See Jeremiah McCall, *GTP Designer Talk Podcast – Jon Shafer*, July 3, 2019, accessed July 15, 2019, https://gamingthepast.net/2019/07/03/gtp-designer-talk-2-jon-shafer.

on builds daily.[239] Beta testing specifically, however, typically refers to making a beta (unfinished but playable) version of the game externally available to a limited server or limited number of players. Developers can test for technical issues as well as player experiences. These so-called "betas" or "beta tests" can be open or closed, denoting how players may gain access to the beta testing process. Open beta typically means that anyone with the right equipment may access the testing servers and play and test the game at their leisure. Closed beta typically means a player needs some kind of invitation to be able to play. Which beta test format is used depends on what kind of game it is, and what company traditions, needs and marketing strategies apply. The arrangement is based on an agreement between studio and player that the product they are testing is not a finished game and that there might be bugs and issues that testing will help solve before the actual release of the game. In return for testing, players gain access to the game early and get a sense of the product.

In the case of Paradox Development Studio, the aim of beta testing is similar, but the process looks different. Furthermore, the role of Paradox Development Studio beta testers is quite specific, compared to a broader industry perspective. Adhering to the definitions above, Paradox Development Studio essentially conducts ongoing closed betas. The Paradox Development Studio beta testers consist of handpicked community members who have continuous access to the development process and communicate personally with developers to provide their feedback. In many ways, the Paradox Development Studio beta testers' work resembles that of any quality assessment team in a game company, except the work is voluntary and varies in intensity. Importantly, Paradox Development Studio beta testers also do design work, not just testing.

Paradox Development Studio beta testers are not employed by the company. They contribute to game design, content design and bug hunting on a voluntary basis. The process could be compared to a form of crowd sourcing of material and content that Paradox Development Studio does not mobilise the resources to research internally. Beta testers tend to have an interest in and focus on a specific historical era, area or theme. They work remotely and communicate with developers and other beta testers online. Beta testers are sometimes given tasks to test specific aspects of the game and to create content. Sometimes the testers bring ideas or issues to the developers. Beta testers appear to have been a signif-

---

239 Developer informant Dylan (June 29, 2018).

icant part of the Paradox Development Studio workflow since at least around the release of the first *Europa Universalis* game.[240]

Beta testers are, in the words of developer Dorian, "completely essential" to the production of *Europa Universalis IV* and *Hearts of Iron IV*. Dorian even goes so far to say that *Hearts of Iron IV* could not exist in the way that it does without them: "We would need very big teams. The type of work they do – we would have to hire historians and people with special interests, and it is extremely collaborative. I am very open with them [and they] understand the way we think, and our rationalisations."[241]

It is difficult to assess the number of hours of work on average the beta testers perform. All beta testers say it varies a lot and that they regularly break away from beta tester work for up to six months. Work intensity also fluctuates over time. The smallest amount mentioned in the interviews is approximately two hours per month.[242] Others estimate doing approximately one month of full-time work in total over the course of a year.[243] One beta tester approximates that they have, on one occasion, for a specific task, done up to 100 hours of beta tester work over the course of a single month.[244]

Developer perception appears to be that beta testing is always available as a resource, although they acknowledge that there is never any guarantee that beta testers available will be able help with very specific issues or research.[245] The amount of work produced by beta testers appears to vary with who the individual beta tester is and when Paradox Development Studio needs to activate them for a project. As previously mentioned, communication between beta testers and developers happens primarily online on the Paradox forums or on a dedicated Slack server, and it appears that there is some form of constant communication going on between beta testers and developers but with varying intensity. All beta testers, however, give the same impression: whenever a release is coming up, the possibility to get involved with testing and contribution increases, and beta testers are called upon more frequently.

Paradox Development Studio developers reach out to beta testers for many different reasons, one of the most important being to help and provide expertise with particular historical content. As an example, historical culture and conno-

---

[240] Henrik Fåhraeus, *Crusader Kings 3 – PDXCON Berlin Keynote* (video resource, 2019); beta tester Blue (August 20, 2018).
[241] Developer informant Dorian (June 29, 2018).
[242] Beta tester informant Brook (February 21, 2018).
[243] Beta tester informant Bobbie (February 20, 2018).
[244] Beta tester informant Bay (February 2, 2018).
[245] Developer informant Dorian (June 29, 2018), Devin (June 28, 2017).

tation is often local and beta testers in certain regions are engaged to provide context and help make decisions with regards to, for example, content design, the naming of historical provinces in English and cultural context for a specific culture and region. Blaine says they make a lot of use of sources in their native language, which they feel are inaccessible to other developers and beta testers.[246] Bobbie mentions using their localised expertise to help navigate topical sensitivities, such as how perspectives on colonialism and post-colonial discussion differ in their home country compared to, for example, the rest of Europe and the United States.[247]

Beta testers are perceived by developers as both driven and able to take initiative, as well as available to be given specific tasks. This usually depends on the situation, how far along the design process is and what kind of issue the teams are facing. Tasks vary. The most generic ones are bug and stability testing, balance testing and content creation. As put by Dorian: "We have a lot of testers who are interested in fleets and similar things, and they have information that is difficult to find online. [So I ask] them to look through their books. 'We could do with some help. Please, research these African countries and figure out what alternate flags for them could look like.'"[248]

Beta testers are selected based on their experience with Paradox Development Studio games and their interest in history, often a narrow special interest that is useful. Beta testers can also be selected based on what languages they speak, in order to help out with quality assessment of game localisation.[249] Developers generally appear to put a lot of responsibility and faith in their beta testers but are equally aware that they represent a core group of avid players and history whizzes who might not fully represent the other hundreds of thousands of players.[250] Having said that, most beta testers as well as developers are quick to underline the amount of influence beta testers have on the games themselves. Quoting beta tester Brooklyn: "There are some beta testers who started recently, that are very surprised at the amount of influence they have. [For me], that means really embracing [this influence] as well."[251] They elaborate on this influence, stating that it gives them more immediate access to the processes at Paradox Development Studio and that their suggestions are considered much more promptly than suggestions given by players on the regular forums. The beta test-

---

246 Beta tester informant Blaine (July 4, 2018).
247 Beta tester informant Bobbie (February 20, 2018).
248 Developer informant Dorian (June 29, 2018).
249 Developer informant Dallas (June 26, 2017).
250 Developer informant Dorian (June 29, 2018); beta tester Brett (July 5, 2018).
251 Beta tester informant Brooklyn (October 22, 2018).

ers describes themselves as "ambassadors of sorts, to keep up with what [non-beta tester] players discuss and what appear to be the biggest issues."[252] This notion is confirmed by developer Devin who, when asked about the influence of the public forums, said that beta tester suggestions are easier to work with because it is possible to track the person behind those ideas and have longer discussions about them if necessary.[253] When research is done by beta testers, developers fact-check their work, perpetuating the notion that historical authenticity is a baseline criteria, whether or not it is implemented as such, or functions as a point of reference for counterfactual gameplay.

Beta testers can focus on either balance and bug hunting or research, but most informants state that it is usually up to themselves to take on tasks they find interesting.[254] They discuss using the same channels and tend to bounce their work off one another regardless of speciality.[255] Brooklyn illustrates a third category, that of "advising," "discussion partners" or "sounding boards" for Paradox Development Studio developers, meaning beta testers who are not specialised in creating content, or testing the game, as much as discussing historical events, context and application into the game.[256] Beta tester Bay, who is associated with both *Europa Universalis IV* and *Hearts of Iron IV*, says they contribute primarily by bug hunting for *Hearts of Iron*, and content creation, as well as bug hunting, for *Europa Universalis*. Bug hunting, or balance testing, includes, for example, checking that in-game resources are acquired and spent the way they are intended by each playable nation.[257]

In terms of content creation, it appears beta testers can be assigned chunks of content to deliver, usually related to a topic or a region in the game. As an example, beta tester Bay talks about "delivering" a set of national ideas for several playable nations, and a major portion of the map work for the random new world setting.[258] Content creation, for example national ideas, is described as entailing doing research, "find[ing] interesting historical stuff that can relate to in-game mechanics."[259] In other words, this process includes evaluating the histor-

---

[252] Beta tester informant Brooklyn (October 22, 2018).
[253] Developer informant Devin (June 28, 2017).
[254] Beta tester informant Bay (February 2, 2018).
[255] Beta tester informant Bobbie (February 20, 2018).
[256] Beta tester informant Brooklyn (October 22, 2018).
[257] Beta tester informant Bay (February 2, 2018), Brooklyn (October 22, 2018).
[258] Beta tester informant Bay (February 2, 2018). Random new world (RNW) is an optional setting available in the *Conquest of Paradise* DLC, in which continents are randomly generated from a set of tiles. Tiles are given a variety of statistics and modifiers to create dynamics. Gameplay in RNW is centered around historically plausible as well as fantastical scenarios.
[259] Beta tester informant Bay (February 2, 2018).

ical content found during research in order to make sure it makes sense in the context of the game (or DLC), giving, for example, National ideas a reasonable bonus but not making them too overpowering. This again indicates that developers place a lot of trust in beta testers going into a process.

Beta tester Bailey lays out a few different ways developers can activate beta testers. Bailey describes an occasion when they were given a task with specific guidelines from a developer regarding new provinces that would go into a *Europa Universalis IV* expansion. They were provided with a target number of provinces to create but otherwise had free reign. On a different occasion, Bobbie gave the Paradox Development Studio design team a couple of suggestions for the map that were then contemplated by the developers, who picked their favourites and suggested a few changes of their own. Communication and iteration went on from there. In a third scenario, Bailey's suggestions for National Ideas were rejected or modified by developers to a large extent before implementation. According to Bailey, the task in the third scenario had to do with in-game bonuses and balance to a larger extent than the previous two. They say developers have a better understanding of these particular design elements and are thus more than welcome to veto such things.[260] This, of course, is a striking example of design imposing itself on the representation of the past. Bailey's work is done from the perspective of history, but the issue of balance is a gameplay value that is, ultimately, external to historical considerations.[261]

Even though there is trust and developers, in fact, seem to fully depend on beta testers, every contribution to the game by beta testers will be carefully evaluated by Paradox Development Studio developers before implementation. Beta testers assert that they are always taken seriously and everything they create is considered by Paradox Development Studio even if it does not end up being implemented.[262] Blue underlines that good ideas that are not immediately used can be brought back at a different time for revaluation.[263] As previously mentioned, developers perceive beta testers as both driven and able to make independent and creative suggestions, as well as execute specific tasks. This dynamic appears to be reciprocal to some extent. For example, beta tester Bobbie says that their main driving force is to be able to contribute to their favourite games, but also to be allowed to learn about game making and design work from interacting with Paradox Development Studio developers.[264]

---

260 Beta tester informant Bailey (March 13, 2018).
261 McCall, "Historical Problem Space Framework."
262 Beta tester informant Bailey (March 13, 2018); beta tester Blue (August 20, 2018).
263 Beta tester informant Blue (August 20, 2018).
264 Beta tester informant Bobbie (February 20, 2018).

Notes on Game Industry Labour

As suggested by digital humanities researcher Xinge Tong (building on design scholar Bill Moggridge) the extensive practice of having players provide direct feedback, for example via *Steam*, seems to create a certain connection between developer and player beyond seller-buyer, or producer-consumer, relationships.[265] Similarly, Dominic Arsenault notes that these communicational practices foster a special mode of participation and influence over game development.[266] This investment and multifaceted relationship is certainly the case for beta testers in the Paradox Development Studio context, having been granted access behind the scenes to participate directly in the development of *Europa Universalis IV* and *Hearts of Iron IV*. In fact, it is worthy of note that the responsibilities of a Paradox Development Studio beta tester go well beyond the generic understanding of the term, to the point where the distinction between player, beta tester and game worker becomes less clear. One such indication is the long-term, standing relationship between beta testers and the studio. Some beta testers have been a part of the Paradox community for close to 20 years at this point. Paradox Development Studio do perform controlled and contained testing that do not include beta testers specifically. These are "playtests" or "user tests" that provide the studio with information about the status of their games but that ultimately do not afford play testers the status of "beta tester." As such, the role of "beta tester" is exclusive to those with increased insight as well as the opportunity to actually create parts of the games, not just give feedback.

I say "opportunity" but the practice of keeping a roster of beta testers must also be discussed in the context of the precarity of game labour. The game industry has long had to negotiate the concepts of play and fun in relation to the notion of work. Perhaps more so than most other industries, the game industry is positioned to blur the lines in what Olli Sotamaa phrases as "fluid organizational models typical of networked creative industries."[267] Sotamaa also notes that the binary distinction between work and play can certainly be problematic when discussing the day-to-day in the game industry. To be sure, playing can for a game developer be as instrumental to their job as reading is for a historian.[268] Never-

---

265 Xinge Tong, "Positioning Game Review as a Crucial Element of Game User Feedback," 2.
266 Dominic Arsenault as cited by Tong, "Positioning Game Review," 2.
267 Olli Sotamaa, "Game Developers Playing Games: Instrumental Play, Game Talk, and Preserving the Joy of Play," in *Game Production Studies*, ed. Olli Sotamaa and Jan Svelch (Amsterdam: Amsterdam University Press, 2021), 103.
268 Sotamaa, "Game Developers Playing Games," 113–114.

theless, some distinction needs to be made since the present study includes an indication that game development at Paradox Development Studio partly hinges on voluntary, i.e. unpaid, efforts – certainly on the part of beta testers, but also on the part of developers. Whether this entails doing research on the subway to keep up, or playing and analysing *Europa Universalis IV* at home after work, there is a discernible fluidity to formal work practices at play.

For beta testers, the production aspect becomes even more poignant. Beta testers at Paradox Development Studio collectively do hundreds, if not thousands of hours, of unpaid work that goes directly into the game. The significance of this is expressly acknowledged by developers. According to previous research, the game testing role comes with a unique set of conditions in the game industry overall. Ergin Bulut argues that games testers occupy a particularly precarious position in the game making ecosystem – an often hugely underappreciated and understated role that requires few other formal skills beyond having played a lot of games and being passionate about doing so. It is also often considered a convenient entry point to the industry. This position, in turn, can have a host of negative connotations including "degradation of fun" (contextual processes that ultimately reduce the feeling of fun), feeling easily replaceable, and earning less.[269] Paradox Development Studio beta testers—the group of selected volunteers, not in-house quality assessment employees or playtest participants—are indeed in a different position to what Bulut describes, perhaps most importantly because their role is not limited to testing. On the contrary, beta tester work in this study often takes on the hue of historical expertise and content design alongside testing. Beta testers also contribute with ideation and suggestions for game design. In certain instances, modding efforts from the beta testing community have been inspirational to work on *Europa Universalis IV* and *Hearts of Iron IV*. Beta testers in turn cherish this access to games-in-progress as a venue to discuss their favourite games, to learn and talk about history, to benchmark for modding the games in question and/ or to engage with this tight-knit community of core players and developers.

Nevertheless, with the existing reciprocities in mind, it bears mentioning that these practices, including fluid work-time practices among developers, risk perpetuating what Bulut calls the discourses of passion and dedication in game work.[270] That is, the alluring image of game work being a dream job which in turn may obstruct the realities of certain unfair structures and condi-

---

269 Bulut, *A Precarious Game*, 123–124; 134–135.
270 Bulut, *A Precarious Game*, 64–65.

tions.[271] Furthermore, whilst I cannot speak to the exact quantitative balance between hired and unhired work here, the open reliance on unhired work for content creation, scripting and research drastically highlights the contradiction behind using historical themes in games as a shorthand, and the de facto laborious reality behind making them. This practice bears some theoretical semblance to what Julian Kürcklish calls "playbour" – a hybrid space between formal and informal forms of work in the game industry, including modding, that benefits all parties in some way.[272] Notably, this principle allows developers to benefit not only from the quality assessment and content creation of beta testers, but on their ideation and creative work as well.

Design Practices Framing History and Vice Versa

As suggested by the Paradox pillars and supported by the developer and beta tester interviews, design practice at Paradox Development Studio serves two specific values above all. Firstly, to make games that provide the best possible history-and-gameplay experience for as many as possible. Secondly, to create games that are, in one way or another, engaging. Both values sound obvious, but as will be discussed further in the coming chapters, developers and beta testers frequently come across instances in history as well as game design challenges wherein said values contradict one another and effective strategies must be employed to make design decisions. These framings, that are here referred to as player-centred design practices and entertainment-centred design practices, provide fruitful frameworks for describing and exemplifying game design practice with regards to fulfilling these goals, and what it does to historical representation.

Player-centred Design Practices

Game philosophy scholars Douglas Wilson and Miguel Sicart note in their 2010 article "Now it's personal: On Abusive Game Design" that there was a recent shift in game design motivations and practice among developers, going from virtuoso designer presences behind the finished product to designers acting as advocates

---

271 Sotamaa, "Game Developers Playing Games," 104.
272 Julian Kücklich, "Precarious Playbour: Modders and the Digital Games Industry," *The Fibreculture Journal* 5 (2005).

of the player and putting them first throughout the design process. This resulted in what they call the "accessibility turn."[273] According to Wilson and Sicart (building on Jesper Juul and Raph Koster) the accessibility turn happened because games and gaming started to appeal to an increasingly mainstream audience. With that transition from authorial statement design to more accommodating design values, design practices, too, have changed. This argument appears to be consistent with Paradox Development Studio's ambition to broaden the player-base, going from a historically niche crowd of hard-core strategy game fans (as discussed in chapter one) to becoming more broadly accessible and less intimidating. That is, they hope to make games that are appealing for a wider, and, of course, larger segment of gamers.

Annakaisa Kultima and Alyea Sandovar build on this notion posited by Wilson and Sicart in developing a taxonomy for player-centric design values in the 2016 article "Game Design Values." Here, the value of player-centrism is expressed through the ideas of players' advocacy, co-creativity with users, user inclusion and focus on usability and playability.[274] As explored throughout this book, Paradox Development Studio's design practices expressed in the interviews echo most of these values, both with regards to creating specific user experiences as well as the representation of history and counterfactuals. Making a Paradox Development Studio game as user-friendly as possible for as wide an audience as possible is bumped up the hierarchy of design ambition. Furthermore, developers draw heavily on influence and feedback from players primarily through beta testers, but other channels as well. In doing so, they adhere notably to player-centred design practices, in considering players to guide as well as to influence their work.

Explicit indicators that developers and beta testers advocate for the player base are indeed found in the interviews. Developers are aware of the duality that comes with catering to players' presuppositions about history in addition to providing them with enough counterfactual gameplay. Developers gain an understanding of player desires by consuming what they perceive as mainstream consumption of historical tv-series, podcasts as well as books and periodicals

---

273 Wilson and Sicart, "Now It's Personal," 2.
274 Annakaisa Kultima and Alyea Sandovar, "Game Design Values," in Proceedings of the 20th International Academic Mindtrek Conference (2016), 5; See also: Wainwright, *Virtual History*, 41–42; Rolfe Daus Peterson, Andrew Justin Miller and Sean Joseph Fedorko, "The Same River Twice: Exploring Historical Representation and the Value of Simulation in the *Total War*, *Civilization*, and *Patrician* Franchises," in *Playing with the Past – Digital Games and the Simulation of History*, ed. Matthew W. Kapell and Andrew B.R. Elliott (London: Bloomsbury, 2013), 44–45; Apperley, "Modding the Historians' Code," 194–195.

on history. As developer Dorian notes: "I want to make sure that a lot of these things [that are in the games] are recognized by people. One of the major things people like about our games, from my point of view, is the recognition factor. They feel smart because they go 'Oh, I know about this stuff, and I can learn more!'"[275] This is an example of developers tapping into player expectations – the veritable opposite of collecting player reaction to existing design – that in-and-of-itself supports the idea of player-centred design practice.

Despite the interest in building off players' understandings of history, Paradox Development Studio does not seem to expect players to be able to navigate the games and their systems based solely on historical knowledge. As a reminder, the *Nerd Out!* Paradox pillar suggests that players who have real world knowledge might benefit from it in comparison to others, but not that it is a prerequisite for successfully playing or learning the games. In other words, ideally, the player should not have to be an expert in history to comprehend what is going on in the game, or how to progress. Motivated by this principle, designers aim to balance challenging gameplay and verisimilitude, making sure the latter does not become an obstacle in and of itself. This includes making sure the user interface can transmit to the player what the AI is doing in a sensible way.[276] Some systems and explanations of historical change are complex and difficult to explain to players in a coherent and intuitive manner. Having a user interface designer on the team helps the finished design explain to players what rulesets and mechanics correspond to what actions, especially when the effect of player action is not explained explicitly. Thus, in this case, catering to players entails not just simplifying history in general, but also communicating through interface in non-literal ways the working of complex systems.[277] By doing so, it is possible to keep the intent and function of a mechanic but at the same time make it easier for a player to understand it.

Another aspect of player-centred design is design driven by player input. As previously discussed, developers and beta testers amply testify to the influence of discussions on the Paradox Plaza forums or other interactions with players, such as fan gatherings and conventions. Including player opinions from the forums usually means reading ongoing discussions without necessarily engaging in the discussion. It is a form of co-creativity without any formalised communicational process.

---

[275] Developer informant Dorian (June 29, 2018).
[276] Developer informant Delta (June 27, 2017).
[277] Developer informant Drew (June 28, 2018).

As discussed in chapter one, both games are in part defined by their open-endedness and sandbox nature. From a player perspective this includes a notion of self-determination. In spite of this, there are historical events and processes that are expected to be within each game, to the point where events must be forced onto the player. This is called railroading. Railroading, in strategy game jargon, means forcing a key moment by scripting it, or, alternatively, limiting agency through balance or mechanic design with the intent of forcing a particular perspective or outcome.[278] The term is particularly important in the context of digital strategy games as the genre itself offers a promise of high-level player agency and influence with regards to progression and narrative, which, in contrast, may be lacking in many other game genres.[279] For example, the only way to avoid a Second World War in *Hearts of Iron IV* is to play as a non-aggressive Germany (in other words, Germany, if left to its own devices, will commence the Second World War roughly as history dictates). However, the player is still likely to end up with unrest due to other European countries exercising power projection in the wake of the First World War, and this railroads the inevitability of another Great War.

As part of the player-centred design practice and principles, railroading events follows two guidelines: how significant was the event in question, and do players absolutely expect it to happen?[280] It is worth underlining that Paradox Development Studio rarely railroads or force specific historical events in the game in order to preserve player agency, and when it does happen it is exceptional. This, once again, underlines the opportunistic way Paradox Development Studios purposefully cater to player expectations. Developers will, if deemed necessary, veto an event in the game, although this usually only happens if they think players expect it.

From a rules-perspective, then, the inherent structuralist perspective could theoretically constitute a form of railroading too. Like the inevitability of the Second World War in *Hearts of Iron IV*, another example is the case of Spain going bankrupt in the 1600s in *Europa Universalis IV*. A player who colonises Mexico and Peru to obtain gold will not – according to Dylan – inevitably be faced with a (historically predetermined) bankruptcy event at a specific date. They elaborate on this saying:

---

278 For examples of railroading in games see for example Melissa Kagen, "Walking, Talking and Playing with Masculinities in *Firewatch*," *Game Studies* 18 (2018); Matthew George, "Lesson: Railroading," *RPG Theory Review*, February 15, 2007, accessed on July 20, 2019, available at http://rpgtheoryreview.blogspot.com/2007/02/lesson-railroading.html.
279 Köstlbauer, "The Strange Attraction of Simulation," 172–175.
280 Developer informant Drew (June 28, 2018).

We don't want you to suddenly be told that it's 'Bankrupt O'clock!' We want the mechanics in our game to model that. We have this almost responsibility to history, to have it be and feel reasonable. So, if you play it out as our mechanics are there for, you get all this gold income and it's actually going to increase your inflation. This could lead you to disaster where you end up bankrupt and really weakened from this. So, if you're going down the full-on historical path you are going to feel the historical disasters that they fell for.[281]

Notably, then, the notion of railroading events is dismissed by some developers as something that is disruptive to gameplay and to players. However, there is a clear overall message, also expressed in the above statement, that railroading through mechanics can be acceptable or even desired. In other words, by aiming for certain expected historical outcomes (and, presumably, historical reference) to steer the overall message and historiography of the game, Paradox Development Studio games allow themselves to hit certain story beats, not least in the thematical key mechanics pertaining to colonisation and the Second World War.

There is one topic of historical content, however, that Paradox Development Studio say they will not include despite instances of player requests: the Holocaust. Firstly, developers state that they believe the number of players who would truly like to see the Holocaust represented in *Hearts of Iron IV* is "a loud minority" and dismiss them on a blanket basis.[282] In fact, discussions about events like the Holocaust (including topics like the Nanjing Massacre, and use of chemical weapons in the game) are banned from the Paradox forums due to their usually "repetitive and sometimes inappropriate nature."[283] Secondly, all developers and beta testers agree that due to the core design of *Hearts of Iron IV*, focused the way it is on resource management and the military effort, the Holocaust would not contribute to meaningful gameplay. Furthermore, even if it made sense to implement such historic atrocities on a mechanics level, there is nothing to suggest that it would be fun to play through, in the words of Drew.[284] This last point leads into the paradoxical relationship between game culture and historical culture. As will be discussed in more detail in the following, as well as in chapters three, four, and five, historical atrocities are treated quite differently in these games (within each game, but also between them as wholes) depending on where the topics sit as part of the games' design legacies, and in relation to historical institutions beyond games. To contextualise this, the following segment lays out developer and beta tester understandings and rationale behind

---

281 Developer informant Dylan (June 28, 2018).
282 Developer informant Devin (June 28, 2017).
283 Developer informant Devin (June 28, 2017).
284 Developer informant Drew (June 28, 2018).

some of these decisions, how they pertain to other game design practices and some initial thoughts on the implications that follow.

Entertainment-centred Design Practices

When talking to developers and beta testers and discussing the efforts they go to in researching their games, it seems clear that they all take history – recorded history and historical facts especially – seriously. However, as I have described previously, developers also take their players very seriously. As such the practices of player retention, and advocating for the player experience, become compounded with practices pertaining to historical representation and design. I call these balancing-acts entertainment-focused design practices in order to point to this specific interplay. These practices influence the inclusion as well as omission of content, deal with balance issues and difficulty levels, and determine what historical components, including mechanics, make it into the games. Entertainment-centred practices become the most distinguishable when talking about what would constitute that which is not fun. In avoiding designing something that is not fun, developers and beta testers navigate this interplay specifically. Further on, the complex implications of including or not including historical atrocities, and their role in the games, will be laid out, also regarding what this means for the representation of counterfactuals. For now, the focus is on the motivations and historical cultural understandings surrounding these sensitive uses of history in *Europa Universalis IV* and *Hearts of Iron IV* as expressed by developers and beta testers.

First, a note on the topic of entertainment-centred game design practices and the notion of fun versus challenge. Difficulty levels are an important tool for developers to be able to manage engagement and replayability on a design level. Replayability and player retention, as discussed above, are measurements of success and ways to get players to keep investing in the Paradox monetisation model. Ensuring that players feel sufficiently challenged without being discouraged is one of the game designer's primary objectives. Again, the learning curves for *Europa Universalis IV* and *Hearts of Iron IV* are already quite steep, and players could easily give up because they find it difficult to grasp the mechanics of the games. However, the latest iterations of the games take entertainment-centred design practices especially to heart and explicitly create games with a lower threshold for beginners.[285] However, as players become more competent,

---

[285] Developer informant Dallas (June 26, 2017); Dylan (June 29, 2018).

design needs to complement players' variations in skill and cater equally to experienced players as well as casual ones. As expressed by Drew: "That's why we have difficulty levels, because some people find fun in challenge, and other people just find fun in conquering the world."[286] As exemplified by this quote, fun is at the centre of design practice concerning difficulty – high or low – because it is the developer's perception that players enjoy Paradox Development Studio games in different ways.

Notions of not fun, or what not to design, then, as perceived by developers and beta testers, boil down to three items: 1) implausibility, 2) things that hinder replayability and 3) war crimes and historical atrocities. Regarding the former two, players crave a level of counterfactual gameplay in order to stay interested.[287] However, the counterfactual history contained and made possible within the game must be reasonable and made with caution.[288] There are individual players who prefer to blur the lines between counterfactual history and fantasy, but developers insist that their vision of the games stays within the realm of plausibility because that notion of realistic, reasonable historical alteration is the most engaging for the greatest number of players.[289] Similarly, developers assert that players do not want history in the games to be predictable to the point where they can foresee what is going to happen and thus lose the element of challenge in the game. Developers and beta testers perceive these two influences similarly in both games, and they motivate design practices that help balance the fine line between the familiarity of history and the unpredictability of what-ifs.

Regarding historical atrocities, then, developer statements follow a similar pattern to a more general one about violence, games, and play. The notion of agency in videogames complicates the depiction of dark themes, especially from an entertainment-centred perspective. As argued by Adam Chapman and Jonas Linderoth, games are surrounded by at least two kinds of discourse that reframe the dark history subject matter in a problematising way. Firstly, agency can be perceived to transfer responsibility to the player. Secondly, the frivolous cultural framing of games and play can appear to trivialise the subject matter.[290]

---

[286] Developer informant Drew (June 28, 2018).
[287] Developer informant Dorian (June 29, 2018).
[288] Developer informant Dale (June 15, 2017), beta tester informant Bobbie (February 20, 2018).
[289] Developer informant Devin (June 28, 2017), Dale (June 15, 2017). Developers see these players being active in the mod community and encourage such ventures, but developers themselves stay within the designated conceptual framework of the base game.
[290] Adam Chapman and Jonas Linderoth, "Exploring the Limits of Play – A Case Study of Representations of Nazism in Games," in *The Dark Side of Gameplay – Controversial Issues in Playful*

As already established, the Holocaust is not portrayed in *Hearts of Iron IV*, and probably never will be. Entirely in line with Chapman and Linderoth's argument, the Holocaust specifically causes a very distinct design problem for Paradox developers and beta testers. Developers offer two reasons for this:
1) The Holocaust cannot be made into meaningful mechanics or content within the current scope and gameplay focus of *Heart of Iron IV* without becoming problematic.
2) Developers and beta testers cannot conceive of playing the Holocaust and staying in line with the fun criteria at the same time.

From this perspective, the understanding of entertainment is partly defined by developers' views on the relationship between the systemic rule sets, content and the notion of trivialising. That is, they agree that the rulesets and gameplay might obscure the severity of the event at hand. Furthermore, Developer Drew anticipates that anyone making the argument that omitting the Holocaust per definition is also the same as trivialising or suppressing the memory of it probably does not understand game design and the relationship between mechanics and content very well. "And," he concludes his argument, "it's just not my idea of a good time."[291] To the earlier point on player-centred design practice and player expectations, omitting the Holocaust from a game about the Second World War can also be seen as a divergence from the practice of catering to historical cultural understandings. From a historical cultural perspective, the two are oftentimes inherently connected. In contrast, developers argue that it would probably seem worse to try and quantify the Holocaust for no other reason than shoehorning it into a game that is, in their opinion, about something else.[292] Paradox Development Studio is, to be sure, not the only game company to decouple the Holocaust from the Second World War. As argued by Giaime Alonge, this practice can also be found in the wargaming tradition wherein decoupling the German army from Nazi war crimes was the norm for most wargames in the 50s, 60s, and 70s.[293] Furthermore, as found by Eugen Pfister,

---

Environments, ed. Torill Elvira Mortensen, Jonas Linderoth and Ashley M.L. Brown (London: Routledge, 2015), 143.
291 Developer informant Drew (June 28, 2018).
292 Developer informant Dorian (June 29, 2018), Drew (June 28, 2018), Delta (June 27, 2017).
293 Giaime Alonge, "Playing the Nazis: Political Implications in Analog Wargames," *Analog Game Studies* 6 (2019), available at https://analoggamestudies.org/2019/09/playing-the-nazis-political-implications-in-analog-wargames/. Along the same lines, Ulf Zander notes that depicting the Holocaust in literature, let alone television and film, was long near-impossible during the same period due to, for example, fear of trivialising or fetishising the event. See Ulf Zander,

when the Holocaust is, in fact depicted in Second World War games, it is usually done by setting it in a fictional or counterfactual world and calling it something else; or, it is merely hinted at but never called by any of its common names.[294] As will be discussed further in the coming chapters, *Hearts of Iron IV* does neither, but rather extends its blanket decision not to depict Second World War war crimes to include a discussion ban on any such topics at the Paradox Plaza forums, as well as in all sanctioned mods to the game. As previously mentioned, developers note that this was done because of previous experiences wherein some users would, in the words of Daryl, present the event as something other than thoroughly abhorrent.[295]

The idea of play as purely entertainment has been problematised by historians and game scholars alike by pointing to the fact that play has many different purposes, and the potential to illicit any number of emotions and behaviours, not just playful, or positive, ones. In addition, the meaning of play, even within specific contexts, most certainly means different things to different people.[296] However, cultural understandings of games, and historical games in particular, are continually conflated with notions of "trivializing" and "making light of." This causes implicit and explicit moral problems for developers and players alike, and the Holocaust has long been treated as a taboo in games for this reason.[297] However, the Holocaust is not the only historical atrocity at play here. Corresponding discussions for *Europa Universalis IV* tend to focus on slavery and colonial exploitation, which, unlike the Holocaust, are in fact represented in the game. Slavery is part of the trade mechanic. When asked about this potential contradiction between the implementation of difficult historical topics in the two games, developers and beta testers gravitate towards three distinct explanations. Firstly, the events of the Second World War and the events of Early Modern global history are not comparable due to the difference in period and their sustained

---

"*Holocaust* at the Limits: Historical Culture and the Nazi Genocide in the Television Era," in *Echoes of the Holocaust: Historical Cultures in Contemporary Europe*, ed. Klas-Göran Karlsson and Ulf Zander (Lund: Nordic Academic Press, 2003), 255–257.
294 Eugen Pfister, as cited by Thomas Z. Majkowski and Katarzyna Suszkiewicz, "Cardboard Genocide. Board Game Design as a Tool in Holocaust Education," *GAME – The Italian Journal of Game Studies* 9 (2020), available at https://www.gamejournal.it/cardboard-genocide/.
295 Developer informant Daryl (June 26, 2017).
296 For an exhaustive discusson about the notion of play, see Jaakko Stenros, "Playfulness, Play, and Games: A Constructionist Ludology Approach" (Phd. diss., University of Tampere, 2015).
297 Thomas Z. Majkowski and Katarzyna Suszkiewicz, "Cardboard Genocide. Board Game Design as a Tool in Holocaust Education," *GAME – The Italian Journal of Game Studies* 9 (2020), https://www.gamejournal.it/cardboard-genocide/.

impact on current historical culture. Secondly, slavery and colonisation have been part of *Europa Universalis* game design since its first iteration. Thirdly, slaves are a trade good in *Europa Universalis IV*, and colonies provide slaves as well as a number of other quantifiable resources that are mechanically viable in the game.[298]

In discussing this, developers and beta testers emphasise that slavery is not in the game because it is fun or entertaining, but that it is a design legacy and an integrated part of an important mechanic. However, this design practice underlines that the consequences of colonisation and slavery are somehow not problematic enough to be taken out altogether. *Europa Universalis IV* is fundamentally about European colonisation, and, as discussed in chapter one, despite the scope of content, struggles to produce nuanced representations of non-European histories of war and expansion. As noted by Rhett Loban and Thomas Apperley, given *Europa Universalis IV*'s focus on colonialism, the lack of, for example, Indigenous perspectives on this history, and the perspectives of victims of trans-Atlantic slave-trade for instance, are particularly remarkable.[299] This contradiction, that it is possible to depict the historical exertion of power in an uneven dynamic with detrimental consequences for the other in *Europa Universalis IV* but not in *Hearts of Iron IV*, speaks to the significance of design legacy and genre convention here.

Summarily, then, Paradox Development Studio's rationale here appears to be as follows. Since the Holocaust would not be fun to play, including it in *Hearts of Iron IV* does not serve a worthwhile purpose. Nor could it, in a meaningful way, tie into existing mechanics and contribute to gameplay in *Hearts of Iron IV*, the way for example slaves-as-a-good and colonisation appear to do in *Europa Universalis IV*.[300] In addition, games do not have an obligation to the betterment of mankind, notes Drew, underlining that it is not within the role of these games to critically address historical atrocities specifically.[301] This reasoning aligns with previous observations and discussion among historical game scholars such as Thomas Z. Majkowski and Katarzyna Suszkiewicz who note that the game industry, as part of a larger digitized memory culture, tends to leave it up to other institutions to own these kinds of questions. Interestingly, as argued by Majkowski and Suszkiewicz, in doing so, the games inadvertently

---

298 Developer informant Dale (June 15, 2017); beta tester informant Bailey (March 13, 2018); beta tester informant Brook (February 21, 2018).
299 Loban and Apperley, "Eurocentric Values at Play."
300 Developer informant Drew (June 28, 2018); Dallas (June 26, 2017).
301 Developer informant Drew (June 28, 2018).

become a part of such regimented historical cultures.[302] This can also be understood as intertextual behaviour among developers in a larger discursive context – what Eugen Pfister calls "the reproduction of dominant discursive statements."[303] As I have begun to show, and continue to discuss further in chapters three and four, developer and beta tester statements support this analysis and emphasise that the impact of historical culture in this structural way is significant to design.

Chapter Summary

This chapter discusses external and internal frameworks and circumstances of game design practice at Paradox Development Studio, including beta testers, for *Europa Universalis IV* and *Hearts of Iron IV*. Based on interviews with developers on *Hearts of Iron IV* and *Europa Universalis IV*, as well as Paradox Development Studio beta testers for both games, I have outlined the varying motivations and facilitations that provide the framework for design practice and decision-making, as they pertain to the representation of the past and counterfactuals.

The analysis builds on the underlying assumption that game developers, in their work, are prompted and guided by values attached to the ecosystem of the game industry, as well as by historical culture. This notion is supported by the findings in interviews with some interesting outlying findings. Certain practices are tied directly to professional roles and job descriptions, such as the depth to which content designers and beta testers can delve into historical readings compared to other developers. This is ultimately a time-and-resource issue. Paradox Development Studio developers unanimously express a desire to have more time to research the games' content, and some of them note that they take work home with them. This indicates that developers' and beta testers' personal interest in researching and engaging with the content of the games and historical reference constitute an important underpinning of development.

Beta testers are ultimately fans and players of the games, who volunteer their time and energy to Paradox Development Studio with de facto development to a significant extent. Beta testers provide research, content creation, testing and brainstorming. Work as a beta tester is voluntary and is not compensated. Beta testers are accepted through an application process based on their knowledge

---

302 Thomas Z. Majkowski and Katarzyna Suszkiewicz, "Cardboard Genocide."
303 Pfister, "Why History in Digital Games Matter," 66.

and interest in the games. Developers perceive beta testers an indispensable asset due to the special interests and bulk of work they contribute to development. Beta testers, in turn, express that they feel appreciated by developers and that they have a good relationship with them. Beta testers put in varying amounts of work, depending on what sort of state a project is currently in. Beta testers also function as unofficial ambassadors of players, and tune into their perception of, for example, a newly released feature. They also engage with players to explain why certain things are not possible to implement in the games, for example, due to technical constraints.

Researching the past for *Europa Universalis IV* and *Hearts of Iron IV* share a number of practices, but *Hearts of Iron IV* stands out in terms of available resources, likely due to the extensive research and documentations available on the Second World War specifically. Doing research for the benefit of the games must be considered a primary design activity at Paradox Development Studio. However, it does not solely direct their game design. Getting to know the past and finding reference points for mechanics and balance is an essential part of design practice, but the resulting artefact, i.e. the games, will always be designed according to gameplay goals and adjacent values first and foremost, which ultimately mitigates the need to verify the accuracy of the content.

Technical conditions determine the scope, fidelity and intricacy by which historical representation hinges, such as for example legacy design practices and heritage technology, and game engine. The *Europa Universalis* series has been in development since the mid-1990s, and some elements of the design – events and similar content – have been imported from every iteration to the next. This sometimes means that historical depiction and representation appears outdated. Developers express a desire to go through old content and update it based on new historical scholarship and ideological, societal sentiment.

Circumstances for game design practice also include a level of opportunism, i.e. tuning into the larger ecosystem of game development for clues on desires and inclinations in a player that will yield more sales. This has generated the perception that history is a fruitful backdrop for meaningful gameplay. Players, according to developers, enjoy playing with the past due to a perceived familiarity with the history contained in the games. Designers also know that counterfactual gameplay and the ability to play with historical change within certain parameters appeal to players and that players expect such from their games. Paradox Development Studio have built their monetisation model around core game releases and subsequent incremental DLC releases. This practice partly supports the notion of supplementary design practice – the aim to continue to add content to an existing game system in order to cover as much history as possible without changing the core mechanics of each game.

Opportunism is present primarily on occasions where external needs and pressure outweigh primary gameplay goals. One such example is the Blitz, the bombings of London, where historical presupposition (however misguided) better fits game design logic and thus takes precedent over historical verisimilitude. However, overall in design practice, opportunism appears to be less prevalent, possibly due to genre. Digital strategy games by Paradox Development Studio belong to a long tradition of analogue and digital war gaming that has not only seen less change over time, but is also less sensitive to changes in industry, paradigm changes and progress. As such, Paradox Development Studio design legacy and genre convention, in part, dictate design practice. Firstly, by employing practices that pertain to player expectations, i.e. what denotes a typical Paradox game, and how to adhere to players' historical presupposition. Secondly, Paradox games, through iteration, preserve and reiterate content, UI, mechanics and rules across the individual games in each series over time.

Design principles in both *Europa Universalis IV* and *Hearts of Iron IV* are implemented on the specific terms of player expectations, as well as previously acquired experiences from earlier iterations in the games' series. The retention and appreciation of the–seemingly large–percentage of players who seek an exploratory, less challenging, gameplay experience are currently at the forefront of decision-making. Developers continuously balance designing a historical experience against design logic; making sure history itself does not cloud the gameplay experience for future play-throughs.

Furthermore, development is facilitated by a rigorous research effort, which is primarily conducted by content designers and beta testers, the latter usually upon request from the former or other developers (game direction, creative direction, game designers) at Paradox Development Studio. The research and content creation processes appear to begin online, and take different paths from there, most commonly to other parts of the internet, or to books. Paradox Development Studio allocate funds to support research for the benefit of design for their employees, but most developers and beta testers prefer to do research on their own time and with their own money.

Lasty, understandings of what can and cannot be a part of these games seem to vary. In terms of desirable gameplay values, plausibility and replayabiliy are mentioned among the most important. Furthermore, each period covered by the games come with their own dark history, instances of which are ultimately treated in a somewhat contradictory manner. Design practices dictate that the Holocaust will never be implemented in *Hearts of Iron IV*, whereas, for example, slavery is present in *Europa Universalis IV*. The rationale for this discrepancy is consistently design concerns. The main difference between the two, according to developers and beta testers, is whether or not the game concept, from a player perspective, can accommodate an event or not.

As such, game design practice at Paradox Development Studio is motivated and framed by the following factors:
1. Developer and beta tester interest in history.
2. Supplementary design practice as a monetisation model.
3. Player appeal to counterfactual gameplay.
4. Design legacy and genre convention.
    a. Player-centrism.
    b. Entertainment-centrism.

In the following chapters, the games and developers will be discussed further in order to deepen the discussion on what these frameworks mean for the depiction of the past, and, importantly, counterfactual scenarios. I intend to further illustrate how developers and beta testers balance gameplay values and pragmatism to rationalise game design choices. The next chapter focuses on counterfactuals as uses of history by discussing selected examples as wishful thinking, possible world and future fiction counterfactuals. In doing so, representations in *Hearts of Iron IV* and *Europa Universalis IV* are positioned as artefacts of design and of historical culture.

Chapter Three
Counterfactuals: Uses, Shapes and Problems in *Europa Universalis IV* and *Hearts of Iron IV*

As discussed in previous chapters, *Europa Universalis IV* and *Hearts of Iron IV* are the two longest running Paradox Development Studio titles to date. Both game series have been in development since around the turn of the millennia in one form or another, which makes them interesting examples of games that have seen game development and game design practice change over a considerable period. Additionally, both games' developers explicitly and consciously deal with counterfactuals as an integral part of the gameplay experience.

The previous chapter shows that developers and beta testers at Paradox Development Studio are guided in this by values and frameworks of game design practice. These values and frameworks delimit the representation of history in the games. The surrounding ecosystem, the game industry, the player base and third-party actors consciously and inadvertently shape the games according to at least the elements described in the previous chapter.

This chapter further explores counterfactual history in *Europa Universalis IV* and *Hearts of Iron IV* according to the theoretical framework presented in the introduction. As outlined in the introduction, this part of the book builds on a theoretical framework that positions counterfactuals as uses of history, and their inherent connection to historical culture. This approach is helpful to distinguish between the different ways that *Europa Universalis IV* and *Hearts of Iron IV* deal with counterfactual history, following the premise that not all counterfactuals are designed in an equal manner, from the same point of origin, or to the same effect. By operationalizing the concepts of wishful thinking, possible worlds and future fictions – each representative of a theoretical lens on the framing of counterfactual scenarios, and uses of history therein – we gain a more granular understanding of how mechanics and content design facilitate counterfactual history in the games based on historical culture. Despite building on the same design legacy, and partly sharing developers, the two games approach counterfactual history and historical verisimilitude differently. *Hearts of Iron IV* has a more compact, linear approach to counterfactual scenarios, whereas *Europa Universalis IV* relies more heavily on emergent story-making and gameplay-generated counterfactuals. Importantly and despite these formal differences, both games' counterfactuals, ultimately, rely heavily on historical reference.

In other words, *Europa Universalis IV* and *Hearts of Iron IV* facilitate counterfactual scenarios on two main levels that will also be explored here: as 1) counterfactuals in relation to emergent story-making, and 2) designed counterfactual scenarios that present special goals for each game. The chapter discusses how specific design choices alter the historical arguments that the counterfactuals make with particular regard to goal-setting.[304]

Counterfactuals as Historical Culture and Uses of History

For the analysis of counterfactual history as historical culture and uses of history, the conceptual framework used here is inspired by the reflections of Richard Evans and his essay volume *Altered Pasts – Counterfactuals in History*. Four ways to frame counterfactuals emerge from his essays: wishful thinking, possible worlds, future fictions, and virtual history. Based on Evans, I argue that these types of counterfactuals constitute uses of history and can be distinguished by the motives and questions that produce them. In digital strategy games, the motives and questions are specific to the game context, and need to be understood as such. Naturally, the game context, in turn, is inherently connected to broader social and cultural understandings of history and such understandings underpin the games' design.

In the above-mentioned book, Richard Evans explores and criticises the biases and agendas surrounding counterfactuals on a broad spectrum of origins and contexts. Essentially critical of counterfactuals and their usefulness in scholarly contexts, he notes: "The choice [between possible counterfactuals] is the outcome of the historian's intention, political orientation, factual knowledge and contemporary context. It also reflects to a degree the aesthetic purposes of the author, striving to produce the most satisfying, the most coherent and, often, the most entertaining counterfactual scenario."[305]

Historical counterfactuals, Evans argues, are biased and subjective, and this separates them from what he calls the serious study of the past. Having a track-record of defending history and historical scholarship against abuse, misuse and Holocaust denialism,[306] Evans has a vested interest in maintaining a clear distinction between academic study of the past and the application of history beyond scholarship. He is well aware that there is a historical cultural layer to

---

[304] As much as I would have liked to cover the entirety of the games' content here, it is simply not possible due to the qualitative nature of the study, and the scope of these games. Instead, I have selected examples to present as counterfactual scenarios and gameplay that represent the conceptualisations of counterfactuals.
[305] Evans, *Altered Pasts*, 124.
[306] See Evans, *Telling Lies About Hitler*.

counterfactual history and describes this as "most useful, and most interesting, as a phenomenon in itself, as a part of modern and contemporary intellectual and political history, worthy of study in its own right, but of little use in the serious study of the past."[307] In other words, Evans acknowledges that counterfactuals are meaningful, albeit not for historical scholarship.

Counterfactuals, however, are indeed quite serious about history, just not in the way we sometimes think. As noted by Christopher Prendergast, "the counterfactual is a category of thought and language, but its instantiations are plural, not merely because there are lots of them about, but because their types and functions vary greatly."[308] Prendergast is especially helpful in pointing to the common, and in his words "lazy," assumption that counterfactuals and historical fact are to be understood as polemic concepts, at odds with one another. He astutely notes that the invocation of "fact" (as intrinsic to "counterfactual") distracts from the actual circumstance that the opposite of fact is a non-fact (or, indeed, the absurd notion of alternative fact), not a counterfactual. Counterfactuals, he argues, are supplementary to fact, and "entirely derivative" of the notion of fact.[309] In accordance with this assertion of counterfactuals, and simultaneously adhering to Evans' observations that counterfactuals are shaped by external motives, I argue that counterfactuals in games are wont to be the making primary argument about the application and illumination of history, without claiming to have any sincere empirical consequence for historical fact. In other words, in thinking and speculating about counterfactual outcomes of, for example, the Second World War, games are equally, if not primarily, in engagement with the notion of the war as it happened and its place in our understanding of the past, as they are with the scenario that did not.

By replacing the historian's intention with that of game designers in the quote by Evans above, it can be argued that the same sentiment holds true for game design practice: that counterfactuals are uses of history meant to produce the most satisfying, coherent and entertaining counterfactual scenarios as games. In taking a functional perspective on counterfactual history as a form of engagement with the past, a more nuanced, and precise, understanding of the concept is called for in order to extract and contextualise what Evans refers to as author bias and intent. The notion of historical culture is therefore especially useful to bridge between the theoretical understanding of counterfactuals as

---

[307] Evans, *Altered Pasts*, 125.
[308] Prendergast, *Counterfactuals*, 2.
[309] Prendergast, *Counterfactuals*, 49–50.

derivative of fact and the obvious but often hugely understated importance of collective understandings of historical references in this context.

Historical culture, again, defined as (amorphous) systems of historical references with contextually attributed meanings, requires some degree of relatable key objects and framings. Furthermore, as discussed in the previous chapter, the notion of historical familiarity – i.e. the application of historical cultural understandings – is a central guiding design principle among developers. To the same point, Catherine Gallagher explores the distinctions between historical, fictional and counterfactual depictions of Napoleon Bonaparte, and argues that "the divergence in meanings [between the historical, fictional and counterfactual character], relies on the sameness of the referent."[310] Without a common point of reference, she notes, we would be unable to measure the distance between the various depictions of Bonaparte in her materials. The historical reference, with what I call attributed meanings, centres the counterfactual scenarios.

In digital strategy games, the past is represented through such chosen references, drawing on historical cultural understandings and meanings. In the context of historical culture and uses of history, however, we can also use this relationship to point to the notion of intent beyond factual discussion. As discussed in previous chapters, these choices are far from arbitrary but build on a similar argument as that of Gallagher – counterfactuals as playing with, and reframing, canonical, historical culturally viable references. In other words, by looking at counterfactuals as pluralistic and functional we can observe in detail the meaning of such references in the chosen context, and place them in the larger discussion on what kind of history game history is.

Theoretical Framework

The theoretical framework, then, covers four types of counterfactuals: *wishful thinking, possible worlds, future fiction, and virtual history*. It is intended to function as an aid to nuanced, and precise, discussion on the topic, and it is therefore important to note that counterfactuals of different types can overlap and coexist in the same instance. Furthermore, this framework does not claim to be exhaustive. It is used to discuss the construction of counterfactual scenarios as authored with underlying intent, as well as to discuss counterfactuals through the lens of uses of history. One way to distinguish between the four types is to consider what questions they ask and for what purpose. Standing on an imagi-

---

[310] Gallagher, "What Would Napoleon Do?," 317.

nary timeline, wishful thinking, possible worlds and future fictions represent a focus on the past, present or future, respectively. Virtual history, in turn, represents a specific intellectual exercise wherein counterfactuals are used to undermine determinism and structuralist thinking in history. As will be discussed below, virtual history is at odds with the way counterfactual history is designed and implemented in *Europa Universalis IV* and *Hearts of Iron IV*. Nevertheless, all four categories are here outlined to provide the theoretical scaffolding of the analysis of counterfactual history in the games that follows.

Wishful thinking counterfactuals deal with notions of hindsight and continuity. They connect the past with the present by referring to glory days, or lamenting past events. In depicting counterfactual scenarios in which history is repaired, glory days reinstated, past horrors reconciled or revenged, wishful thinking deals with questions and statements such as: What if the British Empire could be revived? What if the consequences of the Civil War could be undone? In most cases, wishful thinking is about repairing or reconstituting (a subjective) understanding of past state of matters.

Possible world counterfactuals deal with notions of counterfactual causality and speculative synergy between historical events. They experiment with changes in certain causes, and how such counterfactuals allow one to reimagine outcomes of events. Unlike wishful thinking scenarios, possible world counterfactuals are not focused on events that predate the events at hand, nor do they deal with the long-term consequences of said interplay of events. They explore the notion of change itself, by evaluating questions such as: Under what conditions could the Byzantine Empire have persisted beyond the 1450s? Under what conditions could the Thirty-Years War have been avoided?

Future fiction counterfactuals deal with notions of counterfactual contingency and consequence by detailing the repercussions of altered outcomes. Future fictions are generally not concerned with what changed at the point where a scenario deviates from the recorded path, but are primarily interested in what the properties of counterfactual futures (relative to the point of departure) might look like. They evaluate questions such as: What would the world have looked like if the First World War had never happened? What if Nazi Germany had conquered the United States in the 1940s? In scenarios such as these, the focus is not on how Germany might have achieved such a counterfactual, but on the properties of the world in the aftermath of the event.

Virtual history counterfactuals deal with the role of chance and chaos, with the specific intention of reassessing established historiographical interpretations. Virtual history can be seen as a method for critiquing understandings of historical causality as determinist or structuralist, for example by searching for a point in time where chance and chaos played a role in the outcome of events. Virtual history counterfactuals evaluate questions such as: What was the probability of the Second World War happening? Beyond the Second World War, what were some other truly possible outcomes of the Molotov-Ribbentrop pact? Notably, such counterfactuals make any number of contradictory assumptions about how things did come to pass.

Having applied these concepts to the games at hand, I assert that counterfactual history in *Europa Universalis IV* and *Hearts of Iron IV* are representations of wishful thinking, future fictions and possible worlds, but not virtual histories. Ultimately, virtual history counterfactuals make arguments to the epistemology and nature of scholarly history – a trait that sets them apart from the other three types. As previous chapters have shown, developers dismiss any claims to making historical arguments that purport to be factual or scholarly in and of themselves. They are ultimately driven by a different set of values such as gameplay focused design, opportunism and replayability. In the following, this chapter discusses how counterfactual history, from a game design perspective, is not a principal method for evaluating historical evidence. Instead, counterfactuals in this context reflect historical cultural signalling by applying a hindsight perspective on causality, continuity and consequence.

The Problem of Virtual History in this Context

Richard Evans names one of his essays after Niall Fergusson's anthology *Virtual History – Alternatives and Counterfactuals* in which Ferguson considers counterfactuals a "necessary antidote to determinism."[311] Virtual history represents a method of highlighting what Ferguson sees as the "near-miss" nature of historical change. Whereas wishful thinking, possible worlds and future fictions represent uses of history and historical culture, virtual history claims to empirically embrace the uncertainty of knowing the past for the benefit of better knowing a chaotic past.[312] In other words, the suggestion by Ferguson is that counterfactual history should be considered a valid method for critical historical scholarship. Ferguson argues that the (scholarly) narrative of the past is already a concoction of evidence-based fact and imaginary causation and narration, and that the world is so complex that alternative historical outcomes must be seen, and treated, by historians, as having been equally likely to occur.[313] Furthermore, he

---

311 Ferguson, *Virtual History*, 89.
312 Evans, *Altered Pasts*, 31.
313 Ferguson, *Virtual History*, 89–90.

argues, this mind-set can meaningfully be applied to empirical study, something he attempts himself in *Virtual History*, by assessing the truthfulness of the claim that the First World War was inevitable, and what might have been if "Britain had stood aside in August 1914."[314]

Thus, Ferguson's definition of virtual history is closely associated with historical probability and an emphasis on epistemological truth. He writes, "the counterfactual scenarios we therefore need to construct are not mere fantasy: they are simulations based on calculations about the relative probability of plausible outcomes in a chaotic world (hence 'Virtual history')."[315] For Ferguson, this is a way to describe the chaotic reality of historical actuality. In digital strategy games, chaos, chance and probabilistic outcomes constitute ways of creating a balanced and enjoyable gameplay experience based on both historical verisimilitude and, importantly, unpredictability. While in doing so, the games make certain arguments about possible outcomes worthy of study from a variety of perspectives, this is not an act of engaging in the reassessment of historical research. The result is similar, but the intention and application are different.

Counterfactuals in Games and Emergent Stories

Mechanics and content in *Europa Universalis IV* and *Hearts of Iron IV* are modular. That means, firstly, that there are core mechanics through which all playable nations in the game follow the same rules in the same (or very similar) manner.[316] Secondly, it means that on top of the generic systems, there are nation-specific content, missions, events and other scripted elements that dictate the parameters for the development of each playable nation. The nation-specific elements are easy for developers to hook into and out of the core systems. Rigidity in the core systems is therefore mitigated by modular design structures, and through synergy between mechanics, balance design and player agency. The design is weighted so that events in the game gravitate towards a historical path, all the while leaving room for counterfactual instances caused by player and AI agency. As previously noted, this type of game narrative is known as emergent story-making. Likewise, while AI-controlled nations are designed to act in a historically plausible way, the replayability criteria of Paradox design pillars require an element of unpredictability that cause acceptable counterfactual outcomes.[317]

---

[314] Ferguson, *Virtual History*, 228.
[315] Ferguson, *Virtual History*, 85.
[316] Developer informant Devin (June 28, 2017).
[317] Fåhraeus, *Emergent Stories* (video resource, 2016).

The presence of randomness and a high level of detail in both games show that developers do adhere to the value of unpredictability and replayability. In doing so, they enforce the argument that a conceivable chance of some things going differently makes for compelling thought-experiments and, most importantly, good gameplay. Counterfactual outcomes here are partly designed as balance; counterfactual outcomes are less likely to occur than historical ones in order to keep game events with a sense of verisimilitude. However, in keeping with the focus on replayability, outcomes are, to a point, unhistorical. Combinations of such unpredictable outcomes will create counterfactual scenarios.[318] This balance between the predictably factual and the unpredictably counterfactual, as discussed in chapter two, is ultimately dictated by what developer and beta testers consider reasonable alternatives and probabilities, based on their own research and internal discussions.

Counterfactual outcomes and emergent story-making are more pronounced in *Europa Universalis IV* than in *Hearts of Iron IV*. Going back to their most fundamental differences in design with regard to the representation of the past (that is, scope and historical theme presented in chapter 1), emergent story-making in *Europa Universalis IV* is characterised by the way trigger conditions dictate progress. Each event is given one or several trigger conditions that illustrate developer understandings and evaluation of the context and causality of each event. Railroaded instances – i.e. hardcoded events that do not allow for more than one outcome, or that are bound to trigger under almost any circumstances – are put in place to preserve a minimum of historical believability, but as put by assistant developer at Paradox Development Studio Troy Goodfellow: "history starts going off the rails the moment you press PLAY."[319]

For *Hearts of Iron IV*, the notion of emergent stories looks different because the game is designed to focus on, and rubber-band towards, a single core scenario, namely the Second World War. *Hearts of Iron IV* allows the player to explore the different roles nations can take within this one scenario, a more rigid gameplay framework based on the military aspects of the war. In the words of *Hearts of Iron IV* developer Daryl: "Our primary constraint is that we are focused on the conflict itself, while other projects and games [at Paradox Development Studio] are more focused on everything related to ruling a country. If

---

318 Chapman, *Digital Games as History*, 239–240.
319 Troy Goodfellow, introduction to *Europa Universalis IV: What if? The Anthology of Alternate History*, ed. Tomas Harenstam (Stockholm: Paradox Books, 2014), 2. *Europa Universalis IV: What if? The Anthology of Alternate History* edited by Tomas Harenstam is an anthology of counterfactual essays partly sourced from the Paradox Short Story Contest 2014.

we were to do this for our period, a lot more would be included, and it would give us more opportunities."[320]

At its core level and with regard to counterfactual possibilities, *Hearts of Iron IV* follows the same internal design as *Europa Universalis IV*; content and events are weighted and provided with trigger criteria, facilitating the logic of the game world. While the creative space for emergent stories could be described as less multifaceted and less spacious in terms of quantity of content in *Hearts of Iron IV* compared to *Europa Universalis IV*, counterfactuals do follow the same principal logic.

The sandbox nature of *Europa Universalis IV*, however, emphasises the multiplicity of possible outcomes. The open-ended framing supports creativity in gameplay and the role of counterfactuals are contingent on the way content relates to game rules and their dependencies. Consequently, facilitating emergent story-making in both games is important in order to make clear the cohesive (historical or counterfactual) logic of each game. However, conversely, despite the emphasis on emergent gameplay in digital strategy games, both games make conscious use of coherent objectives and gameplay goals (missions and achievements in *Europa Universalis IV* and national focuses and achievements in *Hearts of Iron IV*) as a tool for offering the player specific and cohesive counterfactual scenarios. In other words, there is a nuanced difference between emergent stories and ready-made scenarios (goals) based on design.

Achievements – Scenarios and Goal-setting

The achievement system is a reward mechanic that exists in both games and ties directly into the digital distribution platform, store interface and game launcher, *Steam*. *Steam* functions as a shop and a depository for people to buy and keep their digital games. In *Europa Universalis IV* and *Hearts of Iron IV* achievements are only completable in Iron Man mode and give players a badge in the *Steam* interface to indicate that they were successful. From this point of view, there is no in-game or gameplay related reward or benefit to collecting achievements.

From a gameplay perspective, however, achievements have a lot in common with the way goal-setting works for both games: they constitute challenges that allow the player to test their skills and to explore specific historical and counterfactual scenarios. As such, achievements are in many ways similar to the mechanics of national focuses in *Hearts of Iron IV* and missions in *Europa Univer-*

---

320 Developer informant Daryl (June 26, 2017).

Figure 13: In-game view of an achievement ledger. Note the tooltip that tracks progress. Cropped screenshot, reproduced with permission.

salis IV. However, as mentioned, achievements do not provide any in-game rewards the way national focuses and missions do: those can alter stats and trigger events – achievements can do neither.

There are close to 300 achievements in *Europa Universalis IV* and around 90 in *Hearts of Iron IV*.[321] A typical achievement has a title, a description and a tooltip which contains the trigger conditions and notes the progress to completion (see figure 13). Achievements can be about anything in the game; sometimes they encourage the player towards a specific mechanic and action such as building a particular unit, and sometimes towards entire scenarios. For example, note the difference in specificity and scope between these two achievements in *Europa Universalis IV*.

NEW_ACHIEVEMENT_7_6_NAME:0 "The Grand Armada"
NEW_ACHIEVEMENT_7_6_DESC:0 "Have 500 heavy ships and no loans."[322]

NEW_ACHIEVEMENT_12_26_NAME:0 "Around the World in 80 Years"
NEW_ACHIEVEMENT_12_26_DESC:0 "Starting as a Custom Nation of up to 400 points in

---

[321] Paradox Wiki, *Europa Universalis IV: Achievements*; *Hearts of Iron IV: Achievements*.
[322] *Europa Universalis IV*. Localisation. achievements_l_english.yml. "The Grand Armada." v1.28.3.

the British Region, own New York, San Francisco, Suez, Bombay, Calcutta, Hong Kong and Yokohama by 1524.11.11."[323]

"The Grand Armada" requires the player to obtain 500 heavy ships without going into debt. These are the only criteria, which means that this achievement can be completed as any country at any point in a game. In contrast, the second achievement can only be completed as a custom nation and the rather complex criteria (that in turn rely on a series of antecedents) must be fulfilled by in-game date November 11, 1524.

Achievements drive motivation and goal-setting within the content and mechanics of each game and allow developers to specify possible scenarios that go beyond the missions mechanic in *Europa Universalis IV* and the national focus mechanic in *Hearts of Iron IV*. As such, it is a rich empirical source of content that contains counterfactuals as a use of history based on all of the available content and mechanics in the games.

Counterfactuals in *Europa Universalis IV*

On Goal-setting and Counterfactuals for *Europa Universalis IV*

Goals are part of any gameplay experience as motivation to overcome a challenge, or an end in and of themselves.[324] For example, in the open-world action-adventure game *Assassin's Creed* (2007), the main protagonist has a clear objective to stop a big corporation from acquiring dangerous historic artefacts and using them for evil-doing. Because the game is open-world, the player may explore the game world freely, but the story only progresses when the player performs very specific tasks and missions. The game is designed to guide the player through a sequence of these missions and tasks to eventually end up completing the overarching challenge. The success of the player becomes the success of the protagonist, and as such, in the case of narrative linearity, the goal of the game aligns with the goal of the player.[325]

---

[323] *Europa Universalis IV*. Localisation. achievements_l_english.yml. "Around the World in 80 Years." v1.28.3. Note that achievements more than any other content tend to be designed in reference to items outside of the historical context of the game such as for example *Around the World in 80 Days* by Jules Verne.

[324] Greg Costikyan, *Uncertainty in Games* (London: The MIT Press, 2013), 61–64.

[325] Jesper Juul, *The Art of Failure – An Essay on the Pain of Playing Video Games* (London: The MIT Press, 2013), 27.

The missions and objectives in *Assassin's Creed* correspond to what Jesper Juul calls "completable goals"; goals that are clearly stated and once they are finished, they do not come back or become available again until one starts from the beginning of the game. Winning a match in a fighting game, or solving for example *Solitaire*, are what he calls "transient goals," the point of which are to solve specific rounds of cards but not the game once and for all.[326]

As discussed in chapter one, *Europa Universalis IV* does not offer ready-made, singular objectives for players to follow and accomplish the same way linear games do. Goals in *Europa Universalis IV* can be both completable and transient, to use Juul's terminology, depending on what challenge is being pursued. As designed elements in the game, national ideas, missions and achievements are implemented as completable goals.[327] Although important, they are not obligatory in order to progress in a play-through. Indeed, players are able, and encouraged, to create their own goals for playing.[328] Thomas Apperley has found that Paradox player communities of *Europa Universalis II* and *Victoria: Empire Under the Sun* negotiate goal-setting, internally determining what constitutes "winning conditions" for what most often amount to counterfactual scenarios. In his study, players had noticed that *Europa Universalis II* favours historically "successful" nations, and so the player base would place caveats on specific actions in order to increase the gameplay challenge and define what it means to "win" a game. *Victoria: Empire Under the Sun*, like most Paradox titles, has a score system to rank player nations and AI-controlled nations based on performance in different areas during a game. Player communities discuss and evaluate their skill depending on how challenging it is considered to rank high with a specific nation within this score system.[329] *Europa Universalis IV* has a similar score system which functions as a score board and is utilised as a mechanic by a complex framework of community, as well as individual, goal-setting. It

---

326 Juul, *The Art of Failure*, 85. This context deals with goals related to *Europa Universalis IV*, whether they are designed by developers through mechanics or invented by the player. I do not discuss goals that do not directly relate to this specific gameplay experience in some way.
327 See chapter 1 for details on National Ideas, Missions and Achievements. The Missions mechanic was partly overhauled in patch 1.25 (January 2018), in which mission events were turned into mission trees and introduced to create a greater clarity, bringing the design of *Europa Universalis IV* and *Hearts of Iron IV* closer together (what with the similarity between mission trees in *Europa Universalis IV* and national focuses in *Hearts of Iron IV*). At this point, missions in *Europa Universalis IV* read as if they break down the paths to specific scenarios such as for example the wishful thinking-scenario of reconstructing the Roman Empire (*Basileus*) or the possible world of the Aztecs invading Europe (*The Sunset Invasion*).
328 Developer informants Dale (June 15, 2017), Devin (June 28, 2017), and Dylan (June 29, 2018).
329 Apperley, "Counterfactual Communities," 8–9.

is of interest to note that players in Apperley's study negotiate these goals around their own historical knowledge and criticism of it, as well as their "counterfactual imagination, which may be informed by highly localized knowledge and concerns."[330]

Transient goals in *Europa Universalis IV* are facilitated by the arbitrary sandbox nature of the game's genre, and the randomization and AI behaviour as designed by developers. The rules in the game are persistent, but the causal outcomes within it are not. Like the way a deck in *Solitaire* is unlikely to stack the cards the same way twice, the chances of a *Europa Universalis IV* playing out exactly the same way twice are minimal. Likewise, players can abandon goals at any time, leaving any completable goal unfulfilled without it having any game-breaking consequences for the progression of the session. As put by Drew, "We created more, shall we say, counterfactual mechanics rather than [events]. They're taken from history and then sort of repackaged to become emergent, rather than rigid."[331] This fluidity and open-endedness of historical processes (as opposed to railroaded linearity) – while it constitutes an expedient platform to make historical arguments on a macro scale – embodies a certain amount of chaos which can make it difficult to spot discrete counterfactual history among the less specific sprawl of emergent gameplay. As beta tester Blaine notes on this topic: "These games themselves don't really offer a way to conceivably record your changes. [...] There's not a particular way to, like, document all this stuff."[332] This also points to the lack of cohesiveness of the counterfactuals in the games in terms of grand narratives. Understanding goal-setting (how do players pick their goals?) and designed objectives (how do developers design for those goals and other contingencies?) is therefore a good place to start looking at the design and depiction of counterfactual history in *Europa Universalis IV.* Principles of goal-setting intersect with counterfactuals at the points where counterfactuals are made explicit, and make specific arguments about historical causality and contingency through design.

---

330 Apperley, "Counterfactual Communities," 16.
331 Developer informant Drew (June 28, 2018).
332 Beta tester informant Blaine (July 4, 2018).

Basileus – Restoring Lost Empires

> "As Byzantium, restore the Roman Empire."[333]

As noted in previous chapters, national ideas and missions constitute the metaphorical personality of each nation inside the game. These build on what developers refer to as qualified guesses and arm-chair theories on how nations would have developed had they not developed the way that they did.[334] The personality and actual past of each nation are the primary inspiration in writing and designing possibly crucial events and counterfactual outcomes for each playable nation building on hindsight.[335] A relatively popular nation to play is Byzantium as it offers players a comparably challenging start.[336] Keeping in mind that the 1444 start of a game always mimics a historically adequate baseline (to the best of the developers' ability and as much as game balance allows), the Byzantine Empire consists of a single core province and a vassal province, and is about to meet its demise by the hand of the Ottomans unless the player can avoid it.[337] There are different possible strategies for accomplishing this, most of which entail making suitable alliances ("The enemy of my enemy is my friend") and fabricating claims on nearby provinces while building an army to prevent the Ottomans from conquering Constantinople. If left unchecked, the process of the Ottomans eliminating Byzantium will start immediately and the game will likely soon end for the Byzantine player or AI.

The topic of the Roman Empire is generally speaking a frequent theme within gaming.[338] *Europa Universalis IV*, given its time frame, does not actually take place in classical times, but does make possible the enactment of a reconstruction of the Roman Empire – connecting the in-game present to a longer, cohesive

---

333 *Europa Universalis IV*. Common. achievements.txt; Localisation. achievements_I_english.yml. v1.28.3.
334 Developer informant Daryl (June 26, 2017), Delta (June 27, 2017). Beta tester informant Blake (August 20, 2018).
335 Zerubavel, *Time Maps*, 12.
336 Paradox Plaza, *Top 23 Most Played Countries* by Wiz, June 23, 2015, accessed August 21, 2019, https://forum.paradoxplaza.com/forum/index.php?threads/top-23-most-played-countries.865345/. Byzantium was the fourteenth most popular nation among players according to statistics posted by a Paradox representative.
337 On later starting dates, it is not possible to begin playing as Byzantium since the playable nation is effectively erased in the game by the 1450s.
338 Cassone and Thibault, "The HGR Framework." See for example games *Imperator: Rome* (2019) and *Rome: Total War* (2004–).

Counterfactuals in *Europa Universalis IV* — 135

Figure 14: The Byzantine mission tree. Cropped screenshot from https://eu4.paradoxwikis.com/Byzantine_missions. Reproduced with permission.

and counterfactual timeline.[339] To give Byzantium more playability, developers have designed a mission tree which – just as for any playable state or nation – provides the player with long and short term goals. At the end of the Byzantium mission tree are two counterfactual scenarios that refer to Byzantium's golden days as the remnant of the Roman Empire. The left side of the mission tree focuses on restoring the Western Roman Empire by accumulating provinces in the Balkans and in Anatolia, while simultaneously re-establishing the Catholic faith as the dominant one. The right side leads towards rebuilding the East Roman Empire by conquering provinces in today's Greece and Italy (see Figure 14). The middle part of the mission tree focuses on conquering provinces in Africa and Iberia.[340] Altogether, the entire mission tree and the provinces obtained

---

[339] Zerubavel, *Time Maps*, 18–19.
[340] *Europa Universalis IV*. Missions. PP_Purple_Phoenix.txt. v1.28.3.

therein resemble the Roman Empire at its height, essentially covering the Mediterranean coastline.

Reassembling what once constituted the Eastern Roman Empire by conquering the Balkans and Anatolia will trigger an achievement called *Basileus*.[341] In the similar cases of the *This is Persia!* achievement and restoring the Mongol Empire, the player will have to utilise the Formable Nations mechanic. A formable nation is a feature that under given criteria forces the formation of nations in a counterfactual manner. Formable nations can, on the one hand, be historical but anachronistic in the sense that they are designed and named based on present day nations (for example Japan, Iceland, Romania, Germany and more). On the other hand, another type of formable nations are inherently counterfactual constructions such as United Central America (a unified playable nation consisting of Central American core provinces) or Scandinavia (a unified playable nation consisting of Danish, Norwegian and Swedish core provinces).[342]

As an example of what explicit counterfactuals in *Europa Universalis IV* look like, the *Basileus* achievement embodies the wishful thinking principles of remembering, repairing and maintaining former greatness. On top of the ones already mentioned there are a number of achievements in *Europa Universalis IV* that build on the principle of wishful thinking, exploring, celebrating or lamenting turning points in a country or people's past including, for example, Hungary (*Take that, von Habsburgs!*), Sweden (*Lion of the North*), The Cherokee (*No Trail of Tears*), Delhi (*Emperor of Hindustan*) and Venice (*Venetian Sea*).[343] The shape of the national mission tree, it is worth noting too, elaborates on the idea to reconstruct the Roman Empire in not just one instance, but three, in varying times and to varying extents (Western Rome, Eastern Rome and the Roman Empire). The Byzantium counterfactuals ask the player to turn back time and re-establish an empire according to certain geographic criteria through employing military and diplomatic mechanics *par excellence.*

The use of the Roman Empire as wishful thinking counterfactuals in Paradox Development Studio games is expansive. Beyond *Imperator: Rome* which is set in classical antiquity, *Crusader Kings II* and *Hearts of Iron IV* both have achieve-

---

341 *Europa Universalis IV.* Common. achievements.txt. *achievement_basileus.* v1.28.3.
342 *Europa Universalis IV.* Decisions. UPCANation.txt. *upca_nation.* v1.28.3. *Europa Universalis IV.* Decisions. ScandinavianNation.txt. *scandinavian_nation.* Patch 1.28.3.
343 *Europa Universalis IV.* Localization. achievements.txt. v1.28.3. NEW_ACHIEVEMENT_9_5 (*Take that, von Habsburgs!*), NEW_ACHIEVEMENT_8_1 (*Lion of the North*), NEW_ACHIEVEMENT_6_12 (*No Trail of Tears*), NEW_ACHIEVEMENT_25 (*Emperor of Hindustan*), NEW_ACHIEVEMENT_7_17 (*Venetian Sea*).

ments to the same principle as *Basileus*.³⁴⁴ Beyond this thematic focus, however, *Basileus*, like so many other wishful thinking counterfactuals in *Europa Universalis IV*, taps into what I call a historical cultural canon – historical references that, within certain contexts, are more frequently relied on for counterfactual reasoning and storytelling. From a historical cultural perspective, these upheld historical events, and their use in counterfactual settings, align with principles described by, for example, Angus Mol who notes that "[tropic history] and its ramifications for the 'history of civilization'" perpetuates our understanding of authoritative and highly codified Western histories.³⁴⁵ We play to subvert these histories, Mol argues, not because a game is based on counterfactual history, but because the game allows us to counterplay history.³⁴⁶ Thus, by acknowledging the importance of historical reference as fodder for counterfactuals, *Basileus* can be understood as historical cultural signalling on a broader scale, which, ultimately, has more to do with our understanding and view of the Roman Empire in the present than it does about the past. However, from the perspective of game design practice, it can also be argued that Paradox Development Studio, in turn, signals an awareness of historical cultural positioning by gravitating towards counterfactual scenarios that harmonise with historical cultural canon. Rather than yielding control over the scenario at hand, the developers purposefully pre-empt player expectations also in counterfactual scenarios by framing them as wishful thinking scenarios.³⁴⁷

The Sunset Invasion – Colonising Europe

> "Playing as the Aztec, Own and core
> the provinces of Lisbon, Madrid, Paris,
> London, Holland, and Roma."³⁴⁸

The achievement of *Sunset Invasion* (first available in the *El Dorado* DLC, 2015) turns colonisation, in what the game calls "the New World," around on the Euro-

---

344 In *Crusader Kings II* the achievement is called *Legacy of Rome*. In *Hearts of Iron IV* it is called "I Swear I'm Not a Byzantophile."
345 Mol, "Toying With History," 241.
346 Mol, "Toying With History," 241. My emphasis.
347 For an in-depth look at this period in digital games, see Christian Rollinger, Filippo Carlà-Uhink and Martin Lindner (eds.), *Classical Antiquity in Video Games: Playing with the Ancient World* (London: Bloomsbury, 2020).
348 *Europa Universalis IV*. Common. achievements.txt; Localisation. achievements_l_english.-yml. v1.28.3.

peans. The achievement is linked to a series of missions that explore what happens when Europeans find their way to the Americas, the Aztecs adapt to the situation, run the European nations out of the region and eventually begin colonising European provinces. The achievement gets fulfilled when the above criteria are true in a session. The corresponding mission (also called *Sunset Invasion*[349]) is fulfilled when a playable nation with their capital in the Americas owns any five provinces in Europe. For example, this is the *Drive out the Europeans* mission title, description and tooltip (goal):

> new_world_remove_euro_title:0 "Drive out the Europeans"
>
> new_world_remove_euro_desc:0 "The invading Europeans are rapidly conquering the New World, and are even expanding into our traditional homes. They must be driven back to their ships."
>
> new_world_remove_euro_toolip:0 "No European nation or their colonies own provinces in your capital region."[350]

The logic behind this counterfactual is that the Aztecs utilise their access to gold and aggressive expansion to dominate Meso- and South America during the second half of the fifteenth century. The Aztec playable nation is prevented in hard code from developing the idea of exploration (which in contrast is required by playable European nations to begin the Age of Discovery) as well as the technology (in this case ship building) to travel across the seas. Hence, the critical prerequisite for being able to accomplish the necessary steps in the game is to have Europe make contact with the Americas and introduce both elements to American cultures. The Aztecs are then able to reform and adapt said ideas, which leads them to develop the ability to, for example, hire explorers (contingent on the idea of exploration) and build sturdy enough ships (contingent on ship building technology).

In order to complete the achievement, the Aztec player also needs to prevent European powers (mainly Spain, Portugal, Great Britain and The Netherlands) from establishing strongholds in Meso- and South America. Once the Europeans have left, the game prompts the Aztec player to go after them[351]:

---

[349] The New World mission tree is a generic tree for all playable nations in the Americas. The *Sunset Invasion* achievement is specific to the Aztecs.

[350] *Europa Universalis IV*. Localisation. new_missions_l_english.yml. *new_world_remove_euro*. v1.28.3.

[351] Other digital strategy games have commented on this power relation using the same logic, including *Age of Empires II* and *Medieval II: Total War*. See Joshua D. Holdenried and Nicolas Trépanier, "Dominance and the Aztec Empire: Representations in *Age of Empires II* and *Medieval*

nw_sunset_invasion_title:0 "Sunset Invasion"

nw_sunset_invasion_desc:0 "The invaders have fled from our lands. But is that enough? At any time they might return with even more terrible force. Let us pursue them back to Europe itself."[352]

Sunset Invasion represents an example of a possible world counterfactual. It describes a different but, according to the game logic, possible (if unlikely) outcome to a significant historical cultural backdrop – the initiation of European colonisation of the Americas in the fifteenth century. Through this counterfactual, the game makes the argument that if the player guides Aztecs (or other provinces in the Americas) as a playable nation towards modernisation in the style of Europe, they will be able to colonise.

This scenario is particularly interesting from a representations point of view. Providing the Aztec with the tools and power to fight back against "the invaders," as the event description puts it, is a principal concept in this counterfactual. However, by way of mechanics (reform, idea groups, technology and missions) the Aztecs may only do so while adopting what amounts to a European mind-set and end up mimicking European history.[353] As such, on a design level the game gravitates towards historical actuality on a conceptual level, i.e. the nation which develops these ideas are headed to become colonisers and invaders of other nations, born out of greed or necessity (for instance, the flavour text in the *Sunset Invasion* mission tooltip here suggests the latter).

On the topic of flavour text, it is also worth pointing out that the *Sunset Invasion* counterfactual, despite speaking to the player as the collective voice of the in-game Aztecs, uses "New World" to denote the region they are in. As already noted, the *Drive out the Europeans* description states that: "The invading Europeans are rapidly conquering the New World, and are even expanding into our traditional homes."[354] This of course begs the question: new world for whom? As a term used by Europeans in the fifteenth and sixteenth centuries,

---

II: *Total War*," in *Playing With the Past – Digital Games and the Simulation of the Past*, ed. Matthew Kapell and Andrew B.R. Elliott (London: Bloomsbury, 2013), 115–116.
352 *Europa Universalis IV*. Localisation. new_missions_l_english.yml. *nw_sunset_invasion*. v1.28.3.
353 Early versions of the game had a mechanic called westernisation which was removed in patch 1.18. Paradox Wikis: *Europa Universalis: Institutions. Europa Universalis IV: Patch 1.18*. Westernisation allowed playable nations to introduce a state called western culture to colonised areas and was replaced with the Institutions mechanic.
354 *Europa Universalis IV*. Localisation. new_missions_l_english.yml. *new_world_remove_euro*. v1.28.3.

the game anticipates a Eurocentric perspective on the events at hand. This is partly a technical design issue brought on by the game using generic (game-wide) scripting principles regardless of which nation is currently being played. This has also been noted by Rhett Loban and Thomas Apperley who note that the modular design of the game places indigenous-focused DLCs, such as *El Dorado*, as secondary and supplementary to the principal European-focused core design.[355] To the same point, Elizabeth LaPensée explains this principle by recognising games as "systems of signification,"[356] indicating that inherent Western or Eurocentric design values will impose themselves on the games' ability to represent anything other than this. Ultimately, she argues, this is a question of mechanics rather than for example graphics.[357] In addition to this, the adherence to Eurocentric terminology, in flavour text and in scripting practices, starkly undermine the *Sunset Invasion* counterfactual, specifically, as an effort of historiographic diversity and multiplicity.

As such, the logic of the achievement perpetuates a Eurocentric narrative rather than emphasising the Aztec one by dressing counter-hegemonic potential in hegemonic historiography.[358] While developers agree that *Europa Universalis IV* is Eurocentric (mainly because of design legacy, more on this in chapter four) it is not unprecedented in Paradox Development Studio history to create a counter-hegemonic narrative like this one, i.e. having the Aztecs arrive on European shores first. In 2012, *Crusader Kings II* – the Paradox Development Studio title covering the Middle Ages – released an expansion also called *Sunset Invasion*, in which Europe is invaded by the Aztecs. In the medieval scenario, Europeans have never seen or heard of the Americas before they turn up on European shores. According to developer Dallas, this counterfactual scenario caused heavy backlash from the player community despite being completely optional to purchase and install.[359] In the context of this example, Dallas specifies that players

---

355 Loban and Apperley, "Eurocentric Values at Play," 95.
356 Elizabeth LaPensée, "Signifying the West: Colonialist Design in *Age of Empires III: The WarChiefs*," *Eludamos: Journal for Computer Game Culture* 2 (2008): 18.
357 LaPensée, "Signifying the West," 18.
358 Emil Lundedal Hammar, "Counter-Hegemonic Play, Marginalised Pasts and the Politics of Play in *Assassin's Creed: Freedom Cry*," *Rethinking History* 21 (2017): 383–384. Note that Hammar's study concludes that games that recognise and highlight oppression and marginalisation do have the ability to elicit cathartic moments through counter-hegemonic play, despite inherent design and mechanics issues which perpetuate white hegemony (Hammar, "Counter-Hegemonic Play," 388). The same might well be true for *Europa Universalis IV* from a player perspective but requires more research.
359 Developer informant Dallas (June 26, 2017). Paradox Plaza, *Crusader Kings II: Sunset Invasion DLC – Dev Diary* by Doomdark, *Crusader Kings II* Developer Diary, November 2, 2012, ac-

differ in their critique of what constitutes acceptable counterfactuals in an interesting way: "So [player opinion] very much relies on [what is] down to the player, [to] the AI, or to things that we choose to add to the game."[360] In other words, the developer expresses that players have an easier time accepting counterfactual history if control is yielded to the player. Developers, and the AI, are, as previously mentioned, expected to deliver a plausible historical baseline. Consequently, *Sunset Invasion* embodies one possible limit of counterfactual design, and more specifically designs of possible worlds. Based on the interviews, and as discussed in chapter two, game design practice at Paradox Development Studio partly entails honing designs that work from a sales and consumer perspective. The difference in design between what constitutes a possible *Sunset Invasion* in *Europa Universalis IV* and what does not constitute a possible *Sunset Invasion* in *Crusader Kings II* may perhaps be explained by the contemporary reaction to the latter by the player community, and the relationship between it being an essentially interesting counterfactual and some fundamental issues with execution, according to players.

In contrast, the causal exploration at the heart of the *Sunset Invasion* scenario in *Europa Universalis IV* forces the game to enact historical change by extrapolating historical reference. In other words, the Aztecs must "become" in part "European" in order to fulfil their objective. The counterfactual is dressed in familiarity and as such becomes acceptable. However, while the mission and achievement both promote the idea of a shifted power structure, and possible outcomes thereof, the mechanics and content design must simultaneously harmonise with player expectations. On this, the game analysis supports the findings in chapter two that player presupposition influences developer and game design practice.

---

cessed July 31, 2021. *The Sunset Invasion* minor expansion for *Crusader Kings II* appears to have come about under rather interesting circumstances. From a game design practice perspective, the fact that the entire DLC was made in the developers' private time or extra time between other tasks, or it was outsourced (it is not clear whether this was to beta testers or third-party developers) is noteworthy. The developer diary for the expansion also acknowledges what they refer to as a "passionate" response to the DLC. Alluding to the first two achievements, *Hearts of Iron IV* also has a *Sunset Invasion* achievement in which Japan annexes Mexico before invading Europe from the West.
360 Developer informant Dallas (June 26, 2017).

Counterfactuals in *Hearts of Iron IV*

Two things distinguish *Hearts of Iron IV* from the rest of the Paradox portfolio above all else: scope and theme. As a digital strategy game made by Paradox Development Studio, it stands out in that it only covers two entry points to the same scenario: the Second World War and the years leading up to it. This vertical cut in time and subsequent constraints have consequences for gameplay as well as historical representation, including counterfactual scenarios. In the case of *Hearts of Iron IV*, the digital strategy game format is still a structuralist representation of historical change, although it struggles to highlight longer historical processes and notions of slow change. As such the game is more concerned with causality in the immediate and short-term.[361]

Because the game is not specifically designed to make systemic arguments about long-term or gradual historical change, counterfactual history scenarios in *Hearts of Iron IV* are heavily controlled scenarios, anchored in the decisions illustrated by the national focus tree mechanic.[362]

National Focus Trees

In *Hearts of Iron IV*, each playable country has a role in the Second World War. It is up to the player to decide – again within the parameters of the game's design – what that role shall be, and which path a playable country shall take. To facilitate this, each major playable country has a national focus tree – a design element that outlines decisions and events that correspond to potential paths of agency that a playable country can take. They are similar to a *Europa Universalis IV* missions tree, yet typically more extensive.[363]

The generic national focus tree in *Hearts of Iron IV* provides the player (and the AI) with gameplay options that follow the same logic no matter if the player decides play as, say, China or South Africa. It is made up of five paths. As also discussed in chapter one, the starting points for the branches are army effort, aviation effort, naval effort, industrial effort and political effort, respectively.[364] Each military branch comes with a specific set of decisions that, once completed, provide bonuses that boost or improve the statistics of the army, military, naval

---

[361] Chapman, *Digital Games as History*, 240.
[362] Developer informant Dorian (June 29, 2018).
[363] For a discussion on the design legacy of *Hearts of Iron IV*'s National focus trees, see Pennington, "Authentic-lite Rhetoric," 31–34.
[364] *Hearts of Iron IV*. Common. National Focus. generic.txt. v1.6.2.

and industrial efforts of the playable nation. A player may choose to go down a specific national focus tree branch depending on which units they reckon will be the most advantageous to have considering, among other factors, the playable nation's geographical location and terrain. They may also boost research speed and add, for example, building slots in states.[365]

The political branch allows the player to pick an ideology that translates into a mechanic called National spirits. The National spirits mechanic is a set of historical experiences that determine attitudes and motivation, which in turn come with corresponding modifiers. For example, the generic national focus tree starts with the National spirits "Collectivist Ethos" and "Libery Ethos." The former modifies the Daily Democracy Support by −0.02, and the latter creates a 20% increase in the public's opinion on trade deals to reflect the impact of ideologically based reform.[366] As discussed in chapter one, these modifiers ultimately cause opportunity or constraint for player agency; in the case of decreased Daily Democracy Support, a player's chances of maintaining a democratic ideology diminish.

The biggest and, in the game, most important playable countries in the war have their own uniquely crafted focus trees. As discussed in chapter two, these are typically among the new features in each expansion or DLC. A unique national focus tree will have the five core focus branches and individually designed additional branches that represent gameplay challenges, often counterfactuals. For example, the national focus tree of the German Reich has the four military focus branches, one historical path and an extra two branches that each corresponds to counterfactual political scenarios where Germany takes a different political path: "Oppose Hitler" (democratic or non-aligned) and "Return of the Kaiser" (monarchy or constitutional monarchy).[367]

Despite its short timeframe and the limited amount of long-term historical change in *Hearts of Iron IV*, the presence of the in-game-past (pre-1936) is often at the forefront in event description and playable nation decision-making, and it is mainly in these instances that we find wishful thinking in the game. For many European countries, the Great War is designed as a major influence on incentives and motivations for participating in the Second World War (or not) in order to turn back time and pursue, for example, a reinstated Austria-Hungary. For some countries, such as the United States, an even older past is evoked for counterfactual history, building a wishful thinking scenario around the Ameri-

---

365 *Hearts of Iron IV*. Common. National Focus. generic.txt. v1.6.2.
366 *Hearts of Iron IV*. Common. Ideas. generic.txt. v1.6.2.
367 *Hearts of Iron IV*. Common. National Focus. germany.txt. v1.6.2.

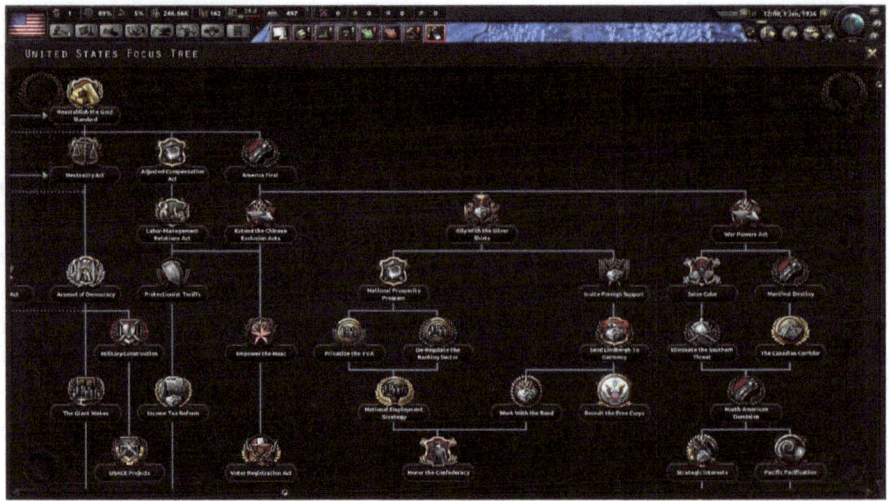

Figure 15: Part of United States focus tree, zoomed in on the branch that ends in "Honor the Confederacy." Uncropped screenshot. Reproduced with permission. *Hearts of Iron IV.* V1.6.2.

can Civil War. The United States has a national focus tree branch that – via its fascism sub-branch, called "America first" – makes it possible to reinstate the Confederacy.[368] The branch outlines a chain of events that tilt political decision-making towards a path that aligns with fascist ideology. Some of those events are scripted to increase the risk of civil war, for example the "Voter Registration Act" and the "Ally with the Silver Shirts."[369] In causally tying these events to the risk, recollection and possible reconstitution of the Civil War, the game connects Second World War-era, far-right sentiments on race, with that of the Civil War-era discourse on slavery.

Counterfactual Rules and Ahistorical AI

A significant part of the gameplay dynamics of *Hearts of Iron IV* resides with the AI and the rules that control the nature of counterfactual scenarios and how the

---

[368] Hearts of Iron IV. Common. National focus. usa.txt. v1.6.2. On top of the national focus called "Honor the Confederacy," there are two achievements that tie into the same theme: "To Arms in Dixie!" and "History repeated itself." The former entails starting a Second Civil War as the southern states, and the latter winning the Civil War as the United States.
[369] Hearts of Iron IV. Common. National focus. usa.txt. v1.6.2. "Voter registration act" and "Ally with the Silver Shirts."

different playable nations respond to each other's actions. This can be described as each non-player nation's behaviour. According to developers, the challenge is for the AI to react appropriately to the player's actions while maintaining historical verisimilitude.[370] Two main mechanics affect the way a game unfolds: country strategy and national focuses. Each major playable nation with a unique strategy and national focus have designed contingencies for a set of counterfactual scenarios. For example, France has four different strategy responses to four different German Reich scenarios including counterfactuals. The French controlled AI also has a game plan for going fascist, communist, or attempting to form the Little Entente.[371]

At the beginning of each game, the player decides if they want the AI to play with "historical" or "ahistorical" focuses.[372] The default is ahistorical but, importantly, this does not mean that it is automatically counterfactual. It means that the AI is more likely to go counterfactual, as opposed to the historical mode in which the AI will pick the same progression of historical focuses every time. Furthermore, each choice the AI makes is weighted towards historical actuality, which means that the likelihood of the game going completely off the rails immediately is small.[373] While the player may set the game to historical, that does not prevent the player from picking counterfactual focuses for themselves. The AI decides which decision to make based on the scripted *ai_will_do* factor. When making a decision, the game takes the factors of all available choices into consideration and rolls a digital die to pick a decision. A higher factor value means higher probability to get picked. For example, in a case where AI controlled Poland needs to decide whether to pick the "Develop Upper Silesia" focus or the "Additional Research Slot" focus, they both have a factor 10, thus they are equally likely to get picked in that particular instance.

```
focus = {
            id = POL_develop_upper_silesia
            icon = GFX_goal_generic_consumer_goods
            prerequisite = { focus = POL_invest_in_the_old_polish_region}
            x = 1
```

---

[370] Developer informant Daryl (June 26, 2017); beta tester informant Brooklyn (October 22, 2018).
[371] *Hearts of Iron IV*. Common. ai_strategy_plans. FRA_alternate_strategy_plan.txt. v1.6.2.
[372] "Ahistorical" or "alternate" are terms often used by developers when discussing counterfactuals in *Hearts of Iron IV*. In practice, this demarcation denotes the default setting in which the AI may lean on its counterfactual options. It just means that it can go counterfactual, not that it necessarily will. Developer informant Daryl (June 26, 2017).
[373] Developer informant Daryl (June 26, 2017).

```
y = 1
relative_position_id = POL_invest_in_the_old_polish_region
cost = 10

ai_will_do = {
    factor = 10
```
[374]

There are some counterfactual paths that alter the foundation of the main scenario (the Second World War) that require strategies, like the ones exemplified by France above. In such cases, the AI has been set to respond in a specific way to certain player actions with the intended goal of maintaining the integrity of Second World War -like scenarios. The same is true from a player perspective. If the player chooses to play according to historical actuality as Austria, the Anschluss event poses a gameplay as well as design problem. Austria represents an example where the game forces the player to consider a counterfactual scenario because the goal of the game is navigating the war in the role of a nation. The minute that playable nation has been destroyed – or in the case of Austria, annexed – the game ends. As such, the only viable choice for a player-controlled Austria is to go counterfactual and refuse the Anschluss when proposed by Germany in 1936 and the game has been designed accordingly. The AI may refuse the Anschluss as well but has a three times higher chance of accepting the union than refusing it (although, 100 % accept rate if in a strictly historical focus game).[375]

A similar principle is the importance of factions in causing the Second World War. On a rules level, the game is designed to always force global conflict when it can. Historically, Germany was the nation that initiated the war. Should Germany take a counterfactual path and become democratic, other nations in Europe will instigate conflict based on other political criteria. If Germany reinstates the Kaiser and allies with Great Britain against the Communist faction, France will play the counterfactual role of a communist threat, providing cause to start what will amount to a world war.[376]

These counterfactual rules that implore the AI to react to their events around them in order to produce a specific dynamic are much less pronounced, when they are at all available in *Europa Universalis IV*. Counterfactual rules gravitate towards future fiction in the way they explore the aftermath of significant events. As Evans notes, Hitler dying before the war, or Hitler winning the Second World

---

[374] *Hearts of Iron IV.* Common. National focus. poland.txt. v1.6.2.
[375] *Hearts of Iron IV.* Common. National focus. germany.txt. v1.6.2.
[376] *Hearts of Iron IV.* Common. ai_strategy_plans. FRA_alternate_strategy_plan.txt. v1.6.2.

Figure 16: Cropped screenshot from *Hearts of Iron IV* playing as Austria (historical AI). Germany wants to annex Austria. The tooltip for the option of joining the German Reich details the consequences. *Hearts of Iron*, v1.6.2.

War, already constitute two of the most common future fictions in counterfactual literature and film.[377] Compared to *Europa Universalis IV* which, to a larger extent attempts to explain how historical development happens, *Hearts of Iron IV* makes little effort to explain, for example, how France came to be communist in the above example. Instead, *Hearts of Iron IV* mainly explains how a Second World War comes to be and develops in such a world.

Counterfactuals in Roleplaying and Descriptive Text

Events are an integrated part of the national focus trees as they tend to fire upon focus completion. Some events, most importantly news events, fire when the AI does something of note like declaring war on another country or holding an election. Events are designed to convey the way the game is going, and are thus either designed to be generic (which allows the game to paste in the relevant playable nation's name to an event template), or they are nation- and event-specific. They all have flavour texts, which contribute to the counterfactual scenario-building in the game when applicable. These descriptive texts outline the

---

[377] Evans, *Altered Pasts*, 65–68.

event itself and are weighted in accordance with the path the player is currently taking. The following event is an in-character ("we" being the country's government) notification, informing a player of a fascist United States that Germany has become an ally of the communist faction. The event comes with the option to abandon fascism and go back to being a democratic nation. It hints that the fascists gaining ground in the United States so far had been a result of fear for a communist revolution, but now that the Germans have switched sides, fascist support in the United States is dwindling.

> usa.14.d:0 "Our great role-model, Nazi Germany, has betrayed their deepest principles and has allied themselves to the great enemy: The Communists. As the knowledge spreads, unrest follows in its wake. The people were willing to follow us this far, through fear of a Communist revolution, but with Germany's defection our great revival is being questioned."
>
> usa.14.a:0 "Return to Democracy."
>
> usa.14.b:0 "Stay true to Fascism."[378]

The player discerns that this event has consequences for the game in that support for the ruling faction is an important way to gain political power that is necessary for most government–related actions. The logic follows that of counterfactual rules throughout the game and is dressed in contemporary role-play.

A series of major cities on the planet have unique descriptions of the consequences of an atomic bombing.[379] Being future fiction, events like these are frivolous compared to most other content and written to echo specific topical and stereotypical aspects of each city. The temporality of the text itself is of particular interest in the way that the flavour subtly incorporates flashes of – in game-time – future events. For example, destroying Stockholm using a nuclear bomb produces the following news event:

> nuke_dropped.13.t:0 "Atomic Bombing of Stockholm"
>
> nuke_dropped.13.d:0 "The beautiful city of Stockholm, proud Venice of the North, was struck by a nuclear bomb today. Despite their best efforts to stay neutral in the past, the Swedes have now paid the ultimate price for international conflict. The epicenter of the blast was in the middle of south central Stockholm, an area intended for future development and grand construction projects, now irreversibly destroyed. Much of the city is beyond recognition, but the old structures at Slussen seem to have survived the blast better

---

378 *Hearts of Iron IV.* Localisation. events_l_english.txt. *usa.14.* v1.6.2.
379 Hiroshima, Nagasaki, Berlin, London, Kyoto, Tokyo, Washington D.C., Rome and Paris. All other cities use a generic event when bombed. *Hearts of Iron IV.* Localisation. events_l_english.txt. v1.6.2.

than expected. It has been decided that it should stand untouched forever as a monument to the city's resilience."

nuke_dropped.13.a:0 "With this, Swedish neutrality will be but a memory."

nuke_dropped.13.b:0 "The Swedish tiger will not lose its stripes!"[380]

This flavour text notes that Sweden has a history of staying "neutral" in global conflict (a common, and contested, theme in Swedish uses of history[381]). The epicentre refers to the Stockholm area Södermalm, where Paradox Development Studio is situated. The Slussen area is an interchange in south central Stockholm built in 1935. Over the years, there have been several attempts at rebuilding the area due to structural deterioration. Because of social and political disagreements, the Slussen reconstruction started as late as 2016, much to the annoyance and amusement of the Stockholm locals. According to the flavour text, if Slussen can survive municipal politics, it could probably survive an atomic hit. While the counterfactual specifics in flavour text like these take obvious liberties with counterfactual description "without," as Evans describes it, "enquiring too closely into how it came into being," they also situate these scenarios on an extended timeline, partly disconnecting the flavour from the graveness of nuclear warfare.[382]

This is not the only instance in which *Hearts of Iron IV* employs humour to discuss historical events.[383] According to Jerome De Groot, laughing at the past may be rooted in a sense of historical difference: "The past is an odd place, and laughable insofar as it is strange and other," he writes, discussing dark humour television on a historical backdrop.[384] The core of his argument is that laughter and pleasure aligns with historiographical insight and that to laugh at history is to gain some notion of control over it in demonstrating how the past is different from the now.[385] This theory lends itself well to the nature of digital strategy games, which embody both a literal and intellectual sense of control, while very consciously and purposefully making a variety of historical arguments in clear contrast to the present.

---

[380] *Hearts of Iron IV*. Localisation. events_I_english.txt. *nuke_dropped.13*. v1.6.2.
[381] See, for example, Ingmarie Danielsson Malmros, *Det var en gång ett land...: Berättelser om svenskhet i historieläroböcker och elevers föreställningsvärldar* (Agerings bokförlag, 2012).
[382] Evans, *Altered Pasts*, 91.
[383] Another example is the occasional use of puns and contemporary popular cultural references. See for example *Hearts of Iron IV*. Localisation. events_I_english.txt. v1.6.2.
[384] De Groot, *Remaking History: The Past in Contemporary Historical Fictions* (London: Routledge, 2016), 169.
[385] De Groot, *Remaking History*, 169–170.

Furthermore, games carry an inherent connotation to be fun, and developers maintain that design practice is driven in part by entertainment value. With regard to the latter, Martin Wainwright notes that "[...] developers misrepresent reality in order to transform what are often some of the least pleasant moments in a person's life into a source of entertainment and pleasure in the virtual world. For there is no denying that violence sells video games, but only because it isn't real."[386] In the case of the example above, *Hearts of Iron IV* includes a humorous mix of present and past in order to create a sufficient amount of distance between the future fiction in flavour and descriptive text, and the abhorrent historical reality upon which it is based. This space is given up to the player who gains control and insight into the scenarios at hand.

Hindsight and Reconstitution (Wishful Thinking)

Even when we cannot fully understand why things go the way they do, we must at least accept that time runs its course and that humans are unable to go back and change history. This unyielding truth is why a typical characteristic of a wishful thinking scenario is the juxtaposition between historical actuality and the counterfactual from a position of if only? – an act of lingering, indulgence, or regret. Wishful thinking allows for one to elaborate on historical outcomes and ponder how they might have gone differently. The indulgent might fantasise about the resurrection of vast empires, and the regretful will lament the horseshoe nail, the absence of which caused the fall of the very same.[387]

As illustrated by, for example, missions and achievements in *Europa Universalis IV*, older history can return incarnated as designed counterfactual depictions of the Early Modern era. The recurring theme of the Roman Empire is just one example of this. In *Europa Universalis IV* a player may reconstruct Early Modern versions of the classical Roman Empire in at least four different missions and achievements, one of which is available to any playable nation.[388] In practice, the player spends their time engaging with Early Modern principles

---

[386] Wainwright, *Virtual History*, 185.
[387] Evans, *Altered Pasts*, 30.
[388] Achievements: *Mare Nostrum* (restore the Roman Empire as any nation) and *Basileus* (restore the Roman Empire as Byzantium). Byzantine missions: *Recover Lombardia* (Restore the Western Roman Empire), *Rome Reclaimed!* (Restore the Eastern Roman Empire and be Orthodox). *Europa Universalis IV.* Common. achievements.txt; Localisation. achievements_l_english.-yml. NEW_ACHIEVEMENT_10_13 (*Mare Nostrum*) v1.28.3; *Europa Universalis IV.* Missions. PP_Purple_Phoenix.txt. v1.28.3.

for historical development in trying to create counterfactual scenarios building on, or referencing, earlier historical scenarios. The same principle is applicable to other empires.

In *Hearts of Iron IV* wishful thinking is based mostly on the same principle: if only the treaty of Trianon had not existed! What if the Confederacy had persisted? What if there never was anything called Greater Austria-Hungary in the 1940s, or the Swedish Empire was revived in the wake of a broken Europe? These are potential outcomes of gameplay and they are made explicit by achievements and national focuses. Wishful thinking counterfactuals in the games are all specific enough to have been curated – that is, chosen and specifically designed – based on historical cultural canon. The scenarios come with a series of cultural, ideological and historiographical implications that will be discussed in the following chapter.

Similarly to *Europa Universalis IV*, the distinguishing feature for wishful thinking scenarios in *Hearts of Iron IV* is the way they draw on historical experience but with a different outcome – for example, the American Civil War and the fate of the Confederacy. In comparison, the communism sub-branch called "Suspend the Persecution" elaborates on a scenario in which the United States ultimately can become allied to the Soviet Union or Communist China. The introduction of a far-left regime in the United States will increase the risk of civil war (just as the fascist branch does). After the point of divergence, neither the fascist branch nor the communist branch builds on historical precedent, but one – the fascists – makes reconstituting arguments based on historical experience, i.e. the U.S. Civil War and its context. The communist scenario builds on speculative contingencies and an entirely counterfactual context towards a historically unfamiliar goal, which I argue weights it towards future fiction. Again, however, these categories tend to overlap.

The building blocks – i.e. historical cultural references – for which scenarios to use as wishful thinking counterfactuals tend to lie outside the games' timelines, either in the past (as is the case with the Roman Empire) or the future (as is the case with formable nations). Rarely do wishful thinking counterfactuals originate from within the timespan of the game itself, which is logical considering that designing for players to consciously destroy an existing empire only to rebuild it within the same session does not resonate with any of the context or gameplay fundamentals for *Europa Universalis IV*, let alone *Hearts of Iron IV*.

Wishful thinking counterfactuals as uses of history focus on hindsight and explore what agents or nations of the past could have done differently – with or without value judgment – but are not dictated by historical context.[389] However, in *Europa Universalis IV* and *Hearts of Iron IV*, a wishful thinking counterfactual is in fact trapped in an anachronistic context as a baseline. In other words, recreating the Mongol Empire in 1650 using only Early Modern mechanics says more about the developers' understanding of Early Modern institutions than the Great Khan. Consequently, wishful thinking renders the details of contingency within a specific scenario unrelated to the concept, survival or revival of the historical Roman Empire itself. *Hearts of Iron IV* contextualises even less as the game's counterfactuals, in particular wishful thinking, are more railroaded in general. Nevertheless, from a game industry point of view, wishful thinking scenarios constitute part of the social and cultural context which, in part, dictates design practice. As such, they represent an important way through which a broader interest in history is translated into game design.

Synergy and Reimagination (Possible Worlds)

What crucial steps are required for making the Holy Roman Emperor the ruler of my playable nation? Would Columbus have needed to find another patron for his travels if Spain had refused him again, or would he have faded, unsuccessful, into oblivion? What key event caused the Swedish empire of the eighteenth century to ultimately collapse? From a design–analysis and technical–readings point of view, the only argument either of the two games make with regard to counterfactual causality, possibility or plausibility is whether or not it is possible and plausible to depict certain counterfactual scenarios within the games. The answer is exclusively yes in such cases where Paradox Development Studio have designed explicit contingencies for the benefit of the player, such as the examples above.

In *Europa Universalis IV*, the answer is very likely yes also in cases of emergent counterfactuals – scenarios where the examination of a scenario is not overtly depicted in game design (yet), but rather hinges entirely on the player's ability to manipulate the game and produce an emergent story. It is worth noting that both *Europa Universalis IV* and *Hearts of Iron IV* have designed generic contingencies for such times where a game goes off the rails, for example, generic events for when a playable nation accepts a new (and possibly counterfactual) culture, or the AI is able to forge a counterfactual *casus belli* (righteous war) against a historical friend. In other words, if something is in the game, it has

---

389 Evans, *Altered Pasts*, 20.

a function, which means it can be a part of gameplay, counterfactual or not, especially if there are missions, achievements or national focuses described as goals for such counterfactuals through for example events, missions and descriptive text. The nature of such possible world counterfactuals is to engage the player in challenge and evaluation of consequence within the context of each event.

From a developer point of view, it is conceivable that the entertainment focus drives this process by latching on to players' desire to explore these counterfactual possibilities. As put by one developer when asked why they design counterfactual scenarios at an increasing rate for *Hearts of Iron IV:* "People really like it. The more we do it, the more popular it gets."[390] Even *Europa Universalis IV* —which continuously builds on 20 years of content creation and development legacy, and sports over 60 different mechanics to describe how development in the Early Modern era happened—does not include themes like ecology, sociology, consumption, family, or childhood. As is arguably true for all sorts of history, as long as there is no name for it, the game cannot emulate it, no matter how much a player might wish to do so.[391] *Hearts of Iron IV* has even more glaring omissions that, on the one hand, can be attributed to scope, not just in time but also in content. On the other hand, civil and social influence on the war effort are largely omitted, not to mention war crimes. Consequently, possible world counterfactuals involving these historical elements are unavailable from both a design and gameplay point of view.

Along the same lines, possibility in the games is one of the main constraints imposed by the digital strategy game genre and the inherent eurocentrism that is present, particularly in *Europa Universalis IV.* A famous gripe in the game's player community is the trade system, which illustrates the shipping of goods across the world – a central aspect to the topic of globalism and colonisation. However, the trade mechanic is designed so that it can only ship wares one-way, mainly towards Europe. Developers acknowledge that this is neither historical nor premium game design, but for technical reasons it is difficult to change.[392] The implications of this rigid system, then, is that it presents a singular historical scenario which does not allow for historical nor counterfactual play with regard to trade. In other words, the mechanic itself is hindered in its ability to become a meaningful piece of the puzzle.

---

390 Developer informant Dorian (June 29, 2018).
391 Unless they mod the game to include new mechanics. This takes considerable effort and skill and only a few overhaul mods are currently attempting it, for example one known as *MEIOU and Taxes.*
392 Developer informants Drew (June 28, 2018), Devin (June 28, 2017).

Consequence and Repercussions (Future Fictions)

In the undercurrent of future fictions rings the question "what potential worlds are we not living in?" This theme is widely present in popular culture in general and in regard to games specifically used in, for example, *Wolfenstein: The New Order* (the United States in a world in which Nazi Germany won the war) and *World In Conflict* (in which the Cold War becomes heated when the Soviet Union and China invade the United States mainland).[393] In *Hearts of Iron IV*, counterfactual future fictions are used to explore conditions on a shorter timeline than the above-mentioned games, and with significant multiplicity. Within the one larger scenario (the Second World War) *Hearts of Iron IV* depicts a variety of contingencies, similarly to a game of rock-paper-scissors: any two ideologies are either compatible or incompatible. Compatible elements form factions that are more or less likely to go to war with other factions. This dynamic ensures that the war happens and also alters the power dynamic of the war itself. It is, however, unable to depict longer, changing historical contexts the way *Europa Universalis IV* does. This inability aligns with one of the basic qualities of future fiction counterfactuals: focusing on context and contingency, and the repercussions for a world altered from ours by some counterfactual event. What happens in a world in which the Soviet Union aligns with Germany under a fascist ideology? How are power balances and the status quo in the game juxtaposed to actual historical development? What is the same?

From a historical cultural point of view, the assumption in the game is that the Second World War is the one event that dictates the rest of the twentieth century. The game is centred on aspects of the '30s and '40s, like ideology and technological development, and the Second World War itself. The relationship between the historical context and causality is not immediately visible in the game, although its design builds on such principles. The consequence of a lack of focus on causality is not less plausible but rather a shift of focus and a more pronounced emphasis on holistic parameters for history and play: "It is actually only really the first half of the game that really matters because you are building up to the war. Once the war happens, that's when it gets dynamic."[394] In the 1936 scenario the player is able to manipulate the preface of the war, and as such the war itself and anything that comes afterwards, effectively nullifying anything that came before 1936, i.e. the Great War, which Zerubavel

---

393 *Wolfenstein: The New Order* 2014; *World in Conflict* 2007.
394 Developer informant Dorian (June 29, 2018).

argues enforces a sense of historical discontinuity.[395] What if Japan was taken over by a communist revolution in 1937 and never declared war on China? Would Japan ever have declared war on the United States? What would that mean for the rest of the war? For the rest of the century? For the present?

As stated by developers, the more time goes by in *Europa Universalis IV*, the less connected the game is to historical actuality and the historical events that shaped the world we live in.[396] The gap between the end of the game in 1821 and our present is already large and distorted by the oddness and strangeness of a different time, which only makes connecting the game to the actual present harder. The game mechanics as well as flavour and description texts reflect this complex application by simulating a historical ecosystem of ideas and development which are an important part of history but irrelevant for modern life. Consequently, *Europa Universalis IV* struggles to illustrate future fictions for the same reasons it struggles with meaningful counterfactuals in the end-game.

Chapter Summary

Counterfactuals in *Europa Universalis IV* and *Hearts of Iron IV* exist in two spaces: as a designed mechanic or goal, and as emergent scenarios based on gameplay. In *Europa Universalis IV* and *Hearts of Iron IV*, wishful thinking counterfactuals as uses of history are depicted through the notion of turning back time to restore former empires. This is exemplified by the noticeable presence of the revival or reincarnation of the Roman Empire in *Europa Universalis IV*. In *Europa Universalis IV* they are presented as gameplay goals, supported by mechanics and content design primarily through achievements and missions. In *Hearts of Iron IV*, wishful thinking counterfactuals are primarily supported by national focus trees which guide the player through specific scenarios dealing with similar principles such as reinstating the Confederacy in the United States.

Possible worlds as counterfactuals represents a use of history to negotiate the historically possible versus the historically impossible. In *Europa Universalis IV*, this is represented, for example, in the way a player may take a generic mechanic modelled on reality and apply it to a new scenario to achieve a different outcome. The achievement *Sunset Invasion* illustrates is colonialism as an inher-

---

395 Zerubavel, *Time Maps*, 95–98. While it is hard to discern how individual players perceive this, in the present study, developers and beta testers state that the Second World War is the most important event in the twentieth century. This is supported by the large number of player mods with extended timelines that explore the aftermath of the war.
396 Developer informant Dale (June 15, 2017).

ently European feature, something that the Aztecs then copy from historical actuality. As such, possible world scenarios concentrate on what specific elements and causality would enable believable counterfactual outcomes. The game alters the power dynamic between the Aztec and the Europeans in an almost opportunistic manner in order to facilitate the scenario in which *The Sunset Invasion* may be fulfilled.

Future fiction is characterised by the way it references the present and tangibly connects the game world with the real, contemporary world. Counterfactuals in *Hearts of Iron IV* are characterised by future fiction in the way they prescribe longevity to the counterfactuals in the game unto the twentieth century. *Europa Universalis IV* struggles with incorporating this category as it is prevented by the distortion of distant pasts.

Based on the interviews with developers and beta testers it is evident that they harbour a sense of what constitutes historical accuracy and what is unacceptable digression from said accuracy, based on player feedback as well as intuition. Developers and beta testers can intricately depict nuances of said past in the games, leveraging them against the player community and their expressed grievances at any given point in time. As a result of this, we see interesting shifts and nuances in design of the same counterfactual speculation over time, as exemplified by for example the *Sunset Invasion* scenario.

There is a poignant contradiction in that *Hearts of Iron IV* appears to have a more pronounced depiction of, and stronger connection to, counterfactual history. Where *Europa Universalis IV* is more abstract and produces counterfactuals in the ephemeral, metaphorical and emergent, *Hearts of Iron IV* takes command of counterfactual history and makes it explicit. Counterfactual history is more elaborate and detailed in *Hearts of Iron IV* than in *Europa Universalis IV*. Design practice for *Hearts of Iron IV* seeks to cover more potential gameplay outcomes and contains description for counterfactual scenarios. This is particularly clear when noting that *Europa Universalis IV* employs the hindsight perspective to a much larger degree than *Heart of Iron IV*. The contradiction lies in what developers themselves express as an abundance of historical information coupled with high expectations on historical accuracy. The Second World War is one of the most well-researched and popular themes for the uses of history, which, in a way, makes the life of developers and beta testers easier, and yet the expectations on counterfactual historical scenarios appears to have led them to a point where development is highly characterised by exploring counterfactuals through national focus trees, AI and content design. The more specific a counterfactual scenario Paradox is trying to make, the more specific they need to be about how players get there. The solution to this is the national focuses which streamline gameplay to a larger extent than missions do in *Europa Universalis*

IV. As such, counterfactual history in *Hearts of Iron IV* can be considered designed instances, not emergent counterfactuals resulting from sandbox play.

The rules of the games denote the constraints for counterfactual gameplay. Regardless of whether players can think them up, a scenario that is not emergent or specifically designed for cannot take place in the game. For *Europa Universalis IV* these constraints are mechanic-bound rather than content bound. For *Hearts of Iron IV* it is the other way around. A typical counterfactual in *Europa Universalis IV* is experimenting with notions of wishful thinking and possible worlds because the game's design allows for elaborating on those notions, for example, by asking "Why did the Roman Empire cease to exist?" and "How does Austria-Hungary come to pass?" In contrast, *Hearts of Iron IV* explores narrative space, utilising wishful thinking and future fiction as a stepping-stone towards questions like: "Where would we be if Germany had not become Fascist in the 1930s?" and "What would the war have looked like, if no one had broken the Molotov-Ribbentrop Pact?" However, it is important to note that the game has a fundamental obligation to provide gameplay, which is why the question "What happens in Austria after they accept the Anschluss in 1939?" becomes harder for the game to answer. In practice, the game locks the player out of the continued game, if they accept as Austria because there are no pragmatic tools available for the player to elaborate on the scenario. It is, of course, a historical scenario, but it does not provide 1) a challenge, because an AI Germany has effectively annexed Austria and taken over all controls of the nation, and 2) the game is not (at this point) designed to facilitate outcomes that do not connect with the war scenario and mechanics.

Richard Evans claims, and rightfully so, that Ferguson's stance on counterfactual history – that counterfactual history underlines the chaotic in human nature, and the influence of chance in the human experience – is explicitly anti-determinist in order to reinsert counterfactuals in historical scholarship as a way to undermine theories that would uphold hindsight as evidence for providence (regardless of whether it is on a theological, political or other, level).[397] With regard to the present study, digital strategy games build on systemic rulesets that, in all but name, resemble structuralist and determinist models of historical change.[398]

---

[397] Evans, *Altered Pasts*, 31–44. Evans argues that counterfactuals and chaos theory in history have primarily been practiced by those who orientate as politically right-wing due to the impulse to disprove left-wing ideologies as humanity's predetermined goal. While I adhere to Evans' analysis of the historiographical and political context building Ferguson's incentive, I am not suggesting that game designers engaging in virtual history as game design practice share Ferguson's views.
[398] Chapman, *Digital Games as History*, 239; Koebel, "Simulating the Ages of Man," 63.

However, these models coexist with player agency and designed counterfactual content, as well as developer contexts that, for varying reasons, disregard academic and epistemological criteria. Thus, virtual history constitutes a theoretical perspective that can highlight and problematise points of contact between the implementation and depictions of determinism and free will in the games, as well as the overlap of academic sentiments and popular history. However, as this study shows, digital strategy games do not engage in probabilistic calculation of outcomes for the purpose of simulating the truth, nor is that their intention. As such, virtual history is considered an important coordinate in the ontology of counterfactual history, but not as a use of history in this context.

In short, the game analysis and technical reading shows that:
1. The study of counterfactuals helps to define the use of history in digital strategy games.
2. Counterfactuals build on the application of historical reference.
3. Different types of counterfactuals make different types of arguments about what and whose history can be employed, and in what way, but only within the given ruleset.
4. Goal-setting mechanics are particularly central for producing counterfactuals in the games.

Going forward, I intend to discuss the implication of these findings for notions of uses and omissions of history from the perspective of historical culture, as well as the pragmatism of game design practice. Counterfactual history is a central aspect, not just of digital strategy games, but of game design practice – something designers consciously take into consideration and construct in line with the design frameworks and practices at Paradox Development Studio. Indeed, this is something that is inherently important for understanding all these elements as uses of history.

Chapter Four
Approximately History and Ambivalent Desires

Previous chapters have demonstrated that game design at Paradox Development Studio is framed and often influenced by the pragmatism and rationale of the game industry on the one hand, and by historical cultural influences on the other. These include monetisation practices, genre convention and design legacy, as well as player-centred and entertainment-centred practices. Chapter three details some concrete examples of counterfactual history in *Europa Universalis IV* and *Hearts of Iron IV* and how design choices interplay to create goal-setting mechanics, emergent gameplay and ready-made counterfactual scenarios. Counterfactuals, regardless of the point of view they are depicting, are thoroughly grounded in historical understandings and inherently tied to historiographical norms. This relative rigidity in historical depiction stands in some interesting contrast to the idea of open-ended, creative sandbox gameplay that Paradox Development Studio identifies with and promotes.

In this chapter, game design practice and counterfactual history are brought together. In describing the relationship between game design practice and historical representation in the games, developers touch on issues of epistemology, verisimilitude, periodisation and ideology – important topics for understanding uses of history and historical culture in this context. Game design practice, decision-making and implementation are framed by more or less practical constraints. So, what happens to historical and counterfactual depiction in this space of practical constraints? What responsibility, if any, do developers and beta testers consider themselves to have when it comes to historical and counterfactual representation? How can discrepancies in historical and counterfactual design practices between *Europa Universalis IV* and *Hearts of Iron IV* be explained?

In other words, this chapter is about the inherent tension between counterfactuals and verisimilitude; about the way developers maintain the balance when players expect to play with a familiar past in digital strategy games, but at the same time expect intricate counterfactual outcomes, possibilities and replayability. There are notable differences in attitude and ideological positioning between developers and beta testers about the vision and implementation of counterfactual history. How, for example, do understandings of game design practices and the requirement of counterfactual gameplay explain the representation and omission of historical atrocities in *Europa Universalis IV* and *Hearts of Iron IV?*

Turning History into Games

When asked about whether the games imitate history, Devin, who is associated with *Europa Universalis IV*, says that they do not feel like that is the actual purpose of the game: "The purpose of the game is that it is supposed to be fun, of course."[399] Although, as they develop their argument, they go on to say:

> The idea is to leave the player in the world as it looked [...], giving you the feeling that you enter the world and take over. [...] I try to think of it as aiming to make the player understand why they would make certain decisions. [...] For example, playing as the Incas... there will be loads to do with religion in the various small states around the Andes. [The player] collects their idols and so on. [...] It is my hope that it will make people reflect upon why these things happened, and tell that story.[400]

Their line of reasoning thoroughly underlines the central whys and what of historical game development, by emphasizing the value of verisimilitude and retelling of past events in order to explain how humanity ended up where we are. The layer in which players are able to engage with the what-ifs of historical strategy games is also present in this comment. However, Devin also says that for *Europa Universalis IV* "[counterfactual history] is not something we actively focus on, but surely something which we encourage a lot [...] and we try to create a space for it."[401] Interestingly, this somewhat contradicts statements of, for example, developer Delta whose job it is, in part, to construct counterfactual contingencies for the games, such as assets for content packs.[402] Similarly, it contrasts statements from several developers and beta testers who attest that all Paradox Development Studio games are counterfactual from the point of pressing "unpause."[403]

This duality could be explained by the importance of emergent counterfactual history in *Europa Universalis IV*. That is, a comparably small amount of time and effort is spent constructing ready-made counterfactual scenarios in *Europa Universalis IV* because counterfactual history is considered primarily an emergent element and, as such, is the responsibility of the player rather than that

---

399 Developer informant Devin (June 28, 2017).
400 Developer informant Devin (June 28, 2017).
401 Developer informant Devin (June 28, 2017).
402 Developer informant Delta (June 27, 2017).
403 Unpause means pressing the play button on the in-game clock at which point the in-game time begins to tick away and subsequently resolve moves and rules in intervals of one day per turn for *Europa Universalis IV* and one hour per turn for *Hearts of Iron IV*.

of the developer.⁴⁰⁴ This notion is supported by Devin who, in contrast to their own approach to development expressed in the quote above, claims that counterfactual gameplay indeed is very important to players.⁴⁰⁵ This logic suggests that developers view game design practice as shaping historical content and plausible rulesets that serve to illustrate the history of the world in such a way that players are able to extract factual and counterfactual meaning from it simultaneously.

It is not clear exactly what historical skills players are expected to learn, for example, from the Inca example in the statement above, or which skills the player is supposed to bring to the game, although some historical presupposition as a baseline appears to be expected. In general, however, it might be worthwhile to consider for a moment who the player developers have in mind is. Historical culture always comes with contextually attributed meanings. It follows, that depending on player background and other criteria, they will come into the games with varying knowledge and presuppositions.⁴⁰⁶ Beta tester Brooklyn underlines that there are macro aspects to *Hearts of Iron IV* and to the Second World War that the player is expected to be familiar with:

> For example, that the French would be completely steamrolled by the Germans early on in the war, and later that the Soviet Union fought without weapons and sacrificed millions of lives [...] Everyone already have their minds made up about the basics of the Second World War, and what the different nations were like. That means that as a game developer, one does not explain anything – there is already an inherent expectation that as the Soviet Union, one needs to play with a large amount of manpower.⁴⁰⁷

---

404 Developer informant Devin (June 28, 2017). Compared to *Hearts of Iron IV* which flavours gameplay with much more specifically counterfactual content and scenarios. Devin here continues: "But we don't do it like *Hearts of Iron IV* who through their focus trees offer ready-made alternative routes for history."
405 Developer informant Devin (June 28, 2017). Grufstedt: "Is counterfactual history important to your players?" Devin: "Yes, I believe it is very important."
406 More research is required to paint a nuanced and reliable picture of the Paradox digital strategy game player-base, but there is at least some evidence to suggest that males typically dominate within the genre (see Robert Houghton, "History Games for Boys? Gender, Genre and the Self-Perceived Impact of Historical Games on Undergraduate Historians," *gamevironments* 14 (2021): 12, available at http://www.gamevironments.uni-bremen.de). Beyond gender, it would be enormously valuable to obtain data on player location, age, identity, playtime, purchases and more, to better understand the archetypes developers cater to in their work, but such statistics are generally treated as industry secrets and are typically inaccessible.
407 Beta tester informant Brooklyn (October 22, 2018).

Considering both the Inca and the Soviet examples above, it is interesting to note that the developers and beta testers in question present differing expectations of players when it comes to historical understanding. The developer, working on *Europa Universalis IV*, stresses that the game can provide a sounding board for developing historical knowledge and consciousness, whereas the beta tester, mainly associated with *Hearts of Iron IV*, expects the player to be able to draw specific conclusions about gameplay based on historical presupposition without having to explain it at all. Other developers, like Delta, underline the importance of having an interest in history but also on being willing to learn more outside the game.[408] Dylan, in turn, asserts that there is no need to know anything about history in order to play *Europa Universalis IV* successfully.[409]

This discrepancy among answers can be attributed to an interplay of the accessibility turn (the accommodation of a broader variety of players) as well as the notion of player-centred design practice and the Paradox Pillar "Nerd Out!" This pillar reads: "If you have real world knowledge about something, it should benefit you in the game."[410] Developer Drew says that if one would compare the importance of understanding the game at face value – learning the mechanics and reading tooltips – against learning the game based on previously acquired historical knowledge, the latter is by far much less important. They argue that they have seen a number of players who have previous knowledge of strategy games in one form or another pick up and play *Hearts of Iron IV* "without breaking a sweat."[411] However, Drew also says they have had discussions with new players who complain that their playstyle is not working and after looking more closely at a player's style, they discovered that the player had attempted to take on the Soviet Union in the middle of winter using heavy tanks in marshlands. The beta tester says that they sometimes have discussions with these players on the forum, explaining why this strategy will not work based on historical and real-life logistics: the tanks would get stuck in the mud and make it impossible to win battles, let alone the Second World War.[412]

When asked about what makes history a good topic for games, Daryl comes back to the rules of historical development and how they correspond with game design: "The framework. I guess I feel that that is the key to what makes history appropriate for games – there is a ready-made framework to build on."[413] How-

---

[408] Developer informant Dallas (June 26, 2017).
[409] Developer informant Dylan (June 29, 2018).
[410] Jorjani, *Ideas Are Useless!* (video resource, 2017).
[411] Developer informant Drew (June 28, 2018).
[412] Developer informant Drew (June 28, 2018).
[413] Developer informant Daryl (June 26, 2017).

ever, representing history, not to mention historical change, is not as easy as implementing historical references at face-value. Both games use normalizing techniques on units, sizes and resources. One example is the ducat, the baseline financial unit – coin, if you will – in *Europa Universalis IV*. Its name is based on the medieval European currency known as *ducats*, but its value is completely made up and constitutes a metaphor for financial resource management in the game. This kind of normalizing is one of the tools necessary to illustrate historical development, particularly to enable relative comparisons over space as well as time.[414]

As another example, *Hearts of Iron IV* needs a system to mimic the growth of the American steel industry over the course of the war. According to beta tester Brooklyn, the actual number of resources produced by each nation is too unwieldy to translate into gameplay, and their solution is to normalise all units and build a system which is based on proportion rather than on actual numbers, i.e. the production of a specific resource for each playable nation is tied to a proportion of the global total in-game. According to Brooklyn, the production of steel in the US in 1936 was about 20% of the global total, largely due to the aftermath of the Great Depression leading up to the start of the game and war. However, as the war progresses, the US production intensifies, and the percentage of the global total escalates to roughly 45%. This escalation is built into the game so that the power-balance between varying playable nations remains historically accurate, no matter what actual numbers are on the table for any given playthrough.[415]

For *Hearts of Iron IV*, core mechanics, according to the interviews, come down to production, military strategy and politics. As discussed, each core mechanic breaks down into smaller, more intricate mechanics. Brooklyn says that their impression, in particular for multiplayer games, is that as soon as the Second World War begins, players forget that they need to keep an eye on production and politics and focus solely on micromanaging their military units. They continue by describing how they find an imagined connection between gameplay and historical reality here fascinating because "one can almost imagine how the leaders of a real nation would find themselves so caught up in [the fighting] that they cannot focus on the other bits to the same extent – building and mobilizing the industry or having the right people in the right place in politics."[416] The counterfactual history in the game creates unlikely scenarios in

---

414 Wainwright, *Virtual History*, 38–45.
415 Beta tester informant Brooklyn (October 22, 2018).
416 Beta tester informant Brooklyn (October 22, 2018).

which players forget to import oil for about six months – something Brooklyn considers an unlikely scenario outside of the game. "Key," they say, "is to make sure that playable actions that cost the same amount of resources have equal impact but varying results in order to ensure interesting decision-making in gameplay."[417]

Considering again that game design practices limit the way historical scholarship influences the games, and the acquisition of historical knowledge for content, it is interesting to note that developers and beta testers express insights on what they consider shortcomings on the topic of accuracy and authenticity. Brooklyn connects issues with game design resources to historical representation: "There are bits that represent history [less] appropriately due to bugs or other problems or because whoever designed the content or code was not up to speed on how things really happened. This is where the beta testing role is to come in [and] help. To fill in the gaps. [...] Although, there are many gaps in our knowledge too. So many things we do not know."[418]

Beta testers and developers are conscious that these types of practical as well as intellectual circumstances influence historical representation in the games. In its first three years of existence, for example,[419] *Hearts of Iron IV* did not have intricate mechanics for naval warfare, which could nuance the way certain aspects of the Second World War played out in the game. The mechanics needed to imitate naval battle in a more detailed and accurate way were simply missing. According to Brooklyn, this absence exemplifies how balance and design choices limit the scope of historical representation and the multiplicity of outcomes.[420]

Therefore, supplementary design practice and player-centred design practice appear to be central to a game's historical accuracy and authenticity. In contrast to this "more is more" mentality, on one occasion, a developer talks about the potential encumbrance of historical content. Discussing mods, the developer notes that there have been occasions when the level of detail in mods has become so high that gameplay becomes impossible to oversee and manage. Such mods have usually dealt with map design, they add, but include mechanics as well. The developer argues that there is a level of anachronism inherent to this kind of design, because there was no administrative system in place at the time, which could potentially maintain the same level of detailed control

---

417 Beta tester informant Brooklyn (October 22, 2018).
418 Beta tester informant Brooklyn (October 22, 2018).
419 *Heart of Iron IV* expansion *Man the Guns* was released on February 28, 2019.
420 Beta tester informant Brooklyn (October 22, 2018).

over large areas. Of course, one could argue that this is true at any point in time. Their point, however, is that there is such a thing as too much detail. "You would be tricking yourself,"[421] they say, underlining that increasing levels of detail do not necessarily constitute historical accuracy. The "more detailed history is more accurate history" argument is here presented as a fallacy when it comes to representation, even though the value of increasing detail is in fact partly embodied in the supplementary design practice and DLC economy. This noteworthy contradiction is likely a conflict between gameplay values and design values in this particular genre. Players – and to a point, beta testers – idealise complexity and historical detail, and developers have successfully turned supplementary design practices involving increasing detail into a profitable monetisation model. However, according to this developer, digital strategy games can only be realistic up to a point before genre convention reaches its limit, as for example in the user interface, whose job it is to convey interaction and meaning to the player.

It seems established that there is a close relationship between notions of historical verisimilitude, even realism, and the game genre of digital strategy games. To explore this relationship in more detail, and to discuss what this means in the context of game design practice, it is worthwhile to place this observation in the context of the game industry. In an extensive study of the relationship between the economy of game making and the depiction of hegemonic pasts in historical digital games, Emil Lundedal Hammar has found that games tend to be more similar in their representations of the past the more expensive the games were to make. Hammar shows a correlation between high budgets and hegemonic depictions.[422] In other words, there is less variety in historical representation among high-profile, big-budget games. Neither *Europa Universalis IV* nor *Hearts of Iron IV* were part of Hammar's study, but according to his classification they would constitute low-budget games. On the one hand, his conclusions do not fit Paradox Development Studio fully, since the player-centred and entertainment-centred design practices tend to make these two games normative in their depiction of the past. That is, the systemic underpinnings of each game promote specific, overarching narratives – that of European colonial dominance in *Europa Universalis IV* and that of imperialist warfare in *Hearts of Iron IV*. However, on the other hand, the DLC monetisation model has provided the games with a large amount of varied content, thus aligning with Hammar's theory.

---

421 Developer informant Devin (June 28, 2017).
422 Hammar, "Producing and Playing Hegemonic Pasts," 50–68.

Firstly, this possible discrepancy between the economic context of Paradox game making and the outcome of historic description in both games is likely explained by genre. Hammar's study is focused on games in what Adam Chapman calls a realist-simulation style. These are defined as games with a high visual fidelity, level of aesthetic detail and playable characters. According to Chapman, the opposite of realist-simulation style games are conceptual-simulation style games. Digital strategy games fall into this second category. Among other things, conceptual-simulation style games do not rely on literal representation but rather abstraction and symbolism to make complex and far reaching arguments.[423] Following this argument, digital strategy games, specifically due to their varied in-game outcomes, employment of counterfactuals and ambivalent relationship to verisimilitude, abide by a different logic in terms of hegemonic memory-making and overall design than games in, for example, realist-simulation style games.[424] This is a different logic in the sense that they accommodate a macro view of the past but not a micro view, like realist-simulation style games do. That is, even if one were to think of Paradox Development Studio games as significantly distinct from triple-A (high budget) development, the games nevertheless fall into normative tracks due to genre convention.

However, arguably, Paradox Development Studio games are not, in fact, low budget. Secondly, and perhaps most relevant to the study of game design practice, it is worth considering the potential impact of beta tester labour in this context. On the one hand, we know from the interviews that development of *Europa Universalis IV* and *Hearts of Iron IV* in certain ways depend on beta testers, and the work they contribute without compensation, rendering the *de facto* budget a hidden, considerably larger, figure. On the other hand, since beta testers tend to represent a variety of linguistic and local historical expertise, it is possible that the use of beta testers contributes specifically to the diversification of content and game design by representation simultaneously, although I cannot here discern to what extent, and the question of beta tester labour requires further research.

Throughout this book, I have suggested that seemingly obvious and mundane aspects of game design practice are fruitful objects of study, because problematizing them can lead to insights and conversations about the fundamental principles of using representations of the past in games. One of those fundamen-

---

423 Chapman, *Digital Games as History*, 61–75.
424 Hammar "Producing and Playing Hegemonic Pasts," 48–49; Chapman, *Digital Games as History*, 70–71.

tals is play. Those of my informants who have a long history as players or beta testers on top of their role as employees of Paradox often move between the role of the designer and the role of a player somewhat seamlessly.[425] One developer states that they will play Paradox games, mods and assist the modding community "after hours" and describes the lines between work and their spare time as "blurry."[426] Another testifies to only being interested in making games they would like to play themselves.[427] Casey O'Donnell notes that the game industry tends to reinvent itself because of a relative lack of institutional memory, in part, because the industry lets itself be driven by a constant influx of new technology, products and services.[428] This notion stands in rather stark contrast to practices at Paradox Development Studio, whose nature is so infused by continuity. In other words, play, here, entrenches tried and tested values and frameworks. Developers can and do include themselves in the practice of facilitating the Paradox legacy of history and counterfactual history by taking on this double role. Simultaneously, this practice underlines the implications of design legacy and genre convention. In other words, it seems that developers and beta testers at Paradox Development Studio perceive designing *Europa Universalis IV* and *Hearts of Iron IV* as near endless projects.

There are, to be sure, elements of opportunism at Paradox Development Studio but overall, developers seem to enjoy the fact that their games are long-haul ventures. In defining game design timeliness and particularity, Kultima notes that "even though experience in game design work is an important factor [...] the lessons learned might not be transferrable to the next project"[429] It is worth noting that developers in Kultima's study appear not to work on the same game series for 20 years at a time, something Paradox Development Studio only have in common with a small handful of other studios, such as Firaxis (*Civilization* series) and, arguably, id Software (*Doom* series). For as long as Paradox Development Studio continue to employ monetisation practices, historical representation and internal strategies in this way, lessons learned, or not learned, will continue to transfer onto the next projects by way of game design practice.

---

425 Developer informants Devin (June 28, 2017); Dylan (June 29, 2018); Delta (June 27, 2017); Dale (June 15, 2017).
426 Developer informant Devin (June 28, 2017).
427 Developer informant Dale (June 15, 2017).
428 O'Donnell, "Work/Play," 109–110; Neff and Stark 2004, 175 cited in O'Donnell, "Work/Play," 109.
429 Kultima, "Game Design Praxiology," 53.

Approximately History – Counterfactuals as Uses of History

In historical game studies, counterfactual history is often discussed in the same vein as scholarly historiographic description. That is, counterfactual history and virtual history – as per the definition used in this book – are oftentimes measured against the same ruler.[430] Adam Chapman, for example, describes the relationship between digital strategy games and history by conceptualising counterfactual history as "narrative history*ing*." Narrative history*ing* (his emphasis) denotes the player or developer's act of producing historical narratives in games.[431] According to Chapman, counterfactuals in digital strategy games specifically are extensions of existing historiographic arguments, embedded in the systemic structure of the game artefact: "Thus, whilst games like *Civilization* are still histories that use opportunities for narrative history*ing* to make their arguments, the value of the counterfactual in these games is as a rhetorical technique to draw out these arguments rather than an end unto itself."[432] While I do not contest that narrative history*ing* relies on the game structures, I propose that the value of counterfactuals be expanded to include uses of history as inherently valuable representations of historical thinking beyond rhetorical technique. I also argue against that the design of digital strategy games is inherently dependent on, or subordinate to, academic tradition and historical scholarship, as developer perspectives show that the shape of counterfactuals are contingent on other factors as well. Delimiting understandings of counterfactuals in this context risk perpetuating the authority of scholarly tradition with regard to design and sidestep counterfactual histories as meaningful aspects of historical culture with nuanced traits and applications.

In the present study, definitions of counterfactuals in digital strategy games as inert is contrasted by two main findings: the value composition of entertainment-focused design practice in general, and developer and beta tester statements on the intentions behind counterfactual game design practice. As discussed in chapter two, developers and beta testers describe ambivalent experiences in their game design practices with regard to historical verisimilitude. They are all aware of the perceived dichotomy between history as known

---

430 See for example Apperley, "Counterfactual communities"; Clyde et al., "Beyond the 'Historical' Simulation"; Tobias Winnerling and Florian Kerschbaumer (eds.), *Early Modernity in Video Games* (Newcastle upon Tyne: Cambridge Scholars Publishing, 2014); Ferguson, *Virtual History*.
431 Chapman, *Digital Games as History*, 231, building on Greg Dening, "Performing Cross-culturally," in Keith Jenkins, Sue Morgan and Alan Munslow (eds.), *Manifestos for History* (London: Routledge, 2007).
432 Chapman, *Digital Games as History*, 239–240.

through historical scholarship, and games and play as history, and when asked about their approach to doing historical research, there appears to be a method: finding credible sources, listening to feedback and for some, drawing on experiences from studying history at university. However, they are simultaneously conscious of the delimitations that the game industry and game genre impose on history in the games, such as the limitation of resources, compression of time and distance, or the simplification of political and trade systems. Furthermore, every now and then the technical parameters of the game engine cannot accommodate a certain design option.[433] Developers are equally aware of external contexts that influence the extent to which historical actuality is emphasised in the games, for example monetisation and related principles such as player expectations and uses of history. Developer and beta testers justify this dichotomy largely by leaning into the otherness of history in games, which serves to fuel the counterfactual nature of both games. Thus, the games are not expected to be or depict the past, but a story-world that resembles history.[434] As such, counterfactual design and gameplay instances in both games are unsuited to make virtual historical arguments in the vein of Ferguson. Instead, they represent the logic of that game world. However, it is important to note that counterfactual scenarios in digital strategy games make detailed viable arguments about the developers and player community's expectations as far as wishful thinking, possible worlds and future fictions, which are all part of the historical cultural canon.

Counterfactual History and Game Design Practice

> [Counterfactual history] is not something we focus actively on for *Europa Universalis IV*, but something we encourage to a large extent. Many small decisions will fork and lead to something entirely new, and we want to provide an opportunity for that, but not like [*Hearts of Iron*] who through focus trees provide ready-made alternative historical paths. It's not the same for us.[435]
>
> Developer informant Dylan

Developers and beta testers are aware that counterfactuals are expected by players, and looking at the Paradox Pillars, the notion of emergent story-making is one of the main attractions of a Paradox game. Beyond this, at a more granular level, developers and beta testers give differing answers to why counterfactuals

---

[433] Beta tester informant Brooklyn (October 22, 2018). See also Wainwright, *Virtual History*, 38–45.
[434] Developer informant Dylan (June 29, 2018).
[435] Developer informant Devin (June 28, 2017).

are important. On the one hand, they agree that counterfactuals play a larger role in *Hearts of Iron IV* than in *Europa Universalis IV*. On the other hand, as noted by the developer in the epigraph, counterfactuals appear to be more integrated in the fundamental game design of *Europa Universalis IV* for the purpose of supporting emergent stories through gameplay. In other words, the application of counterfactual history and gameplay is specific and comes with a series of varied justifications and rationale depending on the setting.

The relationship between counterfactual history and interactivity is frequently highlighted in the interviews. Dallas emphasizes that fun gameplay comes from the player's ability to influence history in the game[436]: "Well, why would we have a feature in a game if one cannot do anything to influence it? Then you definitely end up just watching [the game]."[437] Developers and beta testers agree that interactivity and player influence on history in *Europa Universalis IV* and *Hearts of Iron IV* are essential features of Paradox Development Studio titles. Still, it is challenging to design an approachable game in which a player can accomplish counterfactual scenarios and learn how to skilfully manipulate historical developments. As the Paradox Pillar "Accessibility" states, "a Paradox game should be easy to learn and difficult to master."[438] This is echoed by a developer saying "The challenge should never be to find the information [needed to play] but to learn how to use it."[439] Their perception is that players do not like to be surprised – they like to be in control and have a system in place that is predictable enough for them to be able to react in an appropriate time and way.

Developer Devin muses on why counterfactuals are important for players and say:

> Different players have different approaches. There are those who just want to do everything, of course. Then we have those who role-play various developments. And then there is the middle-road one, who will expand and become an all-consuming 'mushroom' and then try to motivate [their aggressive expansion] by connecting it to historical actuality. To feed the inner conqueror, I guess.[440]

This testimony refers to *Europa Universalis IV* and is consistent with a comment from beta tester Brooklyn on *Hearts of Iron IV*, identifying a single category of counterfactual possibilities that the tester considers on the far end of believable

---

436 Developer informant Dallas (June 26, 2017).
437 Developer informant Dale (June 15, 2017).
438 Jorjani, *Ideas Are Useless!* (video resource, 2017).
439 Developer informant Devin (June 28, 2017).
440 Developer informant Devin (June 28, 2017).

scenarios in the game: smaller countries conquering the world during and after the Second World War.⁴⁴¹ Such counterfactuals are illustrated by a number of achievements designed to inspire players to aim for scenarios in which smaller countries become much more powerful in their counterfactual play-throughs. Some examples include the *Northern Lights* achievement: "As a Scandinavian country form your own faction, and have Denmark, Sweden, Norway and Finland in it,"⁴⁴² or the *Miklos Horthy and the Habsburg Prince* achievement: "As Hungary, restore Austria-Hungary."⁴⁴³ Brooklyn says they do not necessarily prefer this particular style of design for *Hearts of Iron IV*, as most future fiction scenarios in this vein should be considered "highly unlikely."⁴⁴⁴ As such, these "extreme" counterfactuals do not fit within their [Brooklyn's] ideal version of the game. When asked about why they think Paradox Development Studio still makes them, Brooklyn says they think the choice of designing smaller countries this way is to appease specific groups and nationalities of players.⁴⁴⁵

One beta tester discussed the mid-war tension between Germany and the Soviet Union in Hearts of Iron as an example of a counterfactual trigger. This is a specific counterfactual scenario in the game that well exemplifies the perceived closeness to reality most counterfactuals in the games have:

> There is a war-era propaganda poster from the Allied side in which Hitler and Stalin shake hands, with a knife in the other hand behind both their backs. It illustrates the general idea at the time, their own included, that it [the German-Soviet Nonaggression Pact, i.e. the Molotov-Ribbentrop Pact] was never a question of a long-term alliance so much as a matter of dividing Europe between the two of them before setting up for a final battle.⁴⁴⁶

As a rule, counterfactual scenarios in *Hearts of Iron IV* hinge onto historical reference to some degree, and in this case the war-era notion that the pact might not last constitutes the back-drop for the scenario of "what if Soviet backstabs Germany early in the war?"⁴⁴⁷

Beta testers as a group appear to prefer playing and designing realistically. One expresses that they enjoy playing on counterfactuals primarily with a realist historical goal in mind.⁴⁴⁸ Using the game as a trial ground, they say they test

---

441 Beta tester informant Brooklyn (October 22, 2018).
442 Paradox Wikis, *Hearts of Iron IV: Achievements*.
443 Paradox Wikis, *Hearts of Iron IV: Achievements*.
444 Beta tester informant Brooklyn (October 22, 2018).
445 Beta tester informant Brooklyn (October 22, 2018).
446 Beta tester informant Brooklyn (October 22, 2018).
447 Developer informant Dorian (June 29, 2018).
448 Beta tester informant Brooklyn (October 22, 2018).

variables such as resource management and timing in order to explore what would be plausible alternative routes in order to achieve roughly the same outcome as those they perceive as historically accurate, i.e. testing the integrity of determinism and causality in the games' design.

Once a game session has derailed notably from the historical path, which normally happens early on (i.e. for *Europa Universalis IV* in the late fifteenth century, and for *Hearts of Iron IV* between 1936 and 1938), historical development is primarily mediated through flavour and event content design, and also art design. In *Europa Universalis IV*, game progression and historical development become visible in layers that denote possible outcomes for the different playable nations over the course of the game, represented by imagery such as uniforms and flags. There are two distinct categories of game elements that go into generating counterfactual scenarios that players are able to experience visually. Such content that was designed to illustrate a specific counterfactual outcome, i.e. it was envisioned and invented by the developers and beta testers and subsequently created for a particular scenario. One asset of the former variety created for an individual playable nation in a distinct scenario is the Prussian uniform mentioned in chapter two. Another such example is the look and feel of playable nations in the Americas represented in the *El Dorado* DLC for which developers created scenarios in which the European invasion either did not happen or was unsuccessful. In other words, scenarios in which, for example, Mayan cultures were allowed to thrive beyond historical record, and develop in parallel with influential, but non-colonial, powers. These scenarios are visually illustrated in game design through visual assets like uniforms and flags:

> We used the first tier, which was theoretically the technology level they had at the time, as a base. For the second tier, we imagined what they might look like if they had stood their ground against the Spaniards. What would they have looked like if they had obtained firearms? So, the second tier is still very much their own culture still, but other influences seep in.[449]

Developers and beta testers mention possible world counterfactuals like this repeatedly. They also detail how these representations of intercultural development and the transfer of ideas take place in human encounters, presenting a dynamic global history that clearly underlines their view on the meaning of network versus isolation through art design. These counterfactuals are the only visual counterfactual representation of human avatars in the game. From the interviews it seems that this content is very resource heavy, and often out-

---

[449] Developer informant Delta (June 27, 2017).

sources to third-party developers who assist in production.⁴⁵⁰ This is likely why counterfactual animated assets are relatively rare in the game overall, compared for example to counterfactual mission trees, achievements or emergent possibilities.

With regard to counterfactuals as wishful thinking, the underlying starting point is most commonly that of "what would it take to avoid the Second World War?" However, the player will soon become aware that a world war is likely to break out at some point. Based on the content in *Hearts of Iron IV* it appears that the representation of Hitler is that of a codified historical necessity. Starting in 1936, Hitler will already be in place. Playing as Germany, the player has a number of options as far as removing Hitler from power, and the a-historical AI will have a specific likelihood of doing the same. Although considering that the game is trying to replicate the Second World War and that the war needs to happen somehow, the chances are low. Historical AI will always keep Hitler in office and act within a narrow corridor of choices that would resemble that of Hitler and the German Reich during this period.

As explained by game designer and writer Sean Vanaman, "there are points in history, or these points in whatever timeframe you are addressing, that feel like they have to be hard-coded in because no simulation, or at least most realistic simulations, are not likely to get there."⁴⁵¹ His thoughts reflect the issue of simulation and railroading, and how certain issues in historical actuality might be considered so unlikely in and of themselves that a more simulation-focused design would struggle to replicate them. As an example, Vanaman mentions Hitler's rise to power and the impact of "just the one person" on world history. Developers and beta testers on *Hearts of Iron IV* note that the simulator approach would likely cause games in *Hearts of Iron IV* to be fundamentally event-less because simulation requires time.⁴⁵² That is, time to allow historical development to play out, something that the game at its core does not facilitate.

The opposite of simulation, then, is railroading, which, as discussed elsewhere, denotes the act of forcing content and contingencies on the player. The sentiment that certain things need to be railroaded in order to show up in a simulation is partly the case for *Europa Universalis IV*, as exemplified by changes in design practice such as accessibility focus, and the implementation of counter-

---

450 Developer informant Delta (June 27, 2017). I do not have access to information about who or where these third-party companies are.
451 Idle Thumbs, *Three Moves Ahead* podcast, episode 473, July 12, 2019, accessed on July 31, 2019.
452 Developer informant Dorian (June 29, 2018).

factual scenarios and contingencies, but also how events and historical personality and canon is scripted to be put at the forefront.

Historical Atrocities and Consequences of Game Design Practice

The omission of the Holocaust in *Hearts of Iron IV* does not seem to constitute a design dilemma for Paradox Development Studio. At least, it is quite clear what their rationale behind omitting it is. Unlike the case of naval warfare discussed above, developers do not have to navigate aspects of historical and counterfactual gameplay to have the game make sense despite this event. Players on occasion request the Holocaust as a feature, or even just a mention in an event in *Hearts of Iron IV*, but developers sidestep such requests. Developer Devin notes in this context: "Just because one has identified a problem, one hasn't necessarily identified a good solution."[453] Beta tester Bobby notes that counterfactual gameplay has the potential to allow players to explore historical atrocities safely and in dynamic ways, but that this needs to be implemented with great caution and context.[454]

As discussed in chapter two, the Holocaust , reasonably, does not qualify for entertainment-focused design for ideological as well as gameplay-related reasons. In discussing historical atrocities and the limits of play with both developers and beta testers, *Hearts of Iron IV* is presented as fundamentally unsuited to accommodate historical representation of this type. For example, making a comparison to population mechanics and the effects of disease in the player mod *MIEOU and Taxes*,[455] one beta tester says: "I think pops in *Hearts of Iron IV* would be utter madness and legal hellhole for [Paradox Development Studio]."[456] They here refer to the hypothetical implications of having a population based system ("pops") in *Hearts of Iron IV* in which players would be able to manipulate war issues related to population, ergo making civilians a part of the gameplay and mechanics. This beta tester does not see population and civilian targets as any more a viable mechanic than the Holocaust would be. This rhymes

---

[453] Developer informant Devin (June 28, 2017).
[454] Beta tester informant Bobbie (February 20, 2018).
[455] *MIEOU and Taxes* is a major overhaul mod for *Europa Universalis IV* in which the pop mechanics stands for population and emulates population related issues like culture, migration and disease in more detail than the Paradox Development Studio core game. This beta tester is not affiliated with *MIEOU and Taxes*.
[456] Beta tester informant Blake (August 20, 2018).

well with Chapman and Linderoth's findings on dark play. They note that the discrepancy between how television series and games manage representations of the Holocaust (television series being able to depict this particular genocide to a larger degree than games) can be explained by how "different media are subject to different framing processes when dealing with difficult subjects."[457] Games are surrounded by discourses on play, playfulness and entertainment whose connotations, cultural and historical, complicate the use of historical atrocity as subject matter. Agency tends to be at the centre of these judgements.[458]

The same is true, not just for different types of media, but for different genres within the gaming context as well. As discussed, developers and beta testers do not consider *Hearts of Iron IV* a suitable context for historical atrocities such as genocide and war crimes to translate into gameplay, mainly because of constraints related to strategy game convention. Genre and design values dictate the focus of the game, which is military, politics and industry during war. To underline an earlier point that history is used differently in different settings, neither the specific strategy game genre nor Paradox Development Studio design practices leave room for nuanced discussion on the consequences of war, let alone the Holocaust, through gameplay. In comparison then, some recently developed games in other genres do deal with historical atrocities meaningfully through gameplay, for example, the platform puzzle game *My Memory of Us* (2018) that deals with segregation in the Second World War Warsaw ghetto and the survival game *This War of Mine* (2014) that depicts life during the 1990s civil war in the Balkans.[459] To Chapman and Linderoth's point above, some games can tell dark history stories through genre, gameplay and tone, but they do so in ways that are fundamentally different from that of *Hearts of Iron IV*.

Chapman and Linderoth go on to note that framing (such as genre and industry convention) and commonly accepted practices for toning down problematic aspects of conflict in games (such as omission) create this tension between dark content and form.[460] I agree with this assessment and here assert that we can observe how developer negotiations on such tensions happen; between games of different kinds, as well as between similar games such as *Hearts of Iron IV* and *Europa Universalis IV*. In other words, not all games use history the same way, and it is the implementation and treatment of the subject matter

---

[457] Chapman and Linderoth, "Exploring the Limits of Play," 146.
[458] Chapman and Linderoth, "Exploring the Limits of Play," 141–143.
[459] *My Memory of Us* (2018), *This War of Mine* (2014).
[460] Chapman and Linderoth, "Exploring the Limits of Play," 147–150.

that defines the use of history, not the gamic context or agency in and of itself. Nevertheless, historical cultural meanings heavily frame and often delimit uses of history.

The findings in the interviews support this notion also. On the comparison between the implementation of slavery in *Europa Universalis IV* and the lack thereof for the Holocaust in *Hearts of Iron IV*, one developer notes that it is not an arbitrary thing, as if slavery was somehow okay and the Holocaust was not: "I would have loved it if we [...] had been able to emulate why slavery disappeared in *Victoria II*. But because of Modernisation, it didn't work out. The [morally] bad choices would become the best choices to make."[461] This statement, again, highlights the way content and form are perceived to come together in a way that structurally explains a certain historical development – in this case the end of slavery in this context – but makes gameplay problematic, simultaneously. The developer here refers to the way industrialisation caused the dynamics of labour to change. In a following comment, they note that they did design and implement the influence that the ideological anti-slavery movement at the time had on this development. However, their statement underlines the fact that, again, gameplay takes a turn for the cynical insofar as the only incentive to avoid slavery is to avoid the Civil War in the United States, which in turn negatively impacts the economy and stability. For the game to become the message, the connection between content and form must create an incentive for enticing gameplay.[462]

Consider this outcome in the light of Souvik Murherjee's work, which notes that digital games almost always portray slaves and slavery from the point of view of a free person. Because of the importance of agency in games – something which enslaved persons have none of – this phenomenon causes the ambiguity of contemporary historical discourse, towards the horrors of slavery, to persist in games.[463] From this point of view, slavery and the Holocaust share the same ludic framing, as Chapman and Linderoth would put it. They argue that one way to successfully implement dark history into games is to "be very careful about what aspects of the theme are made a topic for play."[464] In comparing *Europa Universalis IV* and *Hearts of Iron IV* on this matter, I would argue that the

---

[461] Developer informant Dorian (June 29, 2018). *Victoria II* covers the years between 1836 and 1936.
[462] Developer informant Dorian (June 29, 2018).
[463] Souvik Mukherjee, "Video Games and Slavery," *Transactions of the Digital Games Research Association* 3 (2016): 253–254, accessed July 30, 2021, https://doi.org/10.26503/todigra.v2i3.60.
[464] Chapman and Linderoth, "Exploring the Limits of Play," 150.

games follow the same logic, and that the discrepancies in design align with Mukherjee's findings on the remediation of slavery-narratives.⁴⁶⁵

However, there are contradictions in Paradox's treatment of dark history in the games. In the national focus for the United States, the "America First" branch allows the player (and AI) to reconstitute historical events and decisions and make possible another Civil War based on similar ideological disagreements. As noted by games journalist Charlie Hall, the counterfactual scenario was considered controversial on its release due to its inescapable connection to the historical experience that is still unresolved in the United States at present. Hall received a statement from Paradox Development Studio and *Hearts of Iron IV*'s game director, Dan Lind, saying:

> The trope of a sustained or revived Confederacy is an old and common one in alternate history fiction, so it makes an easy foil as the Fascist offshoot of an America that was pursuing policies anathema to the [O]ld South. [...] Just as the presence of the Third Reich in *Hearts of Iron* (or many other strategy and war games) in no way indicates an endorsement or promotion of Nazi ideas, the fictional construct of a reborn Confederacy says nothing about Paradox's position on racial equality or the clear injustice of the Secessionist cause in the American Civil War.⁴⁶⁶

Developers and beta testers here appear to be navigating the space between the counterfactual and factual aspects of their design, while also falling back on the pragmatism of game design practice. Lind emphasises that the Confederacy scenario is an "easy foil," not based on its historical precedent but the counterfactual's position as an "old and common trope." I interpret this stance as an instance in which the counterfactual canon is given a specific role in historical culture, indicated by repetition and reiteration. Importantly, one could argue that the trope itself gains its validity based on its historical reference – a step that is not addressed to the same extent by Lind in his statement.⁴⁶⁷ The impor-

---

465 Notably, it seems Paradox Development Studio are on a path to what they call a "respectful" way of designing slavery in the context of colonialism. Developer diaries in September of 2021 suggest that the goal for the – at the time of writing – forthcoming *Victoria III* is to represent "the institution, systems and causes of slavery, as well as the people who lived under and fought against it." Paradox Plaza, *Victoria 3 – Dev Diary #15 – Slavery. Victoria III* Developer Diary by Wizzington, September 16, 2021, accessed November 15, 2021, https://forum.paradoxplaza.com/forum/developer-diary/victoria-3-dev-diary-15-slavery.1490983/.
466 Charlie Hall, "Hearts of Iron DLC lets players revive the Confederacy, decolonize the British Empire," *Polygon*, February 14, 2019, accessed November 20, 2019, https://www.polygon.com/2019/2/14/18224986/hearts-of-iron-4-dlc-man-the-guns-confederacy.
467 Note that I have not interviewed developers or beta testers about this specific scenario as it was released after the interview period had ended.

tance of historical reference does, however, become clear by looking at the "Honor the Confederacy" tooltip and description:

> USA_honor_the_confederacy_tt:0 "These decisions allow us to rebuild the people's trust in the government in the event of a civil war by reconnecting with the past."[468]
>
> USA_honor_the_confederacy_desc:1 "For too long, the story of the Civil War was told from the northern perspective – the story of a doomed rebellion. It is time that the other side is heard as well."[469]

There are two notable strategies at play here. Firstly, as mentioned, the counterfactual specifically enables the player to connect to the Civil War and the in-game past through gameplay and in the tool tip. Secondly, the description laments not the event itself so much as the way historians have written about the Civil War since it occurred. In *Remaking History*, Jerome De Groot notes that items of contemporary historical fiction, especially those that concern themselves with time and rewriting the past, "provide a forum of discussion for the ways that time works and, importantly, how it is constructed as an interpellating and interpretative discourse."[470] Along a similar principle to the counterfactual roleplaying style of the event description above, De Groot notes that the reimagining of the past highlights the malleability of time and the consequences for cultural understanding "of temporality, chronology, memory and narrative."[471] Igniting another Civil War and "Honor the Confederacy" is not framed so much as a second chance at a Southern victory as an ideological critique of mainstream discourse here.

The counterfactual on the Confederacy and Civil War is largely decoupled from slavery, contrary to its historical precedent. In contrast, and as previously discussed, slavery is a part of the trade mechanic in *Europa Universalis IV*. On this point, developers assert that the deeper into the past something happened, the more comfortable we generally are with taking counterfactual liberties. However, the thematical and historical cultural context is equally important for the framing of historical representation and Paradox Development Studio receive criticism on this particular point. This further underlines historical atrocities and dark pasts as one instance in which history imposes itself on design practice, whether the result is inclusion or omission of content.

---

468 *Hearts of Iron IV*. Localisation. mtg_focus_I_english.yml. v1.6.2.
469 *Hearts of Iron IV*. Localisation. focus_I_english.yml. v1.6.2.
470 De Groot, *Remaking History*, 133.
471 De Groot, *Remaking History*, 133.

Notes on Epistemologies and Game Design

From an epistemological point of view in a postmodern context, games that depict history from a structuralist perspective can appear to be on a collision course with the direction historical research has been taking since the '70s. The impact of the linguistic and post-structuralist turn shifted historiographical writing from universalist to individual perspectives. While the universalism of structuralist thinking fits the digital strategy game genre quite harmoniously, a post-structuralist or constructivist perspective would, theoretically, ground the games in contemporary study of the past. However, there is nothing in the interviews to suggest that this might be an inherently ideological decision. Nor is it a design choice made specifically based on readings or understandings of academic history.

One developer had previously expressed a direct intention to build the economic system of *Europa Universalis IV* on Marxist theory. When asked about whether they have implemented any other theorists in *Europa Universalis IV*, they said: "I wouldn't know. I probably have but couldn't name any [...] I probably have but I wouldn't know. There's nothing very specifically targeted."[472] The developer goes on to note that Marx's point of view helped them frame the forces behind colonization because of how it relates to economic exploitation and markets. However, they note, beyond those particular theories, historiographic theorists are not typically used. In fact, when asked to describe how historical development is designed at face value, they describe their method as follows:

> In the case of Europa Universalis trade system, which is one I developed as well, I actually looked at historical empire building. The whole principle of territorial control of trade nodes was based around both the Venetian experience where they build these kinds of bases and seized islands along the Holy Roman Empire and then into the Mediterranean to help to control trade. And the Portuguese imperial experience where they built these forts along to help their trade routes to come along.[473]

Based on this particular interview, it would appear as if in-game systems or mechanics – diplomacy, military, trade, etc. – are designed through extrapolation from a few prominent historical examples and then applied as generic mechanics to the game.

> Ylva: So, just to clarify, and sorry if this is repetitive, but just so I'm clear: Most of these systems or mechanics, diplomacy, military, trade, are based off of one or two or maybe a

---

472 Developer informant Drew (June 28, 2018).
473 Developer informant Drew (June 28, 2018).

few more historical examples and then applied as a generic mechanic?

Drew: Yes.[474]

In light of the above description of game design practice for historiographic description and periodisation for *Europa Universalis IV*, the relationship between form and content – and, by extension, systemic depictions and event design – becomes increasingly tangible. Based on a comparison between *Civilization V* and *Europa Universalis IV*, Greg Koebel argues that periodisation is of particular interest for historical game designers. He considers the fact that Paradox Development Studio dedicate individual game series to specific epochs, and create separate rulesets for each depending on historiographic arguments about theory of change, as an indication that periodization is central to their understanding of the past (i.e. the way *Crusader Kings II* makes different arguments about historical change than *Europa Universalis IV*).[475] Subsequently, Koebel says, Paradox games make metahistorical arguments against historical certainty, in particular when one ruleset is contrasted against another Paradox game.[476]

The academic community has concerned itself with the representation of historiography to a large extent. The underlying assumption appears to be that this game genre is representative of historical change and systems. It is worth looking more closely at the implications of these kinds of assumptions in tandem with the material. Koebel as well as Chapman note that developers appear particularly concerned with periodisation.[477] When asked about their perception of historical depiction in *Europa Universalis IV*, the following exchange took place:

Ylva: Whose history is *Europa Universalis IV* based on?

Devin: The game systems are generally built around Western Europe, definitely. For example, our one-way trade routes. Everything moves in one direction, either to the English Channel or Northern Italy. All of the trade in the game world moves towards them, and it is a one-way trade as well, meaning only one party benefits from the exchange instead of two.

Ylva: Would it be technically possible to implement different game systems for different parts of the world? For example, would it be possible to have a different trade system for South America than for Europe?

---

[474] Developer informant Drew (June 28, 2018).
[475] Koebel, "Simulating the Ages of Man," 68–69.
[476] Koebel, "Simulating the Ages of Man," 70.
[477] Koebel, "Simulating the Ages of Man"; Chapman, *Digital Games as History*.

Devin: It's a little bit outside of my area, but I don't see why not. The trick is to figure out a way to do it well – so that it works when the regions interact. Because there is danger in exceptionalism [...] We try to keep this in mind when we do expansion packs for different parts of the world – and this is something I feel is one of *Europa Universalis IV*'s strengths – to show that all of these things happen at the same time, in the same world. [They're comparable because] humans are humans and states are states.[478]

This statement points to the intricate balance between portraying historical peoples and cultures as ultimately human and simultaneously wanting to explain how interactions between said cultures and communities have played out.[479] The developer elaborates on how the systems are based on European examples, and blanketed across the game world, but that the modular shape of content implementation in the games enables giving each playable nation a specific personality, doing so with the expressed intention of making an argument about the multiplicity and sameness of historical development in different parts of the world.[480] This content-form sensibility is likely one of the most important game design practices for the representation of historical change in both *Europa Universalis IV* and *Hearts of Iron IV*. The described practice is another example of how developers and beta testers work with the historical information at hand in a way that is particular for the specified purpose of making games. While it is an admirable goal to emphasise similarities between peoples and societies over time, this practice also runs the risk of erasing the experience of the victims of, for example, colonization. The experience of European expansion and exploitation from the perspective of Indigenous peoples in the Americas, Africa, or Australia, is often one of oppression, revoked agency and in some cases genocide. Design practice here aligns with Loban and Apperleys assertion that "Indigenous peoples are often depicted in an ahistorical, generalized way, that ignores their unique cultures and histories as sovereign people."[481]

Overall, there are significant differences between the way historical continuity and change are represented in *Europa Universalis IV* and *Hearts of Iron IV*. Again, these are mainly due to differences between the games' scope in time and concept. For example, the short timeline and immediacy of the Second World War as the focus of the game's design and gameplay makes representa-

---

[478] Developer informant Devin (June 28, 2017).
[479] For an elaborate discussion on this issue in *Assassin's Creed III*, see Shaw, "The Tyranny of Realism."
[480] The notion of providing each country with as much unique content as possible is echoed by other developers as well. Developer informant Dylan (June 29, 2018).
[481] Loban and Apperley, "Eurocentric Values at Play," 87.

tions and arguments about long-term change less visible. Having said that, longer historical cultural perspectives are indeed present in *Hearts of Iron IV*, and observable on two levels. The first level is represented by references that the game makes to history before the Second World War, and the second to historical events that, historically, took place after the Second World War.

For *Europa Universalis IV*, although the timeline is significantly longer and content more plentiful, the lack of representation of historical change is evident in the way certain mechanics fail to develop over the course of the game. That is, the game mechanics do not always change in parallel with the historical development of the game world. For example, the trade system is fundamentally the same in 1444 and 1821. The fact that the trade mechanic does not in fact invoke change over time is perhaps one of the most notable arguments against the notion of grand historical narratives in the game, epistemologically speaking.[482]

Summarily then, as laid out in chapter two, developers and beta testers rely somewhat on scholarly history and literature in their design work. However, their ultimate concern is not to make a methodologically or epistemologically viable historical argument. As regards the actual meaning of historical reference in an epistemological context then, Eviatar Zerubavel provides a rather fitting explanation of the role of historical cultural understandings in design: "The historical meaning of events basically lie in the way they are situated vis-à-vis other events. Indeed, it is their structural position within such *historical scenarios* (as 'watersheds,' 'catalysts,' 'final straws') that leads us to remember past events as we do."[483]

Using the example of the Blitz as described in chapter two, we note that developers re-situate the impact of strategic bombing to fit the gameplay logic. To Zerubavel's argument above, contextually speaking, the event gains its meaning in the way it is situated vis-à-vis a gameplay objective. It is not strictly false or counterfactual, but the use of history is clearly influenced by the setting. To go back to the Lego analogy in chapter one, developers build – from a game design perspective – functional history in a defined-by-genre framework using the Lego bucket. Historical reference is organised to facilitate story-making on a test-and-balance basis, with an emphasis on causality, outcomes and how events interplay. Exactness and historical accuracy are encouraged, but ultimately become ancillary values rather than an end unto itself.

---

[482] Koebel, "Simulating the Ages of Man," 68. Beta tester informant Brook (February 21, 2018).
[483] Zerubavel, *Time Maps*, 12. His emphasis and parenthesis.

Verisimilitude – Accuracy, Probability and Game Design

> If you were to simulate history, you might not end up with a fascist dictator who defines the first half of the 21st century. You might not end up with a violent liberal revolution in the late 1700's, but I feel like if I'm playing with history – if my goal is to have a historical experience in a video game – I kind of need for those things to happen. [...] I do kind of crave those iconic-like, mythologised story-beats.[484]
>
> Leana Hafer, Game journalist.

Beverley Southgate argues in his book *History meets fiction* that "history and fiction at once benefit and stuffer from their cohabitation: aspiring to inhabit at least some of the same territory, they have a relationship characterised by periods of tranquillity interspersed with more aggressive competitiveness."[485] Southgate argues that fact and fiction might look representative of two intellectual fashions or cultural emphases that have somewhat come to grow together under the critical methodology of postmodern thinking. In his book, Southgate partly focuses on the meaning of scholarly history for the purpose of fiction – much like historical game scholars do. He asserts that there is little to be gained from looking at these concepts as a "binary opposition"[486] and refutes any claim that this blurred condition would represent the decline of rationality and scientific progress. With regard to the present study, this dynamic between factual and counterfactual history is central to the way perception and understanding of history with regard to game design practice is described. Game designers can seamlessly move between discourses of fact and not-fact for the benefit of constructing believable systems and scenarios in *Europa Universalis IV* and *Hearts of Iron IV*. For the design of games, the perception and application of historical actuality is not situated in the empirically rational but in manufacturing something authentic. In the words of Southgate: "In practical terms, we do still contrive to make distinctions – not so much between the strictly fictional and the 'merely' fictional, but on the basis of varying degrees of *probability*."[487]

Game developers' perception of historical accuracy in digital games has previously been researched by Tara Copplestone. Based on 125 interviews with three groups of what she calls stakeholders in games and cultural heritage (players, cultural heritage professionals and game developers), her findings indicate that the developer segment of her informants takes authenticity seriously but

---

484 Idle Thumbs, *Three Moves Ahead*.
485 Beverley Southgate, *History Meets Fiction* (London: Pearson Education Limited, 2009), 22.
486 Southgate, *History Meets Fiction*, 173.
487 Southgate, *History Meets Fiction*, 175.

will, in most instances, focus on gameplay over accuracy in content, compared, for example, to cultural heritage professionals, who would aim to uphold a notion of accuracy to a larger degree. Copplestone attributes this particular difference to the way developers take business risk-management into consideration, with regard to, for example, profits and copies sold.[488] About 2% of her developer informants say historical accuracy is always important, whereas 54% state that accuracy in games is never important. Finally, 41% state that whether accuracy is important depends on what type of product is being produced.[489]

Copplestone's results resonate nicely with how developers as well as beta testers in the present study talk about historical accuracy, when asked specifically about the meaning of accuracy and authenticity in *Europa Universalis IV* and *Hearts of Iron IV*. In terms of game design, concerns with accuracy never stand in the way of fun and interesting gameplay, i.e. being historically accurate has no inherent value in game design unless it serves a particular design purpose. "I think imitation is a strong word. It's caricature,"[490] says one developer. With regards to developer and beta tester perception, the notion of accuracy is expressed as two different potential game design goals.

Firstly, accuracy is expressed as a function of the DLC monetisation strategy in game design practice. While the absence of an event is not in and of itself indicative of a non-accurate (or counterfactual) scenario,[491] there appears to be a connection between perceptions of accuracy to plausibility and relevance, which in turn is connected to content creation. One beta tester muses on this phenomenon as "we actually had a lot of these events, which [...] were hard to see, or trigger. Basically, they were very historical, but required a very narrow range of requirements to happen."[492] In these games, the player does not get to see every event, every play-through. The chance of seeing specific events is tied to a) the nation one is playing as, and b) a series of trigger criteria. As such, the actual prevalence of content is contingent on design, but the prevalence and probability of experiencing content in a play-through is contingent on gameplay.

One developer elaborates on this phenomenon by talking about the importance of accuracy in terms of relevance to gameplay.[493] In their view, the importance of historical events becomes increasingly difficult to anticipate because of the way the game forks. As such, historical events that take place, historically,

---

488 Copplestone, "But That's Not Accurate," 20.
489 Copplestone, "But That's Not Accurate," 16.
490 Developer informant Drew (June 28, 2018).
491 See also Ferguson, *Virtual History*, 18–19.
492 Beta tester informant Blake (August 20, 2018).
493 Developer interview Dale (June 15, 2017).

closer to the end of the game, become increasingly irrelevant from a design perspective. In this example, they talk about the historical partition of Poland in 1772, saying:

> One event, which happened historically, was that Poland was divided at the end of the eighteenth century – this is not something we really pay any attention to at all. Because if you have played the game through 350 years – you very likely do not even have a Polish state, or [you will not have] Russia, Prussia, or Austria bordering it, or wanting to divide it. [...] It is a historical event which becomes less important for us to simulate.[494]

They imply here that the event is less worth spending designer time on, due to its decreasing probability of occurring in the game.[495] Towards the same end, beta tester Blaine describes the process of designing for late-game content as it simply being "really difficult to predict what conditions should be fulfilled [in counterfactual late-games]."[496] Forcing events to trigger in the name of accuracy would entail either large amounts of railroading to ensure a plausible path, or trigger criteria which would seem implausible in a counterfactual context (for example, by hypothetically forcibly triggering a historical partition in a scenario where no stakeholder is motivated to do so for any conceivable reason), both of which in turn go against player-centred design practices.

In some cases, player expectations appear to have required workarounds. To make sure that events are seen more often by players, the trigger criteria for events have been adjusted. According to one beta tester, Paradox "loosed up a lot of those requirements so people see them more."[497] In order to discuss the potential of pushing accuracy through expected events by making them more visible, we must understand the purpose of trigger criteria. Trigger criteria denote a set of game states that constitute the point at which an event occurs. For example, in *Europa Universalis IV*, Protestantism can only occur in a country if it is a) catholic, b) not the papal state, c) has at least 50% reform desire and d) hasn't already promoted Protestantism.[498] In other words, trigger criteria denote causality for a specific event to occur and changing them is in theory the smallest basic component in counterfactual game design. However, it is not clear whether developers and beta testers consider changing the trigger criteria for an otherwise

---

494 Developer interview Dale (June 15, 2017).
495 In *Europa Universalis IV*, the earliest a game can start is 1444 and ends in 1821, which means that 1772 occurs late in most campaigns.
496 Beta tester informant Blaine (July 4, 2018).
497 Beta tester informant Blake (August 20, 2018). It is not clear which specific events the beta tester is referencing.
498 *Europa Universalis IV*. Events. Catholic.txt *A New Confession of Faith*. v1.28.3.

historical event, counterfactual design or not. It would appear, rather, as if it is conceivable to them to interfere with causality in order to facilitate game design practice on the basis of player expectations for the sake of communicating accuracy and authenticity through events.

On the same topic, the second way accuracy and authenticity are expressed is the baseline to which counterfactual history is juxtaposed on a systemic level. In the words of a beta tester: "I think that's why [Paradox Development Studio] does their anchoring of everything at a specific start date, because it gives them that baseline from which they can slowly build upon. And if they got that baseline built up properly and authentically enough, then it makes it much easier for them to build the next thing authentically enough, and they just keep on making a chain of hopefully authentic enough things."[499] This is supported by developers at Paradox Development Studio who state that at the beginning of *Europa Universalis VI*, the intention is to display content and rulesets as historically accurately as possible.[500] The starting point is meant to be perceived as historically accurate, as if to send a message to the player that this is where they take over – that this is where they begin their history.[501] Developers and beta testers seem to largely share a view on diminishing importance of authenticity. The gap between perceived importance of accuracy and authenticity on the one hand, and counterfactuals on the other, increases in proportion to the proverbial distance the player moves on an in-game linear timescale.

Going back to player-centred design practice, one beta tester elaborates on the notion of gameplay over content privilege by explaining how the AI can work in comparison to how it is supposed to work. They say that an AI that always tries to win has the opportunity to act contrary to known mistakes in history, although if developers create an AI that is historically correct, it will also become more predictable.[502] According to this logic, an optimal AI that adheres to the gameplay over historical content rule is likely more challenging and plays as skilfully as possible, and should therefore be as unpredictable as possible, which in theory goes against the idea of having players benefit from real-world knowledge. However, this logic goes two ways, because something that is unpredictable does not necessarily guarantee good gameplay.[503] Jesper Juul argues, and rightfully so, that challenge constitutes both a negative and a positive feeling at the same time. He suitably calls it the paradox of play and notes, "the

---

499 Beta tester informant Blake (August 20, 2018).
500 Developer informant Dallas (June 26, 2017).
501 Developer informant Delta (June 27, 2017).
502 Beta tester informant Brooklyn (October 22, 2018).
503 Juul, *The Art of Failure*, 52.

combination of more failures and smaller punishments adds up to more frequent opportunities for having failure force us to reconsider our strategies, to learn from our mistakes."[504]

There are situations, particularly in *Hearts of Iron IV* but also in *Europa Universalis IV*, where historical inaccuracy does not lead to plausible counterfactual history, but to illogical chaos (a disconnection between cause and consequence). As expressed by Brooklyn:

> For example, if France had been scripted to always be democratic, always 'the good guys', [the game] simply would not make sense if the player creates the Kaiser's democratic Germany. You would end up with a scenario where Germany has no adversaries except Soviet – everyone else would be their friend. This is why the AI is scripted to create Communist France in case of a democratic Germany, in order to ensure a two-front war in Germany.[505]

According to the beta tester, this type of railroading focuses on forcing a few select events in the game that are considered so central to the gameplay experience that any alternative paths require immense skill or extreme chance in order to occur, here exemplified by the Second World War with a two-front military effort. Another example for *Hearts of Iron IV* is the Anschluss of Austria, which ties into the same requirement (fuelling the start of the war, i.e. the fundamental baseline for the war).[506] Typical examples for *Europa Universalis IV* are exploration events for playable nations like Portugal and Spain that are very likely to occur, and then commit to the game's fundamental theme of colonisation[507] and The Reformation, which fuels internal European conflict and development in the era. Or, as put by beta tester Blaine: "[The] Reformation [is] not outside of your agency, but it happens despite you."[508]

Negotiating the Past and Game Design Frameworks

In the chapter "The Game is a Medium: The Games is a Message" in the edited volume *Early Modernity and Video Games*, Rolf F. Nohr describes a shift in media theory paradigms over the last century that he describes as "an effort to re-write

---

504 Juul, *The Art of Failure*, 72.
505 Beta tester Brooklyn (October 22, 2018).
506 Developer informant Drew (June 28, 2018).
507 *Europa Universalis IV.* v1.6.2.
508 Beta tester informant Blaine (July 4, 2018).

this radical dictum of the loss of content for the benefit of the form."[509] This dichotomy of content and form is of particular interest, and a recurring theme when focusing on the practice and context of fusing what designers and players know about the past with the sandbox nature of digital strategy games. Industry parameters and Paradox-specific prompts and pressures described in the previous chapters shape the motivations and factors, which support historical game design practice. The consequences for historical representation, historiographical rulesets and counterfactual gameplay become apparent in the marriage between game design practice, content generation and developers' understanding and interpretation of history, and its subsequent implementation in the games.

The interdisciplinary analysis becomes a methodological exercise in juxtaposing research from perspectives that are inherently difficult to compare. I have tried to include and compare the findings here with previous research on similar topics, but it is worth stating that due to the lack of previous research in this particular intersection of scholarly fields – historical game studies and game design research – developer and beta tester intention and their personal as well as professional understanding of the implementation of history in digital strategy games are not automatically comparable to, for example, close-readings of historical arguments made through games. On the one hand – in the words of Nohr – the game, as a technological structure that imposes a form on the content, is the medium. Simultaneously, on the other hand, the game, being a "communicative [...] machine for social integration,"[510] is the message.

This phenomenon, and methodological dilemma, is highlighted by a similar ambivalence: developers negotiate their understanding of historical content, and the reality of game design practice, with genre conventions. As noted by history didactics scholar Marianne Sjöland in reference to popular history magazines: genre, in order to be a vehicle that is meaningful beyond its content, "cannot take just any shape."[511] Just as with any other form of historical mediation, there are rules that dictate what history to emphasise and how to do it.[512] In doing so, the rules construct both the media and the message, simultaneously. These convergences of content-and-form issues can be observed in the interviews and concretized by the way historical content gets transformed through design to

---

509 Rolf Nohr, "The Game is the Medium. The Game is the Message," in Tobias Winnerling and Florian Kerschbaumer (eds.), *Early Modernity in Video Games* (Newcastle upon Tyne: Cambridge Scholars Publishing, 2014), 9.
510 Nohr, "The Game is the Medium," 7.
511 Sjöland, *Historia från tidskriftsredaktionen*, 249. My translation.
512 David Harland in Sjöland, *Historia från tidskriftsredaktionen*, 249–250.

accommodate, for example, entertainment-focused design practice, player accessibility and game balance.

A core aspect of the interdisciplinary approach to historical game studies, this dichotomy has also been observed by historical games scholars before, most relevantly here by Clint Hocking and Adam Chapman. Chapman deals with this peculiarity on a conceptual level in his chapter about ludo-narrative dissonance which describes the tension of expectations on games as both "systems for play and as systems for the communication [of] historical narrative."[513] Ludo-narrative dissonance is described as a kind of failure to harmonise between a particular tone and content on the one hand and the interactivity and vehicle for agency on the other. Chapman exemplifies using *Medal of Honor* (1999) and the way the game's bullet-time camera sequences show the player a gory slow-motion representation of the assumed violence their in-game actions cause. Dissonance is found in the way close-up violence clashes with the moral and honourable rhetoric of the over-arching plot of the game.[514]

Historical game scholars are well-versed in exploring this kind of analysis.[515] However, the use of terminology ("dissonance," "tension," "clashes") often gives the impression that a harmonious relationship between content and form is the most desirable design objective.[516] Arguably, there is plenty of opportunity here to question the normative position of the historian's beaten path and explore ways in which game rhetoric communicates conceptual notions of history through game designs and gameplay itself, without shoehorning it into a normative framework conforming to the traditions of humanities research. With regard to this study, this distinction serves to highlight the core benefit of studying de-

---

513 Clint Hocking, "Ludonarrative Dissonance in *Bioshock*," *Click Nothing*, October 7, 2007, accessed October 25, 2019, https://clicknothing.typepad.com/click_nothing/2007/10/ludonarrative-d.html, cited in Chapman, *Digital Games as History*, 161.
514 Chapman, *Digital Games as History*, 161.
515 The duality of system versus content has also been observed in studies on player behaviour, for example in Apperley, "Counterfactual Communities." Apperley finds that players are nimble in their positioning as players, often going between game-focused and history-focused states. Any speculation about the relationship between the nature of ambiguity in game design practice and any subsequent ambiguity in players are outside the scope of this study, but should be considered as a potentially fruitful topic for future research.
516 This notion of the relationship between game content and form, and how to study it, has been discussed at length. See for example Ian Bogost and Will Wright, *Persuasive Games: The Expressive Power of Video Games* (Cambridge, MA: The MIT Press, 2007); Miguel Sicart "Against Procedurality," *Game Studies* 11 (2011), http://gamestudies.org/1103/articles/sicart_ap; Jan H.G. Klabbers, "Tensions Between Meaning and Construction and Persuasion in Games," *Game Studies* 11 (2011).

veloper perception and understanding this dichotomy, namely the irrelevance of such normative terminology to the understanding of game design practice. As already established, developers and beta testers act within a framework consisting of other values and express the work they do in different terms. In other words, it would be empirically dishonest to assume that the goal of game design, in the minds of developers, would align with a harmonious relationship between content and form. Having said that, it would appear as if developers and beta testers are aware of this tension.

As Chapman keenly notes, but does not elaborate upon, "it may well be that these kinds of tensions actually have a role to play in the development of a game-based language of historical representation."[517] From the historical game scholar's point of view, this tension, I would argue, is crucial for the understanding of any unique qualities games as representations of history might have. The digital nature and structure of *Europa Universalis IV* and *Hearts of Iron IV* allow us to rethink the way we understand clusters of knowledge about the past. In turn, the tension between content and form constitutes another systems-based rhetoric to historical discussion, which could very well align with the concept of procedural rhetoric. The term was originally coined by game scholar and game designer Ian Bogost in 2007 and denotes the way programming and games are able to convey statements and ideology persuasively through rules, interactivity and procedure.[518] Much like learning to read takes practice, acquiring procedural literacy, then, does too. Bogost argues that "part of that practice is learning to read processes as a critic. This means playing a videogame or using procedural system [*sic*] with an eye toward identifying and interpreting the rules that drive that system."[519] In the interviews, developers touch on this notion repeatedly, in particular with regard to issues of player-centred design practice, entertainment-centred design practice and accessibility. This is so in the sense that, firstly, developers emphasize slightly more the importance of mechanics and rules than they do content in terms of player progression. In other words, it is their understanding that players who have learned the game mechanics and rules progress faster, and become more apt at the game, than those who only know the content of the games well.[520] Secondly, this is so in that they stress the important role of counterfactual history in both games and the way it consti-

---

517 Chapman, *Digital Games as History*, 162.
518 Bogost, *Persuasive Games*, 1–64.
519 Bogost, *Persuasive Games*, 64.
520 Beta tester informant Brooklyn (October 22, 2018).

tutes a challenge on a systemic level, mainly for *Europa Universalis IV* but *Hearts of Iron IV* as well.[521]

Chapter Summary

Game design practice in relation to historical representation at Paradox Development Studio is driven by design goals. In other words, these games are shaped and framed by player-centred and entertainment-centred design practice, from testing, balancing and feedback, not primarily according to a grand historical narrative. Philosopher and game scholar Luis de Miranda writes: "Artists are not philosophers: They sense more than they quote or analyze."[522] This I find to be representative of the negotiation developers do between historical experimentation and verisimilitude. The developers' intention is to make an argument about how history can be fun and interesting in the form of a game, not about history itself. Nevertheless, sometimes these perspectives collide. Beta testers, who have more ideological leeway, argue much in the same way but maintain a more critical perspective on the possibilities and limitations of the content and form dynamic.

An important conclusion here is the extent to which counterfactuals rely on historical logic. The inherent systemic logic of the games supports the exploration of counterfactuals to the point where they are still recognisable. I have not found counterfactual scenarios that are not extrapolated from historical actuality or somehow function as a foil for historical culture, nor do the interviews support this mentality or design practice. Game designers are aware and intimately connected to their internal discussions and players' discussions about fact and fiction for the benefit of constructing believable systems and scenarios in *Europa Universalis IV* and *Hearts of Iron IV*. For the design of games, the perception and application of historical actuality is not situated in the empirically rational but in the building block for manufacturing something authentic, which, in turn, is based on player expectation (and profitability). What constitutes authenticity appears to be a touch-and-go process although gameplay and notions of fun are always the priority.

As such, representations of history and counterfactual history are designed according to the following logic:

---

[521] Beta tester informant Blake (August 20, 2018).
[522] Luis De Miranda, "Life Is Strange and 'Games Are Made': A Philosophical Interpretation of a Multiple-Choice Existential Simulator with Co-pilot Sartre," *Games and Culture* 13 (2018): 826.

1. Design is limited by historical presupposition.
2. Player expectation and entertainment focus always take precedent.
3. The historical era and topic of the game inform design practice specifics.
4. Counterfactuals are both a prerequisite of design and a result of design.

Europa Universalis IV is one of the most complex digital strategy games on the market, which can be attributed to decades of accumulated development and an ambition to make the game world as interesting as possible to players who have an interest in the Early Modern era. A notable difference between the Early Modern setting and the Second World War setting is that the greater distance in time allows for a discussion of historical atrocities that *Hearts of Iron IV* does not. Developers are very clear that their game does not and will not include notions of the Holocaust, effectively omitting a critically important historical event of the twentieth century. The most frequent argument is that the scope of *Hearts of Iron IV* does not accommodate it in terms of mechanics due to its narrower scope, although there is reason to look deeper as to why that is. Most notably, other historical atrocities such as carpet bombing and the atomic bomb are not only present, but instrumental in playing the game. Simultaneously, *Europa Universalis IV* employs a pragmatic relationship with dark heritage such as transatlantic slave trade, cultural oppression and exploitation in the wake of colonialism, and developers maintaining the position that as long as it has a playable, coherent function, it has a role to play in the game.

Conclusions

Game Design, Uses of History and Counterfactuals in Games

In the broadest sense, this book is about representations of history in games. Its principal aim is to investigate and further our understanding of games as designed artefacts – of games as games – and dig deep into the implications of such an understanding. The book takes a holistic perspective on history in games, and considers relevant contexts to why and how counterfactual history looks and works the way it does in games. The conceptual focus is the interplay between games and uses of history. That is, the practice of using historical reference for communication, signalling and meaningful application of historical culture in and around games. To this end, the book has considered genre, development practices and historical culture as conceptual frameworks and practices that define the topic. Arguably, the same concepts constitute the outline of the book itself.

The contents of the book, then, have considered two primary texts: interviews with game developers at Paradox Development Studio, and their games *Europa Universalis IV* and *Hearts of Iron IV*. Developers' and beta testers' interest in history is a fundamental aspect of the game design context at Paradox Development Studio. This is visible, for example, in the way developers and beta testers do research and source content for the games. Those who did not already harbour a long-standing personal interest in history state that they have an increased curiosity for understanding and learning about the past since working at Paradox Development Studio. The importance of the drive and volition here may sound obvious, but it is actually not a given. Not everyone, but a significant number of game developers in the present study go above and beyond what is expected of them in their professional roles to seek out, purchase, consume and apply findings from historical literature, podcasts and documentaries into the games' content and mechanics. Even then, development fully relies on beta testers – design and development volunteers – to research and create content for the games in order to meet deadlines and expectations. Beta testers produce bulks of content for both games, and take on a significant portion of the time-consuming reading, research and scripting that is required to make these games.

An underlying factor here is supplementary design practice, also known as the DLC monetisation strategy. This strategy entails continuously adding to the core games by making and releasing expansions and downloadable content. This practice, sometimes known as the DLC economy, since it allows the developers to charge players repeatedly, is an archetypical Paradox characteristic, and this has been the case for decades. Supplementary design practice also means that each new iteration of *Europa Universalis* and *Hearts of Iron* core-games build, to a point, directly on top of the previous game. Looking at the state of the games today, we note that the practice has not only been a financial success, but it has also had some interesting practical consequences. Consider for example that the *Europa Universalis* series (that turned 20 years old in 2021) still contains content that was originally created for previous iterations of the game. This tells us at least two things.

Firstly, in order for the practice of reusing and repurposing content to be a technologically and designerly viable option, the ontology of the games has to have been relatively slow to change. In other words, supplementary design practices are directly plugged into genre conventions and design legacy. Secondly, heritage code in *Europa Universalis IV* is evidence of, and perhaps partly responsible for, the rigid representation of history in the game. This is, of course, likely also due to genre convention as well. Digital strategy games, despite their sandbox nature, tell a comprehensive and common history. As noted repeatedly throughout this book, historical representation adheres quite explicitly to structuralist depictions, alongside the possibility of emergent gameplay and the promise that players can change history. In other words, supplementary design practices allow developers and beta testers to add multiplicity and nuance for the benefit of counterfactual history, whilst adhering to the core rules of the game.

Counterfactuals are designed slightly differently in *Europa Universalis IV* than in *Hearts of Iron IV*, something that, again, can also be explained in part by genre convention and design legacy. Developers appear to adhere to what is known as the accessibility turn – the notion that games overall have become easier to play and understand since around 2010. One of the main impacts of this turn is that Paradox Development Studio made gameplay easier to master, and objectives more straightforward. In terms of counterfactuals, this has translated into an increased focus on ready-made counterfactual scenarios in *Hearts of Iron IV*. That is, the player can rely on the game to suggest a scenario path to follow. Conversely, due to the considerably longer time covered and wider historical focus, *Europa Universalis IV* is not suited to cohesive counterfactual scenarios to the same extent. Instead, counterfactuals in *Europa Universalis IV* rely heavily on emergent story-making and goal-setting mechanics such as missions and achievements. Having said that, the expanded and deepened design of missions and achievements in *Europa Universalis IV* release points in the same design direction as *Hearts of Iron IV* – players are increasingly asking for more counterfactuals to play, as noted by developers.

From a game analysis perspective, we can here note that *Europa Universalis IV* emphasises the importance of event design and trigger criteria in gameplay. The player exerts control over the game by manipulating events and stringing them together to make a story. Understanding cause and effect in the game here translates into skilful gameplay. For example, upon the inception of Protestantism in Europe, an event called "A New Confession of Faith" fires. The player must choose between "Promote it" and "Nay, it will damn everyone." The former option provides the player with, among other things, fresh administrative power; the latter will increase papal influence and devotion. The player must decide which path is the most desirable outcome of the two options, usually based on what their plan is for the session. In other words, goals constitute necessary framings for gameplay in *Europa Universalis IV* to make sense. In terms of historical and counterfactual design in this context, focus is on navigating the interplay – or balance – of trigger criteria, outcomes and synergies of the past in the game.

To the same effect, then, *Europa Universalis IV* produces counterfactuals that, in line with the conceptual framework described in the introduction and chapter three, can best be described as wishful thinking and possible world scenarios. The counterfactual scenarios in the game are often focused on questions of causality and contingency as particularly meaningful elements. As discussed, the game is fundamentally quite rigid. That is, history in *Europa Universalis IV* is ultimately deterministic and Eurocentric, and this includes the design of counterfactuals. It is particularly evident from scenarios in the vein of *Sunset Invasion*, whose trigger criteria depends on the Aztec adopting European technology and turning it against them to become invaders themselves. In other words, explorations of how to reinstate or repair lost empires as in the case of *Basileus*, or, similarly, how to reinvent and counter the historical power dynamics of colonialism as in *Sunset Invasion*, do not tell us what sort of world we would be living in, had these scenarios come to pass. They are, for all intents and purposes, a reflection of historical developments and their significance for the present.

As further noted in this book, developers acknowledge in several instances that *Europa Universalis IV*'s design hinges on specific historical events and developments that are then broadly applied as blanket or model mechanics. This is not always the case, however, as nations, periods and regions are given their own specific set of events and plug-in mechanics through DLC development. Nevertheless, the core systems, such as trade, monarch points, and technological development, perpetuate a standardised, Western historical representation through railroading. In other words, historical content and representation never stray far from what developers call authentic or realistic descriptions of the past. The underlying rules and logic are ultimately meant to seem historically adequate and this logic encompasses counterfactuals as well.

In contrast, then, *Hearts of Iron IV* emphasises outcomes and consequences in its gameplay. The limited timeframe of the game does not allow for synergetic gameplay in the vein of *Europa Universalis IV*. Instead, gameplay in *Hearts of Iron IV* takes place within a narrow historical scenario wherein the player follows a more or less ready-made path due to the importance of the national focus trees. This is not to say that *Hearts of Iron IV* does not have events with trigger criteria that are relevant to, and able to produce, emergent gameplay. It does, but they do not dictate gameplay to the same extent as in *Europa Universalis IV*. Instead, the national focus tree branches function as progression paths that outline very specific scenarios. In fact, decisions in the focus tree appear almost as countdowns, denoting the amount of time before they are implemented. As such, they are not concerned with causality, or how, specifically, events unfold in the game – more so outcomes, and the subsequent states of the world.

Primarily implemented as branches on the national focus trees, counterfactual scenarios are designed as ready-made scenarios too. Due to the limited timeline and scope of the game and the inherent focus on outcomes rather than causality, counterfactuals are usually most easily described as future fictions in *Hearts of Iron IV*. Examples include playing as democratic Germany, or playing as Germany to win the Second World War. Notably, certain scenarios in *Hearts of Iron IV* do have characteristics of wishful thinking and possible worlds. Some draw on historical reference and motivate the counterfactual with wanting to revisit something from the past in the in-game present. One such example is the hindsight perspective employed in explaining why fascism gets a foothold in the United States in the 30s. The descriptive text laments the outcome of the historical American Civil War, and, importantly, how historians portrayed the war since. The ultimate objective in the focus tree is "Honor the Confederacy" – a veritable reimagination of the outcomes and repercussions of the Civil War. As such, this particular counterfactual is equally concerned with the history of the 1860s as it is of the history of the 1930s.

The discrepancy in historical representation between two otherwise quite similar games is, as I have shown in this book, a function of overall game design practices, conventions and design logic. Importantly, it is also a function of historical culture. That is, how the use of historical references with contextually attributed meanings provides either opportunity or constraint in terms of adapting said references into games and design. An often-used example in the book, of how historical culture imposes itself on game design practice, is the Holocaust. I have argued that this is because the event holds a particular, if not unique, place in historical culture and, consequently, in game culture as well. The omission of the Holocaust in *Hearts of Iron IV* is only one example that clearly shows the loaded meaning inherent not just to the event as such, but its remediation and re-contextualisation in the context of games. Discussing the games and their contents as uses of history and historical culture are indeed fruitful in instances such as these, as it allows us to consider notions of authorship, bias and intent in some detail. Importantly, it also highlights historical cultural tension between content and design. Game design adheres to a set of values that in some cases are incompatible with historical cultural norms of how, when and why to use certain historical references. Another example of this is the Blitz. Due to the logic of conflict in games, and contrary to historical fact, players expect strategic bombings to have a negative effect on the opponent in *Hearts of Iron IV*. Here, developers are required to reframe the historical reference in order for the games to make sense.

This book has contextualised the game artefacts and the game studio in this way throughout, producing at least two distinct insights. Firstly, both games build heavily on historical canon. That is, repeating themes, events and perspectives; for example the Byzantine and Roman Empire, Austria-Hungary, the Kalmar Union and Hellas permeate discourse in both games. Secondly, by studying the use of history within game design and the game industry, player-centred practices and entertainment-centred practices emerge as discernible design values and rationale. Developers interpret the relationship between player expectations regarding familiarity and presupposition, and how presupposition and player expectation, in turn, relate to gameplay issues such as goal-setting and replayability, and what constitutes challenge, success and failure, for the benefit of historical game design.

The Remarkable Complexity of Making Games about the Past

Paradox Development Studio is a part of several different important and influential contexts. Perhaps the most poignant is that of wargames and the strategy-genre tradition. Paradox Development Studio has a 20-year tradition of making games in the digital strategy genre, which not only has accrued a certain amount of experience and know-how in terms of strategy game making. This deeply rooted experience also provides an in-house design legacy, which allows developers and beta testers to design in an accumulative fashion. As mentioned, the overt example of this is the monetisation model that allows developers to, incrementally, and over longer periods of time than most developers are able, add and develop mechanics and content for the benefit of complexity and multiplicity in the games. Commonly in game development, the nature of tasks in a project change over time, going from research, writing and scripting at the start to bug hunting and stress testing towards the end. There is no reason to assume this is not also the case at Paradox Development Studio, and that this would be reflected on beta testers as well, although it would at the same time be logical if the cycles at Paradox Development Studio overlap to a larger extent due to incremental DLC and patch production. Either way, it is clear that developers and beta testers take advantage of their niche space in the games industry.

Simultaneously, developers build on top of wargaming tradition, which promotes systems and simulation design over aesthetics. In an often realism and technology focused world of game making (i.e. the increasing visual fidelity of games), Paradox Development Studio direct resources towards other areas in order to cater to the expectations of their quite particular strategy games- and history-oriented fanbase. As a game-making studio, it is of course also a member of a global game-making industry. As such, developers are constrained in practice by elements that dictate, or are perceived as dictating, profitability. Profitability, in turn, is a complex mix of promotional activities and consumer data collection for most game developers. At Paradox Development Studio, while they do perform marketing activities and testing, developers seem to find that the most productive way their practice engages in direct communication with the players is via their online forums and beta testers. This book has established that developers and beta testers keep their ear to the ground through their online forums and connect with their player base as an opportunity to collect their opinions on the games as well as discussion about historical development and how it translates within the game. However, design tradition and legacy affect the way developers navigate the space between opportunism and historical verisimilitude.

The Paradox forums also constitute the infrastructure used to engage and communicate with beta testers. Paradox Development Studio rely significantly on voluntary efforts by fans and players with a specific status called beta testers. Beta testers play a particularly important role in testing, curating and creating content for the games. Beta testers function as a foil for players, as well as communicational proxies for developers when it comes to discussing the games, their contents, balance and other issues with players on the forum. They also perform a variety of balance testing and bug hunting on new iterations of each game. However, most importantly, beta testers help design and produce content for both games and are considered an integrated and invaluable part of studio life.

Furthermore, the beta tester pool appears to be an important source for recruiting mainly content designers and game designers. Multiple informants state that they started out as beta testers and were subsequently recruited to Paradox Development Studio. From a game-design practice and work-practice perspective, this has some potentially important implications for our understanding of expertise and talent-acquisition and -retention policy in certain parts of the game industry. This is especially so if we consider that historical games are often publicly discussed in terms of historical accuracy, and that special credit tends to be attributed to studios who hire professional historians as consultants on their projects. It is therefore noteworthy that Paradox Development Studio – a studio that promotes itself and its games as one of the most historically correct – does not actively pursue or hire people with backgrounds in professional historical scholarship. Instead, they look for historically inclined designers.

The benefit of using theoretical frameworks aimed at game design practices and game production is perhaps mainly to unveil how historical and designerly expertise interplay. In keeping with the framework from the introduction, this book has put the processes, skills and views of developers and beta testers at the forefront to gain insights regarding day-to-day work at Paradox Development Studio. Understanding, for example, the details of who does historical research, at what cost and when, constructively helps to distinguish between game design epistemology (designerly ways of knowing), game design praxiology (study of the practices and processes of design) and game design phenomenology (study of the form and configuration of artefacts). In other words, the pragmatic framings of making games about the past have certain consequences, which in turn, relate to developer understandings of design legacy (design epistemology), of scripting and technical problem solving (design praxiology), as well as player experiences with the games (design phenomenology). By engaging with the games at hand on these varying levels, a more detailed understanding of how games are made emerges, but also of the scaffolding of history within the games. Importantly, by taking this almost mundane approach on game making, some notable tensions between game design practice on an individual level, and the conditions of the game industry, become visible. For example, beta testers repeatedly note that their overall vision for the games is sometimes different than what is deemed the most advantageous path forward by Paradox Development Studio and Paradox Interactive.

Although research practices at Paradox Development Studio appear to be guided by a deep understanding of the material being used, game design practice dictates that player-centred perspectives and entertainment-centred perspectives always take precedence. That entails having to make compromises with historical actuality for the benefit of gameplay. Naturally, developers and beta testers find themselves in another context, too – historical culture – which in turn dictates the viability of notions such as "familiarity" and "fun" for the benefit of game design. Counterfactual history, in turn, is a prerequisite for design, as both genre and player expectations dictate designed space and agency with regard to historical development.

Counterfactuals and the Unremarkable Stringency in Historical Culture

At their core, both *Europa Universalis IV* and *Hearts of Iron IV* are conquest and expansion games whose mechanics, of course, are built in code. This book has made a case for technical readings of game design, and, to a point, of game scripting, as a method for better understanding the relationship between game design practices and historical representation. How history and counterfactual history are mapped onto mechanics and rules in the games is a crucial key to better explaining their roles as uses of history. Game content such as events, national focus tree design, mission trees and AI (just to name a few important elements) all correlate and causally depend on one-another to produce gameplay, and ultimately, histories. This is achieved through a careful use of scripting. By studying this scripting as a design practice (which, in turn, facilitates historical representation), I have framed the games as games, rather than as another historical medium. That is, games always come with very influential material and immaterial scaffolding. For example, until quite recently, Paradox Development games were only available to play on PC, which significantly frames the experience, the intended audience, accessibility and more. By including the perspective on games as different types of infrastructure in the analysis, we gain a nuanced understanding of how historical games happen, what their place is on the map of historical media and where we might find important tensions between design and representation. This technical area, I have argued, is where the virtual Venn-diagram of game design practice, historical culture and counterfactual history overlaps. Through our understanding of games as games, then, we gain a new perspective on games as vehicles of historical culture, as well as vehicles of counterfactual gameplay.

Counterfactual history in *Europa Universalis IV* and *Hearts of Iron IV* has been analysed using the wishful thinking, possible worlds and future fiction conceptualisation. As such, I have taken the opportunity to better understand and explain the technical, as well as historical cultural, prerequisites for counterfactuals. The suggested theoretical categories are in no way mutually exclusive. Their presence in the games partly overlap, although, as already established, it is possible to see a tilt towards wishful thinking and possible worlds in *Europa Universalis IV* as well as a more pronounced occurrence of future fictions in Hearts of *Iron IV.* So, one of the most consequential findings regarding the conceptualisation of counterfactual history as uses of history regards the relationship between mechanics, scripted content and counterfactual scenarios as goal-setting. Especially when it comes to emergent counterfactuals in play-by-play, the conceptual framework lacks a clear application outside of the achievements, missions and national focus mechanics for both games. It is worth underlining that facilitating emergent story-making – and, of course, counterfactuals – in gameplay is an important part of digital strategy games, and it would be beneficial if future studies were able to further our understanding of how players construct and make sense of counterfactual script design in relation to emergent counterfactual scenarios specifically. This book has described its instrumental form but has not captured the intricacies of emergent-gameplay experiences from a player perspective, nor has it offered a comprehensive empirical analysis of emergent counterfactual gameplay beyond its theoretical underpinnings.

Nevertheless, in an effort to explain the role of what-ifs, the focus of the book has been the interplay of game design and history. In doing so, the book combines two genetically related materials – developer interviews about game design and related game design products. At times, such an approach can cause issues with dependencies. The query at the forefront is always to what extent game design shapes history, and to what extent history shapes the games. This is partly a methodological question on how to approach game artefacts for the benefit of untangling the contradictions of counterfactuals. According to developers and beta testers, counterfactual gameplay is at the core of *Europa Universalis IV* and *Hearts of Iron IV*. Simultaneously, verisimilitude is an upheld design value, and the games should strive to be historical, say developers. The insertion of design values to the discussion becomes poignant here. Design practice and design values matter because the games themselves follow game logic dispassionately. The contradictions and tension between the factual and counterfactual can only be explained by looking at the scaffolding that frames it.

Furthermore, the technical reading of code is an interesting challenge to demystifying counterfactual representation. To my knowledge, neither historians nor game scholars have formally studied the scripting and textual content of Paradox Development Studio games in the past. This humble attempt at the method, and its contributions, are twofold. Firstly, there are important insights to how games work that cannot be easily discerned from just playing. One example is the details and logic of AI behaviour in both games. Secondly, the "under the hood" approach provides an entirely new perspective on game artefacts. For example, game scripting contains paracode – scribbles in the margins – that provide additional context and explanations to the code. In some instances, the paracodes speak directly about the rationale behind counterfactual design decisions, unveiling the pragmatic nature of making games about the past.

One such example are historical notes on why the game sometimes is set to having the king's spouse die (counterfactual) rather than divorce him (historical) to keep a game in line with its own inherent logic. This particular phenomenon of paracode will hopefully be explored by future studies, as it captures the immediacy and rationale behind design work in a unique way.

Omission of history, mainly applicable to war crimes and dark history in the games, does not appear related to the design of counterfactual history specifically, but rather to Paradox Developments Studio's positioning of themselves as participants in a wider historical cultural context. The core argument from developers and beta testers, that gameplay logic requires relevance between action and content, appears only partly viable in the game analysis, as the lines between what constitutes historical atrocities and what does not are blurred. However, interestingly, it would seem as if the relationship between historical atrocities and the notion of agency as a trivialising factor does not alone frame this design conundrum. The study indicates that entertainment-focus as a design priority frames decision-making to a larger extent than worrying about trivialisation, and that agency itself is not considered an issue for developers. Instead, genre convention dictates that a systemic ruleset and perspective on the past, when driven by exploitation as an incentive, stop being viable design choices. Based on the available data, the Holocaust, specifically, is treated by developers and beta testers as an extraordinary event even in comparison to other well-known historical atrocities. Furthermore, it seems as though sentiments on era, scale and temporal distance are used to explain, in part, the discrepancies in design practice of, for example, transatlantic slave trade and war crimes.

Importantly, however, the burden of game culture – the widely accepted understanding of play as frivolous – and the cultural inference that games risk trivializing the past is not unwarranted. As I have noted, there is an inherent contradiction between the non-treatment of the Holocaust in game settings and that of trans-Atlantic slave-trade, and colonialist oppression. Developers and beta testers argue that the notion of slavery in Early Modern history is such a significant aspect to the political and economic development of global history that it would be unethical not to include it in the game. Arguably, the same could be said for the Holocaust in the context of the political and ideological underpinnings of the Second World War, especially in considering the more recent history of Holocaust denialism. It follows that these statements about the historical cultural value of slavery stand in rather stark contrast to the stance taken not to include the Holocaust in *Hearts of Iron IV*. It seems implied that historical atrocities are not in fact wholly taboo as playable items in games after all, but that the question of how to do it well remains unresolved in these games. The specific comparison between colonial slave trade and the Holocaust in this book has been examined in the context of the existing design of each game. It is, I argue, reasonable not to shoehorn the Holocaust into a game that is fundamentally and very specifically about resource management and warfare. However, it is equally reasonable to expect design frameworks and practices for depicting other genocides in history with similar amounts of care.

In essence, then, the theme and historical focus of the game and its historical cultural context appear to dictate what history must be included in each game, what absolutely cannot be included, and what counterfactual scenarios are expected. The interplay of these three criteria ultimately comprises the scaffolding of verisimilitude and, by extension, the facilitation and delimitation of counterfactuals as uses of history. A noteworthy principle to take away from the study of development practices, then, is that counterfactuals in digital strategy games do not, and, at least in the present study, cannot make arguments about what was historically possible – only what is possible within each game as per design. That is not to say that games are not theoretically able to make scholar-style, virtual history arguments, but it happens on the behest of developers.

Finally, one could argue that digital strategy games tend to emphasise the contradictory nature of play. The systemic foundations upon which history's likeness is being built, tweaked, and rebuilt over long periods of time offers an immense canvas for designers to work with. Nevertheless, their challenge – perhaps more so than their players' – is reconciling a series of dichotomies which are inherent, not to history itself, but in the historical strategy games genre by virtue of what amounts to historical and technical multiplicity. Game design labour and design practices must be understood alongside monetization models, verisimilitude is related to both complexity and simplification, and, finally, entertainment through play is contrasted by our genuine fear of the past and the awful and wonderful lessons we have learned.

What Kind of History is Counterfactual-game-design History?

A few notes, then, on epistemology. For game designers, counterfactual history is almost never about depicting the historically most probable outcomes. To them, authorship is about determining what the most advantageous outcomes from a design and gameplay perspective are. In other words: how are they to create the most entertaining, challenging and engaging gameplay experience possible for their players?

Shaping history, as it were, happens on several different levels here. Perhaps the most intuitive level is designing the game itself. But the immediacy with which game design practice happens in code, in asset design, in mechanics design, does not extend to next tier contexts such as monetisation models, promotional activity, player expectations, and so on. These industry variables are considerably slower, more rigid and stringent than hands-on development. They are however necessary to consider in a holistic analysis of what contexts and framings influence historical representation in games. Digital distribution, incremental DLC releases, other monetisation strategies, player-retention and accessibility values frame representation considerably. Among other things, these practices support replayability and multiplicity of content. Over time, complexity-reduction and stagnation with regard to mechanics and synergy appears to be one of its casualties, leaving some of the fundaments intact over time. A typical example is the trade-system in *Europa Universalis IV*, which was originally made to showcase the importance of Venice as a trading-hub in the 1400s and to this day largely fails to depict any other kind of trade, or – to be sure – fail to facilitate counterfactual history at all. In other words, game industry practices delimit not only the representation of the past but of counterfactuals as well.

Epistemologically speaking, developers engage with history on two primary grounds: 1) as wranglers of the past for the benefit of game making; and 2) as proficient readers of history. Game developers at Paradox Development Studio, to be sure, are well read on history. But there is a level of historical cherry-picking going on here as well, which I argue stems from the contradictory relationship between the design legacy of conflict-driven gameplay and developer understandings of player expectations, as well as their understandings of the games' position in a greater societal context. Central to this whole discussion is the question of how developers balance their understanding of the past with a delimiting sense of what kind of history is specific to the gameplay experience. Importantly, it must be understood that counterfactual in this context does not mean equally viable. There is not a viable historical argument in which Germany won the Second World War. It simply did not happen. But it satisfies the design goals of Paradox Development Studio and so exists in *Hearts of Iron IV*.

The question of why counterfactuals are meaningful is, to be sure, at least tangentially related to aspects on historical epistemology, especially in terms of uses of history. For example, the discourse on omission, trivialisation and counterfactuals borders on revisionism, and while I argue that game-history is not revisionism, the only reason we can argue this is because we make a clear distinction between the different ways in which the description of historical process is being altered, and to what ends. The main difference between a historian and a game developer here, after all, is method. To reiterate, game developers do sometimes make notable claims to accuracy and use scholarly discourse, but more often than not, they emphasise how they are game-makers and not historians. They do not possess, nor attempt to possess, scholarly values or methodology. Perhaps this is the closest this book comes to answering the question of what kind of history game history really is.

Final Words

They say authors of scholarly ventures should find themselves with more new questions than actual answers. This project is no different. Perhaps the most pressing question is how the findings of this study relate to developers and games in other genres. Not all games are made equal; presumably, there are different considerations in adapting historical depictions to a first-person shooter than to a strategy game. The implications for counterfactuals likely go even further as the entire basis for agency and causation alters. There is no one-size-fits-all formula for how to turn historical research, knowledge and presupposition into game design and play. All designers and studios have their own routines and practices that will reflect on their work. They also have varying amounts of resources and strategies for making the most of said resources. To my knowledge, Paradox Development Studio is one of very few studios who keep a roster of dedicated beta testers in this way. Game-design research as well as game studies will likely benefit from continuing to highlight and contextualise games as made within a creative and commercial space. Similarities and differences in practice, as it pertains to their role in a larger societal context, would likely also interest scholars in the study of practices and design.

Additionally, different game genres have different target groups and audiences and, as such, their content is disseminated differently. Community building happens in many ways and have a variety of influence on the game design process. As noted in the present study, the relationship between designer and consumer already provides plenty of interesting and fruitful transactions and contradictions worthy of further study. In other areas and studies under-way, the abundance of multifaceted promotional material, for example developer diaries, provide great opportunities, but also contribute a possible hurdle in terms of curation and analysis. Perhaps this methodological challenge could constitute a worthwhile overlap with advances in digital humanities. Along the same lines, computational advances in qualitative as well as quantitative methodology might be applied to open-source game code with some likely interesting results.

One of the central findings of this study is the importance and influence of design legacy, both in practice and in terms of the code. This was a partly unexpected outcome that deserves a lot more attention going forwards as it might help explain why game-design paradigms are sometimes fluctuating and sometimes stagnant. As I have shown here, the influence of game-design legacy relates to most levels of game design practice – content, interface, infrastructure, community building and so on – which should warrant it as being relevant to scholars interested in the history of games and the interplay of digital and analogue games (especially considering the board-gaming boom currently taking place).

This book also contributes to issues of historical scholarship, methodology and epistemology. The field of uses of history, popular and public history certainly benefits from acknowledging the authors and producers of historical content, regardless of form. Communication and remediation of historical culture and consciousness have been treated partly as communicational discourse within which origins have been assumed rather than studied at face value. This study does not purport to paint the way humans see themselves as historical beings as any less complex than it is, nor is it exhaustive on the topic of games and historical culture, but the study does show that asking questions about the facilitation, context and practice of historical culture puts the critical reading of the artefacts in a new light and fruitfully adds to the discipline. In addition, this book can perhaps be used as a stepping-stone towards not only problematizing game developers and beta testers as historians, but historians and historical consultants in the game industry as game makers.

Finally, counterfactual history probably remains a red flag for some. Hopefully this book inspires further discussion on how to operationalise the concept in a meaningful way. Conceptually, I see partly uncharted questions on the relationship between counterfactual history and historical fictions. Likewise, the application of counterfactuals as use of history could be applied to historical endeavours in any human discourse for the benefit of capturing meaningful historical reference and historical communication.

Appendix 1
DLC and Content Packs Installed and Used for the Study

Europa Universalis IV

100 Years War Unit Pack
Art of War*
Common Sense*
Conquest of Paradise*
Cradle of Civilization*
Dharma*
El Dorado*
Mandate of Heaven*
Mare Nostrum*
Pre-Order Pack
Purple Phoenix
Res Publica*
Rights of Man*
Rule Britannia*
The Cossacks*
Third Rome*
Wealth of Nations*
Women in History

Hearts of Iron IV

Anniversary Pack
Death or Dishonor*
German Historical Portraits
Man the Guns*
Poland – United and Ready
Rocket Launcher Unit Pack
Together for Victory*
Waking the Tiger*

* Full expansion

Appendix 2
Interviews with Developers and Beta Testers

Paradox Development Studio developers

For this study, nine developers at Paradox Development Studio were interviewed. The interviews were conducted via Skype or in person. In some cases, follow-up questions were sent to the informants via e-mail. One interview was performed via Skype chat, as per the informant's request.

The developer interviews are between 60 and 120 minutes long and consist of a semi-structured conversation between the author and the informants. The interviews were framed by an interview guide. The interview guide is a list of specific questions designed to address the research questions of the study in detail. The intent was to build the interviews on open and transparent communication from the side of the researcher; that is, to ask as many direct questions as possible.[523] The interview questions were compiled into the following primary topics of conversation:
1. Gameplay and agency
2. (Historical) Meaning and representation
3. Counterfactual history
4. Causality and continuity
5. Rules and narratives

Within each topic, subsets of questions were prepared from which follow-up questions were then asked based on the informants' replies. The interviews were performed in Swedish or English. All translations – and, by extension, any mistranslations – are the responsibility of the author.

The informants were initially selected and asked to participate based on their job title and main project assignment. Designers whose job titles corresponded to the relevant game design elements to this study were approached primarily via e-mail, or in person at Paradox Interactive community events. Each informant had the opportunity to read and ask about the project, get permission from their supervisors and legal departments as well as opt out at any point until the actual interviews had taken place. Each informant was also asked to refer informants from their team to the study. The first batch of developer in-

---

[523] Steinar Kvale and Svend Brinkmann, *Den kvalitativa forskningsintervjun* (Lund: Studentlitteratur, 2009), 150–157.

formants were interviewed in mid-2017. A second round of interviews were conducted in mid-2018 in order to include some developers initially unavailable for interviews.

Table 1: Developer interviews. Details.

Code	Alias	Date	Duration	Mode
I:SH:1	Dale	15.6.2017	53:49	Skype call
I:SH:2	Dallas	26.6.2017	1:33:40	In person
I:SH:3	Daryl	26.6.2017	1:19:09	In person
I:SH:4	Delta	27.6.2017	1:22:53	In person
I:SH:5	Devin	28.6.2017	1:25:28	In person
I:SH:6	Dakota	28.6.2017	1:22:44	In person
I:SH:7	Dorian	29.6.2018	1:19:53	In person
I:SH:8	Dylan	29.6.2018	1:57:35	In person
I:SH:9	Drew	28.6.2018	1:19:11	In person

Because this study is qualitative and vertical in nature, the aim for the interviews was to go deep into the topic subjects rather than obtaining a big data sample. In contrast, a survey could potentially have generated a quantitative material of a different kind. However, considering the various obstacles concerning getting in touch with and permission to interview developer informants, securing a large enough sample for a quantitative and statistically significant study would be a tall feat, if at all possible. In an effort to keep informants' identities confidential, especially considering the small sample of informants, their genders, ages and other identifiable traits are not listed.

Beta Testers

Interviewing developers, it was made clear that Paradox Development Studio's beta testers are influential in making both games. Paradox Development Studio were thus again contacted and asked to help facilitate a connection to beta testers to be interviewed for the benefit of the study. In February 2018, an invitation to participate in the study was sent out. Nine beta testers responded and were subsequently interviewed.

Table 2: Beta tester interviews. Details.

Code	Alias	Date	Duration	Mode
I:BT:1	Bailey	13.3.2018	-	Skype text
I:BT:2	Bay	20.2.2018	1:49:54	Skype call
I:BT:3	Blaine	4.7.2018	1:32:53	Skype call
I:BT:4	Blake	20.8.2018	1:50:34	Skype call
I:BT:5	Bobbie	20.2.2018	2:52:36	Skype call
I:BT:6	Brett	4–5.7.2018	1:42:17 + 31:44	Skype call
I:BT:7	Brook	21.2.2018	59:39	Skype call
I:BT:8	Blue	20.8.2018	1:26:32	In person
I:BT:9	Brooklyn	22.10.2018	2:06:42	Skype call

The beta tester informants in this study are associated with *Europa Universalis IV*, *Hearts of Iron IV* or both.[524] The sample of beta testers who volunteered ended up being evenly distributed over the three categories. The interviews with beta testers were conducted primarily over Skype due to geographic distance. Interviews were performed in English or Swedish. The same interview guide was used as with developers with an added segment on background questions specific to the beta tester role. Like the developer interviews, each interview lasted between 60–120 minutes (with one outlier at 2 h 50 min). One interview had to be performed as Skype text, at the request of the informant.[525] The interviews were conducted in English or Swedish and a modified version of the consent form was signed for each beta tester informant. In an effort to keep informants' identities confidential, especially considering the small sample of informants, their genders, ages and other identifiable traits are not listed.

---

[524] Several beta testers also contribute or have contributed to other Paradox Development Studio titles such as *Crusader Kings* and *Stellaris*, although those games were only tangibly discussed in the interviews.

[525] The chat interview format carries specific opportunities and challenges. See for example Kvale and Brinkmann, *Den kvalitativa forskningsintervjun*, 165. In this case, the format seems to have had the most impact on scope, compared to other interviews. The overall word count for the interview is well below average, and provided fewer opportunities to ask follow-up questions.

Appendix 3
Game Analysis and Technical Reading

The game analysis was conducted in two ways: by playing the games, and by studying game files. In playing, I made frequent use of save-games as a way to go back and forth inside the game. Intermittent saving produces a series of save-points in the games that allows the player to study their progress. In comparison to, for example, screenshots or video that can only contain the information currently available on a two-dimensional screen, being able to use the in-game interface to evaluate progress is very valuable.[526] In other words, save-games can be used as a form of documentation of game states and progress and enables the researcher to go back and study the goings-on inside the game without the constraints of the one-dimensional mediums of screenshots or video capture. The outcome of using save-games is primarily the ability to track progress and back-track through iterations of a specific game session.

The other, and for the analysis, most important part of the game analysis is a technical reading of the content of game files, i.e. text files containing scripting that do not open in the game program but in a text editor, as readable text.[527] Paradox Development Studio are well-known for making their games accessible for modding. A prerequisite for modding is making game files available for people to edit. This practice must be understood in the context of commercial game-making where proprietary material is more often than not hidden from the user in order not to reveal industry secrets.[528] The benefit of this for the present study is that due to the open access of game files, all of the game information needed to study the games' content and rules has been collected into a cohesive group of text documents and made explicit (unlike for example gameplay in which the rules of the game will be more or less convoluted). Given the complexity of Paradox Development Studio games in general, convolution and unclear rulesets are commonplace. Studying the script files provides the opportunity to access all po-

---

[526] Researchers commonly use gameplay videos for research purposes. I have opted not to do so here. Video capture of gameplay, especially for digital strategy games, is a difficult material to work with for two reasons: 1) the material is not annotated or in any way searchable without external tools; 2) due to the slow and pondering nature of digital strategy games, videos end up being mostly looking at the same screen from which it is difficult to extract data or meaning due to the lack of access to menus, buttons and other UI elements.
[527] For a complete list of content packs and DLC included in the study, see Appendix 1.
[528] Arakji and Lang, "Digital Consumer Networks," 198–199.

tential scenarios at once in plain text, whereas gameplay will only illustrate the current scenario being played.

The files included in this project are located in the following folders and contain the following information:

Table 3: *Hearts of Iron IV* game files used in the study. v1.6.2.

Hearts of Iron IV

Path	Folder name	Description of content
\Hearts of Iron IV\common	Common	Rule scripting – rules and definitions for assets with a function in the game.
\Hearts of Iron IV\documentation	Documentation	Definitions of triggers and objects in scripts.
\Hearts of Iron IV\events	Events	Rule scripting for events including trigger criteria and consequence.
\Hearts of Iron IV\history	History	Scripts for traits and statistics for historical countries, states and units.
\Hearts of Iron IV\localisation	Localisation	Text for tool-tips, rules, events, flavour, news, names, etc.

Table 4: *Europa Universalis IV* game files used in the study. v1.28.3.

Europa Universalis IV

Path	Folder name	Description of content
\Europa Universalis IV\common	Common	Contains rules and definitions for assets with a function in the game.
\Europa Universalis IV\decisions	Decisions	Contains rules, definitions and prerequisites for national decisions.
\Europa Universalis IV\events	Events	Scripts for events including for example trigger criteria and effects.
\Europa Universalis IV\history	History	Scripts for traits and statistics for historical persons, countries, provinces, diplomats and wars.
\Europa Universalis IV\localisation	Localisation	Textual databases with descriptive non-code text for rules, tool-tips, events, flavour, news, names, etc.

\Europa Universalis IV\map	Map	Assets and definitions regarding the map, terrain, climate, etc.
\Europa Universalis IV\missions	Missions	Contains rules, definitions and prerequisites for missions.
\Europa Universalis IV\patchnotes	Patchnotes	Contains changes and descriptions of updates for each new patch.

Folders "Common" and "History" for both games contain a large number of subfolders with names descriptive of their content, for example Ages, Buildings and Disasters for *Europa Universalis IV* and Ideologies, National Focus and Resources for *Hearts of Iron IV*, to name just a few.

Text in the game files is here defined in two ways for clarity: script language and descriptive text. Deciphering script files as rules for scholarly purposes is what academic and game designer Robert Yang calls technical reading.[529] Scripting in game design in general bridges the content and the game engine. That is, this is where most objects and rules are situated, forming the parameters of every moveable part of the game, including their given names, relationships and traits, and adhering to a game specific logic. As a result of this, Yang argues, the code itself becomes a cultural trace of values descriptive of biases and design processes.[530] This method of analysis requires being able to understand the script language and annotation contained therein. For this purpose, I have familiarised myself with the Paradox script language using online discussion and tutorials for modding.[531]

Occasionally, script writers have added what English and new media scholar Mark Sample calls paracode – "the marginalia of the game"[532] – i.e. in-text commentary on the scripting itself. Comments in code are generally prefixed by a "#" and ignored by the engine. That is, they do not have a function other than talking about what is going on in the script or code. It is only visible to readers of the code, not inside the game. For example, a script containing traits and rules

---

[529] Robert Yang, "On 'FeministWhorePurna' and the ludo-material politics of gendered damage power-ups in Open World RPG video games," in *Queer Game Studies*, ed. Bonnie Rudberg and Adrienne Shaw, (Minneapolis: University of Minnesota Press, 2017), 104–106.
[530] Yang , "On 'FeministWhorePurna'," 104–106.
[531] Paradox Wikis. *Europa Universalis IV: Modding*. Paradox Wikis. *Hearts of Iron IV: Modding*. To my knowledge, this particular script language is developed by Paradox and not used in any other context.
[532] Mark L. Sample, "Criminal Code: Procedural Logic and Rhetorical Excess in Videogames," Digital Humanities Quarterly 7 (2013), 38. Accessed November 1, 2021. http://www.digitalhumanities.org/dhq/vol/7/1/000153/000153.html.

for a national ruler character might have the added comment "# Fictional" which indicates that this particular ruler has been invented by a developer or beta tester, perhaps for lack of a historical figure to model. These comments are typically internal and vaguely directed at other coders, script writers, testers, modders or other readers of the code. Most commonly, comments clarify something in the code or note what the outcome of a specific script is, if it is not immediately obvious. For example, the paracode below clarifies the forking counterfactual outcomes of the event "Oster Conspiracy" in which German officers are plotting to overthrow Hitler. The script writer annotates their code in order to clarify what the details of the event identifiers are (that is, the difference between for example "germany.71" and "germany.73").

> 33 = { country_event = { hours = 6 id = germany.71} } # Conspiracy defeated, but Hitler dead
> 33 = { country_event = { hours = 6 id = germany.72} } # Conspiracy defeated, Hitler survives
> 33 = { country_event = { hours = 6 id = germany.73} } # Conspiracy successful, Civil War[533]

As argued by Sample, this commentary can "help us to develop an understanding of the games as cultural objects and of coding itself as a cultural practice. [...] At the very least, they show that the "inside" of software does not always match the 'outside'."[534] Particularly with regards to studying game design practice, such code and comments complement the developer interviews in an interesting way.

As far as form and references, the game files – scripted code and descriptive text – have been treated the same way a historian would an archive depository. Footnotes and references point towards the game version and the relevant file and object in each game folder. For example, *Hearts of Iron IV* (game) Common. Ideas. Australia (subfolder), *ast_great_depression_1* (national spirit). Anyone looking at the same version of either game will be able to find the same information in their installed game files folder.

---

533 *Hearts of Iron IV.* Events. Germany.txt. *germany.70.* v1.6.2.
534 Sample "Criminal Code,", 38.

References

Primary Sources

Europa Universalis IV. Paradox Development Studio, Paradox Interactive [Win] Game version 1.28.3. 2013. Game files last collected on June 1, 2019.
Hearts of Iron IV. Paradox Development Studio, Paradox Interactive [Win] Game version 1.6.2. 2016. Game files last collected on June 1, 2019.
Interviews with game developers. Paradox Development Studio. Interviews performed between June 2017 and June 2018.
Interviews with beta testers. Paradox Development Studio. Interviews performed between January 2018 and October 2018.
Paradox Wikis. *Hearts of Iron IV.* https://hoi4.paradoxwikis.com/Hearts_of_Iron_4_Wiki.
Paradox Wikis. *Europa Universalis IV.* https://eu4.paradoxwikis.com/Europa_Universalis_4_Wiki.

Video Resources

Andersson, Johan. *PDXCON 2017: Europa Universalis – Around the world in 400 years.* Paradox Extra. Convention talk recorded at PDXCON Stockholm, May 2017. https://youtu.be/giAVw7IZCt4.
Andersson, Johan, and Martin Anward. *Europa Universalis IV – An alternate history of the game.* Paradox Interactive. Panel talk at PDXCON Berlin, October 2019. https://www.twitch.tv/videos/496641130?t=1h18m46s.
Fåhraeus, Henrik. *Emergent Stories in Crusader Kings II.* Paradox Extra. Conference talk recorded at Game Developers Conference, San Francisco, March 2016. https://youtu.be/f1Sc6segX_Q.
Fåhraeus, Henrik. *Crusader Kings 3 – PDXCON Berlin Keynote.* Paradox Interactive. Panel talk at PDXCON Berlin, October 2019. https://youtu.be/aqUZoO8WwK8.
Jorjani, Shams. *Ideas are Useless! Pitch your game to Paradox!* Paradox Extra. Convention talk recorded at PDXCON Stockholm, May 2017. https://youtu.be/_KxF0PqCwEQ.
Lind, Dan. *PDXCON 2017: Heart of Iron: Making a World War Even Bigger.* Paradox Extra. Convention talk recorded at PDXCON Stockholm, May 2017. https://youtu.be/fXIeipKaFPo.
Lind, Dan. *Hearts of Iron IV: News From the Front.* Paradox Interactive. Convention talk at PDXCON Berlin, October 2019. https://www.twitch.tv/videos/496641130?t=6h18m10s.

Bibliography

Alonge, Giaime. "Playing the Nazis: Political Implications in Analog Wargames." *Analog Game Studies* 6 (2019). https://analoggamestudies.org/2019/09/playing-the-nazis-political-implications-in-analog-wargames/.
Apperley, Thomas. "Modding the Historians' Code: Historical Verisimilitude and the Counterfactual Imagination." *Playing with the Past: Videogames and the Simulation of*

History, edited by Matthew Wilhelm Kapell and Andrew B.R. Elliott, 185–198. London: Bloomsbury, 2013.

Apperley, Thomas. "Counterfactual Communities: Strategy Games, Paratexts and the Player's Experience of History." *Open library of humanities* 41 (2018). doi: https://doi.org/10.16995/olh.286.

Arakji, Reina Y., and Karl R. Lang. "Digital Consumer Networks and Producer-Consumer Collaboration: Innovation and Product Development in the Video Game Industry." *Journal of Management Information Systems* 24 (2007): 195–219.

Arnstad, Henrik. "Får man strunta i Förintelsen?" *Svenska Dagbladet*. June 25, 2017. Accessed July 14, 2021. https://www.svd.se/far-man-strunta-i-forintelsen.

Assmann, Jan. "Collective memory and cultural identity." *New German Critique* 65 (1995): 125–133.

Aronsson, Peter. "Historiekultur, politik och historievetenskap i Norden." *Historisk tidskrift* 122 (2002): 189–208.

Aronsson, Peter. *Historiebruk – Att använda det förflutna*. Lund: Studentlitteratur, 2004.

Backe, Hans-Joachim. "A Redneck Head on a Nazi Body. Subversive Ludo-Narrative Strategies in Wolfenstein II: The New Colossus." *Arts* 7 (2018): 76. https://doi.org/10.3390/arts7040076.

Beavers, Sian. "The Informal Learning of History with Digital Games." PhD diss., Institute of Educational Technology. The Open University, 2019.

Bennedahl, Marie. *Fall in Line. Genus, kropp och minnena av det amerikanska inbördeskriget i skandinavisk reenactment*. PhD diss. Linnaeus University, 2020.

Bogost, Ian, and Will Wright. *Persuasive Games: The Expressive Power of Video Games*. Cambridge, MA: The MIT Press, 2007.

Bulut, Ergin. "One-Dimensional Creativity: A Marcusean Critique of Work and Play in the Video Game Industry." *Triple C – Communication, capitalism and critique* 16 (2018). https://www.triple-c.at/index.php/tripleC/article/view/930.

Bulut, Ergin. *A Precarious Game – The Illusion of Dream Jobs in the Video Game Industry*. New York: Cornell University Press, 2020.

Carpenter, Marie, Nabyla Daidj and Christina Moreno. "Game Console Manufacturers: The End of Sustainable Competitive Advantage?" *Digiworld Economic Journal* 94 (2014): 39–66. https://ssrn.com/abstract=2533981.

Cassone, Vincenzo Idone, and Mattia Thibault. "The HGR Framework: A Semiotic Approach to the Representation of History in Digital Games." *gamevironments* 5 (2016): 156–204.

Chandler, Heather Maxwell. *The Game Production Handbook*. 3rd ed. Burlington, MA: Jones & Bartlett Learning, LCC, 2013.

Chapman, Adam. *Digital Games as History – How digital games represent the past and give access to historical practice*. London: Routledge, 2016.

Chapman, Adam, and Jonas Linderoth. "Exploring the Limits of Play – A Case Study of Representations of Nazism in Games." In *The Dark Side of Gameplay – Controversial Issues in Playful Environments*, edited by Elvira Mortensen, Jonas Linderoth and M.L. Ashley Brown. London: Routledge, 2015.

Chapman, Adam, Anna Foka and Jonathan Westin. "Introduction: What is historical game studies?" *Rethinking History* 21, no. 3 (2017).

Clyde, Jeremie, Howard Hopkins and Glenn Wilkinson. "Beyond the 'Historical' Simulation: Using Theories of History to Inform Scholarly Game Design." *Loading. The Journal of the Canadian Game Studies Association* 9 (2012).

Copplestone, Tara. "But That's Not Accurate: The Differing Perceptions of Accuracy in Cultural-heritage Videogames between Creators, Consumers and Critics." *Rethinking History* 21 (2017): 415–438.

Costikyan, Greg. *Uncertainty in Games*. London: The MIT Press, 2013.

Danielsson Malmros, Ingmarie. *Det var en gång ett land…: Berättelser om svenskhet i historieläroböcker och elevers föreställningsvärldar*. Agerings bokförlag, 2012.

De Groot, Jerome. *Remaking History: The Past in Contemporary Historical Fictions*. London: Routledge, 2016.

De Groot, Jerome. *Consuming History: Historians and heritage in contemporary popular culture*. London & New York: Routledge, 2009.

De Miranda, Luis. "Life Is Strange and 'Games Are Made': A Philosophical Interpretation of a Multiple-Choice Existential Simulator with Co-pilot Sartre." *Games and Culture* 13 (2018).

Dening, Greg. "Performing Cross-culturally." In *Manifestos for History*, edited by Keith Jenkins, Sue Morgan and Alan Munslow. London: Routledge, 2007.

Deterding, Sebastian. "The Pyrric Victory of Game Studies: Assessing the Past, Present, and Future of Interdisciplinary Game Research." *Games and Culture* 12 (2016): 521–543.

Devereaux, Bret. "Collections: Teaching Paradox, Europa Universalis IV, Part I: State of Play." *A Collection of Unmitigated Pedantry*. April 30, 2021. https://acoup.blog/2021/04/30/collections-teaching-paradox-univeralis-iv-part-i-state-of-play/.

Domínguez, Federico Peñate. "'Heute gehört uns die Galaxie:' Music and Historical Credibility in Wolfenstein: The New Order's Nazi Dystopia." *GAME – The Italian Journal of Game Studies* 6 (2017): 71–89.

Dor, Simon. "Strategy in games or strategy games: Dictionary and encyclopaedic definitions for game studies." *Game Studies* 18 (2018). http://gamestudies.org/1801/articles/simon_dor.

Dumitrescu, Andrei. "Exclusive Hearts of Iron IV Interview with Project Lead Dan Lind." *Softpedia*. March 3, 2014. Accessed July 20, 2019. https://news.softpedia.com/news/Exclusive-Hearts-of-Iron-IV-Interview-with-Project-Lead-Dan-Lind-430287.shtml.

Evans, Richard. *Telling lies about Hitler – The Holocaus, History and David Irving Trial*. London & New York: Verso, 2002.

Evans, Richard. *Altered pasts – Counterfactuals in history*. Brandeis University Press, Historical Society of Israel, 2013.

Ferguson, Niall, ed. *Virtual History – Alternatives and Counterfactuals*. New York: Papermac, McMillan Publishers, 1999.

Fewster, Derek. *Visions of Past Glory – Nationalism and the construction of early Finnish history*. Helsinki: SKS, 2008.

Fewster, Derek. "Fallout, Memory and Values: Uses of History and Time in a Sci-Fi-driven Video Game." In *The Enduring Fantastic – Essays on Imagination and Western Culture*, edited by Anna Höglund och Cecilia Trenter. Jefferson: McFarland, 2021.

Frasca, Gonzalo. "Ludologists love stories, too: Notes from a debate that never took place." In *Level Up: Digital Games Research Conference Proceedings*, edited by Marinka Copier and Joost Raessen. Utrecht: University of Utrecht, 2003.

Frattesi, Timothy, et al. "Replayability of Video Games." Worchester, Massachusetts: Worchester Polytechnic Institute, 2011.

Gallagher, Catherine. "What Would Napoleon Do? Historical, Fictional, and Counterfactual Characters." *New Literary History* 42, no. 2 (2011): 315–336.

Gallagher, Catherine. *Telling It Like It Wasn't – The Counterfactual Imagination in History and Fiction*. Chicago: The University of Chicago Press, 2018.

Garsten, Tobias. "Europa Universalis IV." *Game Reactor*. August 26, 2013, Accessed June 30, 2021. https://www.gamereactor.se/recensioner/120054/Europa+Universalis+IV.

Gee, James. *What Video Games Have to Teach Us about Learning and Literacy*. New York: Macmillan, 2003.

Georg, Matthew. "Lesson: Railroading." *RPG Theory Review*. February 15, 2007. Accessed July 20, 2019. http://rpgtheoryreview.blogspot.com/2007/02/lesson-railroading.html.

Ghys, Tuur. "Technology Trees: Freedom and Determinism in Historical Strategy Games." *Game Studies* 12 (2012). http://www.gamestudies.org/1201/articles/tuur_ghys.

Golub, Alex, and Jon Peterson. "How Mana Left the Pacific and Became a Video Game Mechanic." *New Mana: Transformations of a Classic Concept in Pacific Languages and Cultures*, edited by Matt Tomlinson and Ty P. Kāwika Tengan. Canberra: ANU Press, The Australian National Library, 2016.

Goodfellow, Troy. Introduction to *Europa Universalis IV: What if? The Anthology of Alternate History*, edited by Tomas Harenstam. Stockholm: Paradox Books, 2014.

Hafer, Leana. "Hearts of Iron 4 review." *IGN Magazine*. June 6, 2016. Accessed October 22, 2018. https://www.ign.com/articles/2016/06/06/1558481.

Halbawchs, Mauritz. *On Collective Memory*, Chicago: University of Chicago Press, 1992.

Hall, Charlie. "Hearts of Iron IV Review." *Polygon*. July 19, 2016. Accessed December 2, 2018. https://www.polygon.com/2016/7/19/12215976/hearts-of-iron-4-review.

Hall, Charlie. "Hearts of Iron DLC lets players revive the Confederacy, decolonize the British Empire." *Polygon*. February 14, 2019. Accessed November 20, 2019. https://www.polygon.com/2019/2/14/18224986/hearts-of-iron-4-dlc-man-the-guns-confederacy.

Hall, Charlie. "Solving Paradox: How the historical strategy game maker stayed alive." *Polygon*. August 7, 2013. Accessed October 4, 2020. https://www.polygon.com/features/2013/8/7/4554042/paradox-interactive-history.

Hammar, Emil Lundedal. "Counter-hegemonic play, marginalized pasts and the politics of play in *Assassin's Creed: Freedom Cry*." *Rethinking History* 21 (2017): 372–395. doi.org/10.1080/13642529.2016.1256622.

Hammar, Emil Lundedal. "Producing and Playing Hegemonic Pasts. Historical Digital Games as Memory-Making Media." PhD dissertation. The Arctic University of Norway, 2020.

Hammond, Phil, and Holger Pözsch, eds. *War Games: Memory, Militarism and the Subject of Play*. London: Bloomsbury, 2020.

Harenstam, Tomas, ed. *Europa Universalis IV: What if? The Anthology of Alternate History*. Stockholm: Paradox Books. 2014.

Hocking, Clint. "Ludonarrative Dissonance in Bioshock." *Click Nothing*. October 7, 2007. Accessed October 25, 2019. https://clicknothing.typepad.com/click_nothing/2007/10/ludonarrative-d.html.

Holdenried, Joshua D., and Nicolas Trépanier. "Dominance and the Aztec Empire: Representations in *Age of Empires II* and *Medieval II: Total War*." In *Playing with the*

Past – Digital Games and the Simulation of the Past, edited by Matthew Kapell and Andrew B.R. Elliott. London: Bloomsbury, 2013.

Houghton, Robert. "History Games for Boys? Gender, Genre and The Self-Perceived Impact of Historical Computer Games on Undergraduates." *Gamevironments* 5 (2016): 8–45.

Houghton, Robert. "Where Did You Learn That? The Self-Perceived Educational Impact of Historical Computer Games on Undergraduate Historians." *Gamevironments* 14 (2021): 1–49.

Hung, Richard. "Hearts of Iron Review." *Gamespew*. June 7, 2016. Accessed May 26, 2019. https://www.gamespew.com/2016/06/hearts-iron-iv-review/.

Hutchinson, Andrew. "Makin the Water Move: Techno-Historic Limits in the Game Aesthetics of Myst and Doom." *Game Studies* 8 (2008). http://gamestudies.org/0801/articles/hutch.

Idle Thumbs. *Three Moves Ahead* podcast, episode 473, July 12, 2019. Accessed July 31, 2019.

Juul, Jesper. "Games Telling Stories? A Brief Note on Narrative and Games." *Game Studies* 1 (2001).

Juul, Jesper. *The Art of Failure – An Essay on the Pain of Playing Video Games*. London: The MIT Press. 2013.

Kagen, Melissa. "Walking, Talking and Playing with Masculinities in *Firewatch*." *Game Studies* 18 (2018). http://gamestudies.org/1802/articles/kagen.

Kapell, Matthew, and Andrew B.R. Elliott. editors. *Playing with the Past: Digital Games and the Simulation of History*. London: Bloomsbury, 2013.

Karlsson, Klas-Göran, and Ulf Zander, eds. *Historien är nu – En introduktion till historiedidaktiken*. Lund: Studentlitteratur. 2009.

Karlsson, Maria. *Cultures of Denial – Comparing Holocaust and Armenian Genocide Denial*. PhD diss. Lund University, 2015.

Kemmer, Matthias. "The Politics of Post-Apocalypse: Interactivity, Narrative Framing and Ethics in *Fallout 3*." In *Politics in Fantasy Media – Essays on Ideology and Gender in Fiction, Film, Television and Games*, edited by Gerold Sedlmayr and Nicole Waller, 97–117. Jefferson: McFarland, 2014.

Kempshall, Chris. "War collaborators: documentary and historical sources in First World War computer games." *First World War Studies* 10 (2020): 225–244.

Klabbers, Jan H.G. "Tensions between meaning construction and persuasion in games." *Game Studies* 11 (2011). http://gamestudies.org/1102/articles/klabbers_book_review.

Koebel, Greg. "Simulating the Ages of Man: Periodization in *Civilization V* and *Europa Universalis IV*." *Loading… The Journal of the Canadian Game Studies Association* 10 (2018): 60–76.

Kücklich, Julian. "Precarious Playbour: Modders and the Digital Games Industry." *The Fibreculture Journal* 5 (2005).

Kultima, Annakaisa, and Alyea Sandovar. "Game Design Values." Proceedings of *AcademicMindtrek'16* (2016). doi/10.1145/2994310.2994362.

Kultima, Annakaisa. "Casual Game Design Research." In *Proceedings of Mindtrek, Tampere, Finland*. 2009.

Kultima, Annakaisa. "Multidisciplinary Game Design Research – Ontologies and Other Remarks." In *Game Design Research*, edited by Petri Lankoski and Jussi Holopainen. ETC Press, 2017.

Kultima, Annakaisa. "Game Design Praxiology." PhD diss. University of Tampere, 2018.
Köstlbauer, Josef. "The Strange Attraction of Simulation: Realism, Authenticity, Virtuality." In *Playing With the Past – Digital Games and the Simulation of History*, edited by Matthew Kapell and Andrew B.R. Elliott. London: Bloomsbury. 2013.
Kvale, Steinar and Brinkmann, Svend. *Den kvalitativa forskningsintervjun*. Lund: Studentlitteratur. 2009.
Liu, Rue. "L.A Noir's Rockstar Teams Up With L.A. Times For Interactive 1947 Crime Map." In *Slash Gear*. May 5, 2011. Accessed April 14, 2020. https://www.slashgear.com/l-a-noires-rockstar-teams-up-with-l-a-times-for-interactive-1947-crime-map-05150481/.
Loban Rhett, and Thomas Apperley. "Eurocentric Values at Play: Modding the Colonial from the Indigenous Perspective." In *Video Games and the Global South*, edited by Phillip Penix-Tadsen. Pittsburgh: ETC Press. 2019.
Madrigal, Alexis C. "The Hardcore Archival Research Behind 'L.A. Noire'." *The Atlantic*. June 6, 2011. Accessed April 14, 2020. https://www.theatlantic.com/technology/archive/2011/06/the-hardcore-archival-research-behind-la-noire/239964/.
Majkowski, Thomas Z., and Katarzyna Suszkiewicz. "Cardboard Genocide. Board Game Design as a Tool in Holocaust Education." *GAME – The Italian Journal of Game Studies* 9 (2020). https://www.gamejournal.it/cardboard-genocide/.
McCall, Jeremiah. *Gaming the Past: Using Video Games in Teaching Secondary History*. London: Routledge, 2011.
McCall, Jeremiah. "Navigating the Problem Space: The Medium of Simulation Games in the Teaching of History." *The History Teacher* 46 (2012): 9–28.
McCall, Jeremiah. "The Historical Problem Space Framework: Games as a Historical Medium." *Game Studies* 20 (2020). http://gamestudies.org/2003/articles/mccall.
McCall, Jeremiah. "Video games as Participatory Public History." In *A Companion to Public History*, edited by David Dean. Hoboken: John Wiley & Sons Ltd., 2018.
McCall, Jeremiah. *GTP Designer Talk Podcast – Jon Shafer*. July 3, 2019. Accessed July 15, 2019. https://gamingthepast.net/2019/07/03/gtp-designer-talk-2-jon-shafer/.
McCarthy, Caty. "Interview with Paradox CEO Ebba Ljungerud." *US Gamer*. March 19, 2019. Accessed May 10, 2019. https://www.usgamer.net/articles/the-paradox-way-paradox-interactive-ceo-strategy-games-interview-dice-summit.
McClancy, Kathleen. "The Wasteland of the Real: Nostalgia and Simulacra in *Fallout*." *Game Studies* 18 (2018).
Mereu, Marco, et al. "Digital Distribution and Games as a Service." *Science and Technology Law Review* 16, no. 14 (2013). https://scholar.smu.edu/scitech/vol16/iss1/14.
Metacritic. "Europa Universalis IV." https://www.metacritic.com/game/pc/europa-universalis-iv/critic-reviews.
Metacritic. "Hearts of Iron IV." Accessed June 30, 2021. https://www.metacritic.com/game/pc/hearts-of-iron-iv/critic-reviews.
Mol, Angus A.A. "Toying With History: Counterplay, Counterfactuals, and the Control of the Past." In *History in Games – Contingencies of an Authentic Past*, edited by Martin Lorber and Felix Zimmerman. Bielefeld: transcript, 2020.
Mukherjee, Souvik. "The playing fields of Empire: Empire and spatiality in video games." *Journal of Gaming and Virtual Worlds* 7 (2015): 299–315. https://doi.org/10.1386/jgvw.7.3.299_1.

Mukherjee, Souvik. "Playing Subaltern: Video Games and Postcolonialism." *Games and Culture* 13 (2016). https://doi.org/10.1177/1555412015627258.
Mukherjee, Souvik. "Video Games and Slavery." *Transactions of the Digital Games Research Association* 3 (2016). https://doi.org/10.26503/todigra.v2i3.60.
Mäyrä, Frans. "Getting into the game: Doing multidisciplinary game studies." In *The Video Game Theory Reader 2*, edited by Bernard Perron and Mark J.P Wolf, 313–329. New York: Routledge, 2009.
Nikolaidou, Dimitra. "The Wargame Legacy: How Wargames Shaped the Roleplaying Experience from Tabletop to Digital Games." In *War Games: Memory, Militarism and the Subject of Play*, edited by Phil Hammon and Holger Pözsch. London: Bloomsbury, 2020.
Nohr, Rolf. "The game is the medium. The game is the message." In *Early Modernity in Video Games*, edited by Tobias Winnerling and Florian Kerschbaumer. Newcastle upon Tyne: Cambridge Scholars Publishing, 2014.
O'Donnell, Casey. "The Work/Play of the Interactive New Economy: Video Game Development in the United States and India." PhD diss. Rensselaer Polytechnic Institute, 2008.
O'Donnell, Casey. *Developer's Dilemma – The Secret World of Videogame Creators.* Cambridge: MIT Press, 2014.
Paradox Interactive. "Paradox Interactive Announces Grand Success for Grand Strategy Titles." Press release, June 21, 2017. Accessed June 30 2021. https://www.paradoxinteractive.com/media/press-releases/press-release/paradox-interactive-announces-grand-successes-for-grand-strategy-titles.
Paradox Interactive. "Hearts of Iron Celebrates One Million Sales with Anniversary Edition." Press release, May 19, 2018. Accessed June 30, 2021. https://www.paradoxinteractive.com/media/press-releases/press-release/hearts-of-iron-iv-celebrates-one-million-sales-with-anniversary-edition.
Paradox Interactive. "Revenue Model." Accessed July 14, 2021. https://www.paradoxinteractive.com/our-company/our-business/revenue-model.
Paradox Plaza. *Victoria 3 – Dev Diary #15 – Slavery.* Victoria III Developer Diary by Wizzington, September 16, 2021. Accessed November 15, 2021. https://forum.paradoxplaza.com/forum/developer-diary/victoria-3-dev-diary-15-slavery.1490983/.
Paradox Plaza. *Crusader Kings II: Sunset Invasion DLC – Dev Diary* by Doomdark. Crusader Kings II Developer Diary. November 2, 2012. Accessed July 31, 2021. https://forum.paradoxplaza.com/forum/index.php?threads/crusader-kings-ii-sunset-invasion-dlc-dev-diary.644976/.
Paradox Plaza. *Our Vision* by podcat. Hearts of Iron IV Developer Diary by podcat. February 7, 2014. Accessed June 12, 2019. https://forum.paradoxplaza.com/forum/index.php?threads/hearts-of-iron-iv-development-diary-1-our-vision.754427/.
Paradox Plaza. *Top 23 Most Played Countries* by Wiz. June 23, 2015. Accessed August 21, 2019. https://forum.paradoxplaza.com/forum/index.php?threads/top-23-most-played-countries.865345/.
Paradox Plaza. *EU4 without monarch points* by Taure. December 30, 2017. Accessed April 16, 2018. https://forum.paradoxplaza.com/forum/index.php?threads/eu4-without-monarch-points.1062864/.
Paradox Plaza. *CK2 Dev Diary #18: Optimization and modding* by Meneth. Crusader Kings II Developer Diary. August 9, 2016. Accessed July 29, 2021. https://forum.paradoxplaza.com/forum/index.php?threads/hearts-of-iron-iv-development-diary-1-our-vision.754427/.

Paradox Plaza. *HOI4 Dev Diary – Patch 1.3.3 Update #2* by podcat. Hearts of Iron IV Developer Diary. February 15, 2017.
Patrick, Stephen J. "The History of Wargaming." In *Wargame Design. The history, production and use of conflict simulation games, including a new completely updated comprehensive wargame directory*, edited by Stephen J. Patrick et al. New York: Hippocrene Books, 1983.
Pennington, Michael John. "Authentic-Lite Rhetoric: The Curation of Partial Historical Interpretations in *Hearts of Iron IV*." PhD. diss. Bath Spa University, 2021.
Peterson, Rolfe Daus, Andrew Justin Miller and Sean Joseph Fedorko. "The Same River Twice: Exploring Historical Representation and the Value of Simulation in the *Total War*, *Civilization*, and *Patrician* Franchises." In *Playing With the Past – Digital Games and the Simulation of History*, edited by Matthew W. Kapell and Andrew B.R. Elliott. London: Bloomsbury. 2013.
Pfister, Eugen. "Why History in Digital Games Matters – Historical Authenticity as a Language for Ideological Myths." In *History in Games – Contingencies of an Authentic Past*, edited by Martin Lorber and Felix Zimmermann. Bielefeld: transcript, 2020.
Plunkett, Luke. "Hearts of Iron IV: The Kotaku Review." *Kotaku*, June 6, 2016. Accessed December 2, 2018. https://kotaku.com/hearts-of-iron-iv-the-kotaku-review-1780258434.
Prendergast, Christopher. *Counterfactuals – Paths of the Might Have Been*. London: Bloomsbury, 2019.
Rochat, Yannick. "A Quantitative Study of Historical Videogames (1981–2015)." In *Historia Ludens – The Playing Historian*, edited by Alexander von Lünen et al. London: Routledge, 2019.
Rollinger, Christian, Filippo Carlà-Uhink and Martin Lindner, eds. *Classical Antiquity in Video Games: Playing with the Ancient World*. London: Bloomsbury. 2020.
Roy, Gilles. "Being historical: How Strategy Games are Changing Popular History." *Play the Past*. September 24, 2014. Accessed April 18, 2019. http://www.playthepast.org/?p=4952.
Sabin, Philip. "Wargaming in higher education: Contributions and challenges." *Arts and Humanities in Higher Education* 14 (2015): 329–348. DOI: 10.1177/1474022215577216.
Salt, Chris. "The History and Future of Paradox Grand Strategy Interview with Johan Andersson." *Space Sector*, February 7, 2014. Accessed July 1, 2021. https://www.spacesector.com/blog/2014/02/the-history-and-future-of-paradox-grand-strategy/.
Sample, Mark L. "Criminal Code: Procedural Logic and Rhetorical Excess in Videogames." *Digital Humanities Quarterly* 7 (2013). Accessed November 1, 2021. http://www.digitalhumanities.org/dhq/vol/7/1/000153/000153.html.
Sicart, Miguel. "Against Procedurality." *Game Studies* 11 (2011). http://gamestudies.org/1103/articles/sicart_ap.
Sjöland, Marianne. *Historia från tidskriftsredaktionen – En komparativ studie av* Populär Historias *och* History Todays *historieskrivning*. PhD diss. Lund University, 2016.
Shaw, Adrienne. "The Tyranny of Realism: Historical accuracy and politics of representation in *Assassin's Creed III*." *Loading... The journal of Canadian Game Studies Association* 14 (2015): 9–24.
Southgate, Beverley. *History meets fiction*. London: Pearson Education Limited, 2009.
Spring, Dawn. "Gaming history: computer and video games as historical scholarship." *Rethinking History* 19 (2015): 207–221.

Stenros, Jaakko. "Playfulness, Play, and Games: A Constructionist Ludology Approach," Phd. diss. University of Tampere, 2015.
Stenros, Jaakko, and Annakaisa Kultima. "On the Expanding Ludosphere." *Simulation & Gaming* 49 (2018).
Säfström, Orvar, and Jimmy Wilhelmsson. *Äventyrsspel – Bland mutanter, drakar och demoner*. Malmö: Bokfabriken. 2017.
Tetlock, Philip E., and Aaron Belkin, eds. *Counterfactual Thought Experiments in World Politics – Locigal, Methodological, and Phsychological Perspectives*. Princeton: Princeton University Press, 1997.
Tetlock, Philip E., Richard N. Lebow and Geoffrey Parker, eds. *Unmaking the West – "What-if?" Scenarios That Rewrite World History*. Ann Arbor: The University of Michigan Press, 2006.
Traynor, Lisa, and Jonathan Ferguson. "Shooting for Accuracy: Historicity and Video Gaming." In *Historia Ludens – The Playing Historian*, edited by Alexander Von Lünen et al. London: Routledge. 2020.
Trumbull, Jack. "Hearts of Iron IV is better than ever but its remaining flaws are becoming more obvious." *Wargamer.com*. March 7, 2019. Accessed July 20, 2019. https://legacy.wargamer.com/hearts-of-iron-4-1-6-ironclad-ww2/.
Vahlo, Jukka. "IN GAMEPLAY – The Invariant Structures and Varieties of the Video Game Gameplay Experience." PhD diss. University of Turku, 2018.
Von Lünen, Alexander et al., eds. *Historia Ludens – The Playing Historian*. London: Routledge, 2019.
van Roessel, Lies, and Jan Švelch. "Who Creates Microstransactions: The Production Context of Video Game Monetizatio." In *Game Production Studies*, edited by Olli Sotamaa and Jan Švelch. Amsterdam: Amsterdam University Press. 2021.
Wainwright, A. Martin. *Virtual History – How Videogames Portray the Past*. London: Routledge. 2019.
Walsh, Richard. "Emergent Narrative in Interactive Media." *Narrative* 19 (2011), 72–85.
Willard, Mary Beth. "Constructing Creativity." In *LEGO and Philosophy, Constructing Reality Brick by Brick*, edited by William Irwin, Roy T. Cook and Sondra Bacharach. Hoboken: John Wiley & Sons, 2017.
Wilson, Douglas, and Miguel Sicart. "Now It's Personal: On Abusive Game Design." Author version. Proceedings of *FuturePlay 2010*. https://www.miguelsicart.net/publications/Abusive_Game_Design.pdf.
Winkie, Luke. "The struggle over gamers who use mods to create racist alternate histories." Kotaku. June 6, 2018. Accessed on July 1, 2018. https://kotaku.com/the-struggle-over-gamers-who-use-mods-to-create-racist-1826606138.
Wright, Esther. "Marketing Authenticity: Rockstar Games and the Use of Cinema in Video Game Production." *Kinephanos* 7 (2017): 131–164.
Wright, Esther. "On the Promotional Context of Historical Video Games." *Rethinking History* 22 (2018): 598–608.
Wright, Esther. "Rockstar Games and American History." PhD dissertation. University of Warwick, 2019.
Yang, Robert. "On 'FeministWhorePurna' and the ludo-material politics of gendered damage power-ups in Open World RPG video games." In *Queer Game Studies*, edited by B. Rudberg and Shaw. Minneapolis: University of Minnesota Press, 2017.

Zacny, Rob. "Hearts of Iron IV Review." June 9, 2016. Accessed December 10, 2018. https://www.pcgamer.com/hearts-of-iron-4-review/.

Zander, Ulf. "Holocaust at the Limits: Historical Culture and the Nazi Genocide in the Television Era." In *Echoes of the Holocaust: Historical Cultures in Contemporary Europe*, edited by Klas-Göran Karlsson and Ulf Zander, 255–257. Lund: Nordic Academic Press, 2003.

Zander, Ulf. "Lee, Charlottesville och statystriderna i södern: försoning, fortsatt förslavande eller främlingsfientlighet?" In *Historielärarnas förenings årsskrift*, 39–50. Lund, 2018.

Zerubavel, Eviatar. *Time maps – Collective memory and the social shape of the past*. Chicago: University of Chicago Press, 2003.

Zimmerman, Eric. "Narrative, Interactivity, Play, and Games: Four Naughty Concepts in Need of Discipline." In *First Person. New Media as Story, Performance, and Game*, edited by Noah Wardrip-Fruin and Pat Harrigan. Cambridge: The MIT Press, 2004.

Zimmerman, Eric. "Gaming Literacy: Game Design as a Model for Literacy in the Twenty-First Century." In *The Video Game Theory Reader 2*, edited by Bernard Perron and Mark J.P. Wolf. London: Routledge. 2008.

Games Mentioned

Assassin's Creed series. Ubisoft Montreal, Ubisoft [Multiple platforms] 2007–.
Battlefield 1. Digital Illusions CE, Electronic Arts. [Multiple platforms] 2016.
Call of Duty series. Infinity Ward, Treyarch, Sledgehammer Games, Activision [Multiple platforms] 2003–.
Cities Skylines. Colossal Order, Paradox Interactive. [Multiple platforms] 2015.
Crusader Kings series. Paradox Development Studio. Strategy First. Paradox Interactive. [Win and Mac OS X] 2004.
Doom. id Software [Multiple platforms] 1993.
Dungeons and Dragons series. Gary Gyrax & Dave Ameson, TSR, Wizards of the Coast [Table top] 1974.
Empire of Sin. Romero Games, Paradox Interactive [Multiple platforms]. 2020.
Europa Universalis. Thibaut & de Scorraille. Azure Wish Enterprise [Board game] 1993.
Europa Universalis I. Paradox Development Studio, Strategy First, Typhoon Games [Win] 2020.
Europa Universalis II. Paradox Development Studio, Strategy First, Typhoon Games, PAN Vision [Win] 2001.
Europa Universalis III. Paradox Development Studio, Paradox Interactive [Win and Mac OS X] 2007.
Europa Universalis IV. Paradox Development Studio, Paradox Interactive [Win, Mac OS X, Linux] 2013.
Fallout series. Bethesda Softworks. Interplay Entertainment. [Multiple platforms] 1997–.
Hearts of Iron III. Paradox Development Studio. Paradox Interactive. [PC and Mac OS X] 2009.
Hearts of Iron IV. Paradox Development Studio. Paradox Interactive. [PC and Mac OS X] 2016.
Imperator: Rome. Paradox Development Studio. Paradox Interactive. [PC and Mac OS X] 2019.
Magicka. Arrowhead Game Studios. Paradox Interactive. [Multiple platforms] 2011.

Medal of Honor series. DreamWorks Interactive et al., Electronic Arts. [Multiple Platforms] 1999–.
My Memory of Us. Juggler Games. Crunching Koalas [Multiple platforms] 2018.
Myst. Cyan (Ryan Miller, Robyn Miller) [Multiple platforms] 1993.
Red Dead Redemption series. Rockstar San Diego, Rockstar Games [Multiple platforms] 2010–.
Stellaris. Paradox Development Studio. Paradox Interactive. [Multiple Platforms] 2016.
This War of Mine. 11 Bit Studios. Crunching Koalas. [Multiple Platforms] 2014.
Valiant Hearts: The Great War. Ubisoft Montpellier. Ubisoft. [Multiple Platforms] 2014.
Victoria: An Empire Under the Sun. Paradox Entertainment. PAN Vision, Strategy First. [PC and Mac OS X] 2003.
Victoria II. Paradox Development Studio. Paradox Interactive. [PC and Mac OS X] 2010.
Victoria II: Heart of Darkness. Paradox Development Studio. Paradox Interactive. [PC and Mac OS X] 2013.
Victoria III. Paradox Development Studio. Paradox Interactive. [Multiple platforms] Forthcoming.
Wolfenstein: The New Order. Machinegames. Bethesda Softsworks. [Multiple platforms] 2014.
Wolfenstein II: The New Colossus. Machinegames. Bethesda Softworks. [Multiple platforms] 2017.

Index

abstraction 166
achievements 33, 35, 86, 129–132, 134, 136 f., 141, 144, 150 f., 153, 155, 171, 173, 194, 201
administration 34, 39 f.
advocate 107 f.
aftermath 3, 12, 125, 146, 155, 163
agency 12, 40 f., 57, 65, 70, 76, 82, 85, 110, 113, 127, 142 f., 158, 175 f., 181, 187, 189, 200, 202, 205, 208
ahistorical 32, 144 f., 181
alternate history 32, 70, 128, 177, 215
ambivalence 188
American Civil War 125, 144, 151, 175–178, 196, 214
American War of Independence 33
animation 37
Apperley, Tom 7–9, 21, 91, 108, 116, 132 f., 140, 168, 181, 189
art 15, 21, 74, 86, 88, 131 f., 172, 186 f., 207, 224 f.
artificial intelligence 13, 30, 38, 40, 44–49, 53, 55 f., 59, 74 f., 86, 95, 109, 127, 132–134, 141 f., 144–147, 152, 156 f., 173, 177, 186 f., 200 f.
Assassin's Creed 78, 131 f., 140, 181, 224
assets 5, 39, 68 f., 74, 80, 86, 89, 160, 172 f., 212 f.
attraction 9, 21, 110, 169
Austria-Hungary 10, 143, 151, 157, 171, 197
authenticity 3, 9, 20, 77 f., 103, 164, 183 f., 186, 191
– authentic 3, 20, 48, 65, 142, 183, 186, 191, 195
Aztec 7, 11, 132, 137–141, 156, 195

Battlefield 1 78, 224
Battle of Varna 33
benchmark 106
beta tester 5, 20, 25, 45, 56, 58, 61, 66, 74–85, 87, 91–109, 111–121, 128, 133 f., 141, 145, 155 f., 159–175, 177, 181 f., 184–188, 190 f., 193 f., 197–199, 201 f., 205 f., 208–210, 214 f.
– tester 99 f., 102, 105 f., 170, 214
bias 6, 9 f., 122 f., 197, 213
books 3, 87, 94, 97–99, 102, 108, 119, 128
brainstorm 99–104, 117
budget 165 f.
bugs 100, 164
– bug hunting 75, 100, 103, 198
– bug tickets 79
Byzantium 29, 33, 134–136, 150

Call of Duty 224
canon 137, 151, 169, 174, 177, 197
causality 5, 9, 11, 41, 57, 59, 65, 83, 125 f., 128, 133, 142, 152, 154, 156, 172, 182, 185 f., 195 f., 208
challenge 6, 11, 21, 29, 35, 51, 56, 64, 70, 90, 95, 107, 112 f., 129, 131 f., 143, 145, 153, 157, 170, 186, 191, 197, 201, 203, 205, 210
chance 7, 15, 34, 42, 59, 125, 127 f., 133, 143, 146, 157, 173, 178, 184, 187
chaos 9, 125, 127, 133, 157, 187
Chapman, Adam 6, 8, 19, 22, 28, 57, 64, 76, 113 f., 128, 142, 157, 166, 168, 175 f., 180, 189 f.
Cities Skylines 67, 224
Clausewitz 22, 79
code 7–9, 14, 24, 61, 78, 82, 89 f., 108, 138, 164, 194, 200 f., 204 f., 209 f., 212–214
colonialism 90 f., 102, 116, 155, 177, 192, 195
colonisation 40, 111, 116, 137, 139, 153, 187
company structure 66
conceptual-simulation style 166
conflict 4, 29 f., 43, 45, 94, 128, 146, 148 f., 165, 175, 187, 197, 204
content design 5, 75, 100, 102, 106, 121, 141, 155 f., 172
– creation 20, 86, 102 f., 107, 117, 119, 153, 184

Index — 227

– designer 74, 82, 87, 117, 119, 198
contingency 5, 12, 41, 59, 62, 65, 125, 133, 152, 154, 195
continuity 5, 10, 27, 63, 125 f., 167, 181, 208
control 41, 43, 45, 64 f., 77, 137, 141, 144, 149 f., 157, 164, 170, 179, 195
counterfactual history 1 f., 4, 7 f., 10, 12, 14, 17, 21, 24, 26 f., 46, 56, 60, 65 f., 73 f., 78, 82, 85 f., 113, 121–123, 125 f., 133, 137, 141–143, 156–161, 163, 167–170, 183, 186 f., 190 f., 193 f., 199–204, 206, 208
creativity 30, 46, 57, 70, 72–74, 89, 94 f., 104 f., 107–109, 119, 129, 159, 205
criteria 13, 35, 41, 58, 62, 103, 114, 127, 129, 131, 136, 138, 146, 158, 161, 184 f., 195 f., 203, 212
Crusader Kings 23 f., 57, 68, 73, 77, 81, 92, 95, 101, 136 f., 140 f., 180, 210, 215, 224

decision-making 23, 41, 53, 73, 79, 85, 95, 117, 119, 143 f., 159, 164, 202
design
– ambition 108
– legacy 5, 26, 63 f., 88, 90, 93, 116, 119–121, 140, 142, 159, 167, 194, 197, 199, 204–206
– practice 1, 5, 16, 19, 21, 26, 80, 84 f., 88, 92, 96, 107–110, 112–114, 116–119, 150, 152, 156, 159, 162, 164 f., 168, 173, 175, 178, 181, 185 f., 189–192, 198, 200–203
– values 3, 8, 14, 16, 21, 25 f., 66, 70, 73, 75, 89, 107 f., 108, 116–118, 121, 126, 140, 165, 167, 175, 181 f., 190, 197, 201, 204 f., 213
– work 82, 100, 104, 182, 202
determinism 86, 125 f., 158, 172
developer studies 6, 17–19, 21
digital distribution 24, 67 f., 79, 129, 204
diplomacy 30, 38, 40 f., 50, 53, 179
discrepancies 159, 177, 202
diversity 13, 166
Doom 80, 167, 224

downloadable content 31, 68, 193
– DLC 45, 68 f., 79, 103 f., 118, 137, 140 f., 143, 165, 172, 177, 184, 193, 195, 198, 204, 207, 211
Dungeons and Dragons 32, 224

Early modern 4, 7, 23, 28, 30, 41, 61, 69, 73, 83, 85, 115, 150, 152 f., 192, 202
economic history 88
education 18, 21, 115, 183
emergent stories 56 f., 70, 127–129, 170, 215
Empire of Sin 23, 224
entertainment 3, 6, 8, 26, 67, 72, 107, 112–115, 120, 150, 153, 159, 165, 168, 174 f., 189–192, 197, 199, 202 f., 224 f.
epistemology 6, 8, 16, 126, 159, 199, 203 f., 206
Eurocentrism 8, 28, 90 f., 116, 140, 153, 181, 195
Europa Universalis 14, 23 f., 32, 66, 69 f., 93, 95, 101, 103, 116, 118, 139, 179, 186, 194, 212 f., 215, 224
– *Europa Universalis I* 224
– *Europa Universalis II* 91, 132, 224
– *Europa Universalis III* 31 f., 65, 224
– *Europa Universalis IV* 1, 4–7, 9, 11, 14 f., 17, 23–37, 39–41, 43–47, 49–51, 53, 57–61, 64–66, 68–70, 73–75, 79–86, 88–91, 93, 95–97, 99, 101, 103–106, 110, 112, 115–121, 125–142, 146 f., 150–157, 159 f., 162 f., 165–167, 169 f., 172–176, 178–185, 187, 190–196, 200 f., 204, 207, 210, 212 f., 215, 224
evaluate 21, 95, 98, 125 f., 132, 211
Evans, Richard 4, 10, 122 f., 126, 146 f., 149 f., 152, 157
evidence 90, 126, 157, 161, 194
expansion 24, 31, 35, 40 f., 43, 45 f., 64, 67–69, 79, 91, 93, 104, 116, 138, 140 f., 143, 164, 170, 181, 193, 200, 207
experiment 8, 72, 125, 128

fact 4, 22, 27, 41, 44, 60, 65, 79, 83, 90 f., 96, 98, 103–105, 111 f., 115, 123 f., 126, 141, 152, 165–167, 176, 179 f., 182 f., 191, 196 f., 202

Fallout 14 f., 224
fans 80, 108, 117, 198
– fan gatherings 109
fantasy 14, 32, 113, 127
feedback 67, 79, 96, 100, 105, 108, 156, 169, 191
Ferguson, Niall 5, 8, 77, 126 f., 157, 168 f., 184
fiction 4, 9, 14, 149, 177 f., 183, 191, 206
First World War 10 f., 21, 78, 110, 125, 127
– Great War 110, 143, 154
flavour text 139 f., 147, 149
foil 177, 191, 198
French Revolution 33, 35
fun 43, 88, 95, 97, 105 f., 111–114, 116, 150, 160, 170, 184, 191, 199
funding 66
future 18, 23–25, 32, 44, 77, 119, 125, 148, 151, 189, 201 f.
future fiction 10–12, 14 f., 120–122, 124–126, 146–148, 150 f., 154–157, 169, 171, 196, 200

Gallagher, Catherine 4, 9, 124
game design 1 f., 5, 13, 15–20, 22 f., 26, 63, 70, 74–77, 82, 84, 88–91, 94–96, 99 f., 106–108, 112, 114–116, 118–120, 126, 152 f., 159, 162, 164, 166 f., 170, 172 f., 179, 182–185, 187–190, 193, 197, 199–201, 203, 205, 208, 213
game design conventions 5
game design practice 1 f., 6, 9 f., 12, 14 f., 17, 19 f., 25–27, 58, 63, 66, 73–76, 78 f., 84, 90, 93, 96 f., 99, 107, 112, 117 f., 120 f., 123, 137, 141, 157–159, 161, 164–169, 174, 177, 180 f., 183 f., 186, 188–191, 196, 199 f., 204, 206, 214
gameplay 4–6, 9, 12–17, 21, 23 f., 26–31, 35 f., 38–42, 44–46, 51, 53, 56–58, 61, 63–66, 69 f., 72 f., 75, 80, 83–86, 92, 103 f., 107–109, 111, 113 f., 116, 118–122, 126–129, 131–133, 142–144, 146, 151, 153, 155–157, 159, 161–164, 169 f., 174–176, 178, 181 f., 184, 186–189, 191, 194–197, 199–204, 208, 211 f.
gameplay values 3, 6, 8, 14, 16, 22, 25 f., 31, 66, 70 73, 75, 89, 107 f., 116–118, 119 f., 121, 126, 140, 165, 167, 181 f., 190, 197, 204 f., 213
game production 16, 20, 69, 79, 94, 105, 199
game studies 6 f., 13–19, 24, 27, 78, 80, 86, 110, 114 f., 189, 205, 213
game world 28, 30, 35, 49 f., 129, 131, 156, 169, 180–182, 192
genre 1, 4, 10, 13 f., 22, 24, 26–28, 33, 63 f., 87–90, 93, 95 f., 99, 110, 133, 153, 159, 161, 165 f., 169, 175, 179 f., 182, 188, 193 f., 197, 200, 202 f., 205
– genre convention 5, 14, 16, 63, 90, 116, 119 f., 165–167, 194, 202
Germany 4, 7, 12, 15, 42, 48, 53, 55, 59 f., 83, 110, 125, 136, 143, 146–148, 154, 157, 171, 173, 187, 196, 204, 214
global history 23, 69, 87, 115, 172, 202
glory days 11, 125
goal-setting 15, 33, 64, 86, 122, 129, 131–133, 158 f., 194, 197, 201

Hammar, Emil 20 f., 140, 165 f.
hardcoded 2, 128
Hearts of Iron 23 f., 43–46, 48, 51, 64, 87, 95, 103, 147, 169, 171, 177, 194, 212
– *Hearts of Iron III* 43–45, 65, 85, 224
– *Hearts of Iron IV* 1, 4–7, 9, 11, 14 f., 17, 23–29, 41–51, 53–58, 60, 62, 64–66, 68 f., 74 f., 79–86, 88 f., 91–93, 95 f., 99, 101, 103, 105 f., 110–112, 114–121, 125–132, 136 f., 141–157, 159–167, 170–178, 181–184, 187, 190–194, 196 f., 200–202, 204, 207, 210, 212–215, 224
hegemony 140
heritage 2, 5, 19 f., 22, 77, 89, 92, 118, 183 f., 192, 194
hindsight 10, 45, 92, 125 f., 134, 150 f., 156 f., 196
historical arguments 63, 75, 89, 93, 122, 126, 133, 149, 169, 188
historical culture 1–3, 5 f., 8 f., 16, 21, 26, 28, 31, 63, 73, 76 f., 91–93, 101, 111, 115–117, 120–124, 126, 158 f., 161, 168, 177, 191, 193, 196 f., 199 f., 206
– historical cultural context 178, 202 f.

– historical cultural signalling   126, 137
– historical cultural understandings   9, 112, 114, 124, 182
historical detail   87, 99, 165
historical game studies   1, 6f., 17–21, 23, 168, 188f.
historical logic   83, 191
historically correct   186, 199
historical reference   3f., 8f., 12, 14, 23, 30, 73f., 111, 117, 121, 124, 137, 141, 158, 163, 171, 177f., 182, 193, 196f., 206
historical representation   2f., 5, 7–9, 14–16, 18f., 23, 25–27, 65f., 73, 81, 90, 107f., 112, 118, 142, 159, 164–167, 174, 178, 188, 190f., 193–196, 200, 204
historical scholarship   7f., 18f., 22, 75–78, 96f., 118, 122f., 126, 157, 164, 168f., 199, 206
historiography   6, 25, 75, 90f., 93, 111, 140, 168, 179f.
Hitler   4, 12, 48, 53, 122, 143, 146, 171, 173, 214
Holocaust   4, 111, 114–116, 119, 122, 174–176, 192, 196f., 202f.
horror   125, 176
Hungary   33, 48, 56, 136, 171

ideation   106f.
ideology   7, 14, 46–48, 92, 143f., 154, 159, 190
imitate   13, 93, 160, 164
Imperator: Rome   23–25, 95, 134, 136, 224
imperialism   11, 87, 165
implementation   23, 90, 104, 115, 158f., 173, 175f., 181, 188
Inca   161f.
infrastructure   42, 52, 198, 200, 206
institutional memory   167
interface   12, 29, 36–37, 38f., 44, 46, 49f., 52, 65, 81, 109, 129, 165, 206, 211
interpretation   49, 62, 125, 188, 191
iteration   14, 65, 80, 87–90, 99, 104, 112, 116, 118f., 194, 198, 211
– reiterate   119, 204

Jira   79
Juul, Jesper   16, 108, 131f., 186f.

Kultima, Annakaisa   5, 15–18, 20, 63, 74, 84, 88f., 108, 167

labour   16, 20, 105, 166, 176, 203
learn   22, 31f., 44, 73, 83, 87, 96, 104, 106, 109, 161f., 170, 187
Lego   182

Macro   40f., 87, 133, 161, 166
Magicka   67, 224
mana   32, 40
map   3, 27, 33, 35–40, 48–51, 74, 77, 80, 93, 103f., 134f., 155, 164, 182, 200, 213
marketing   20, 33, 64, 66, 70, 77, 100, 198
Maya   172
McCall, Jeremiah   22, 27f., 90, 99, 104
mechanics   5, 12f., 15, 24f., 27–29, 31f., 35, 39–41, 43, 46, 50f., 53, 57, 64f., 68f., 74, 80f., 83, 86, 89, 91, 94–96, 103, 109, 111f., 114, 116, 118f., 121, 127, 129, 131–133, 136, 139–141, 145, 152f., 155, 157–159, 162–164, 174, 179, 182, 190, 192–195, 197, 200f., 204
Medal of Honor   189, 225
medium   22, 27, 187f., 200, 211
method   28, 46, 75, 77, 94, 96, 98, 125f., 169, 179, 200f., 204, 213
micro-historical   88
military   6, 12, 29, 34–37, 39–44, 50–52, 74, 80, 84, 86f., 93, 111, 128, 136, 142f., 163, 175, 179, 187
mission trees   47, 74, 86, 132, 173, 200
modding   7–9, 70, 81, 106–108, 211, 213
– community   87, 96, 167
Mol, Angus   65, 137
monarch power   32, 40, 53, 65
monetisation   5, 16, 25, 66, 68f., 72f., 81f., 112, 118, 120, 159, 165, 167, 169, 184, 193, 197, 204
moral   2f., 38, 91f., 115, 189
motivation   61–63, 66, 85, 99, 107, 112, 117, 131, 143, 188
multiplicity   8, 41, 43, 57, 64, 129, 140, 154, 164, 181, 194, 197, 203f.
My Memory of Us   175, 225
Myst   80, 225

narrative   4, 6, 13–16, 57, 60, 64, 76, 92, 110, 126 f., 131, 133, 140, 157, 165, 168, 177 f., 182, 189, 191, 208
– narrative historying   168
national focus trees   46, 48, 56, 65, 79, 85, 142, 147, 155 f., 196
national ideas   34, 40, 103 f., 132, 134
naval battle   164
negotiate   26, 105, 132 f., 155, 188
norms   159, 197

objectives   12, 15, 26, 47 f., 73, 86, 112, 129, 132 f., 194
omission   16, 26, 112, 153, 158 f., 174 f., 178, 197, 202, 204
open-ended   8, 12, 14 f., 24, 51, 57, 64, 129, 159
opportunism   16, 84, 118 f., 126, 167, 198
Ottoman Empire   30

paradigms   16, 88–90, 93, 187, 206
Paradox Development Studio   1, 5, 13 f., 16 f., 21, 23–25, 33, 43 f., 46, 65–68, 70, 73, 75–84, 86, 88–111, 113 f., 116–121, 128, 136 f., 140–142, 149, 152, 158–160, 165–167, 170 f., 174 f., 177 f., 180, 186, 191, 193 f., 197–199, 201 f., 204 f., 208–211, 215, 224 f.
Paradox Interactive   17, 23, 25, 31, 43, 45, 66–70, 72 f., 199, 208, 215, 224 f.
Paradox Pillars   14, 66, 70, 72 f., 89, 107, 169
patches   67 f.
pause
– unpause   160
periodisation   13, 159, 180
Pfister, Eugen   3, 63, 114 f., 117
Pillars of Eternity   67
platform   24, 67, 79, 129, 133, 175, 224 f.
plausible   17, 103, 127, 141, 152, 154, 161, 172, 185, 187
playable nation   7, 13, 28, 33–36, 38, 40 f., 44, 47–51, 55, 58, 61–63, 75, 103, 127, 134, 136, 138 f., 143, 145–147, 150, 152, 163, 172, 181, 187

player
– behaviour   1, 13, 28, 30, 40, 43, 115, 117, 133, 145, 189, 201
– emotion   115
– player-base   108, 161
– expectation   1, 5, 9, 64, 84, 109 f., 114, 119, 137, 141, 169, 185 f., 191 f., 197, 200, 204
politics   2, 8, 14, 35, 52, 62, 78, 140, 149, 163, 175, 213
popular culture   2, 5, 22, 87, 154
possibility   3, 11, 27, 64, 76, 80, 85, 101, 152 f., 194
possible worlds   2, 10, 121 f., 124–126, 141, 152, 155, 157, 169, 196, 200
power   7, 34, 39–42, 48, 50 f., 53, 65, 91, 116, 138 f., 141, 148, 154, 156, 163, 172 f., 189, 195, 213
power projection   38, 41, 110
praxiology   5, 16 f., 63, 74, 84, 88 f., 167, 199
predictable   42, 57, 113, 170, 186
Prendergast, Christopher   7, 9, 123
prerequisite   53, 86, 88, 109, 138, 145, 192, 199 f., 211–213
presupposition   84, 108, 119, 141, 161 f., 192, 197, 205
probabilistic outcomes   127
producer   19, 105, 206
production process   66
profit   40, 69, 184
profitability   5, 191, 198
programming   7–9, 14, 24, 57, 61, 75, 78, 82, 89 f., 108, 138, 164, 190, 194, 200 f., 204 f., 209 f., 212–214
progression   34, 55, 83, 110, 133, 145, 172, 190, 196
province   29 f., 35–37, 39 f., 42, 49 f., 54, 61, 86, 102, 104, 134–139, 212
publisher   66 f., 69 f.
publishing   25, 66 f., 168, 188

quality assessment   75, 99 f., 102, 106 f.

railroading   110 f., 173, 185, 187, 195
ready-made scenarios   129, 196

realism 9, 20f., 32, 78, 113, 165f., 171, 173, 181, 195, 198
reassessing 125
reception 25, 28, 31, 33, 40, 43, 45, 79f.
reconcile 16, 18, 46, 92
reconstitute 11, 177
recruiting 87, 99, 198
Red Dead Redemption 77, 225
reimagine 125, 152, 196
religion 12, 30, 34, 41, 58, 160
replayability 70, 72, 112f., 126–128, 159, 197, 204
research 5, 15–20, 42, 47, 50, 52f., 61, 74–78, 82, 90, 92–107, 117–119, 127f., 140, 143, 145, 161, 166, 169, 176, 179, 188f., 193, 198f., 205, 208, 211
responsibility 102, 111, 113, 159f., 208
restore 134, 150, 155, 171
revisionism 204
rhetoric 2, 48, 92, 142, 189f.
Robert E. Lee 3
Roman Empire 4, 11, 23, 40, 132, 134–137, 150–152, 155, 157, 179, 197
rubber-band 128
rule 6f., 10, 12, 27–30, 34f., 51, 57f., 60, 65f., 69, 74, 95, 110, 114, 119, 127, 129, 133, 144, 146, 148, 152, 157, 160, 162, 168, 171, 186, 188, 190, 194, 196, 200, 207f., 211–214
– ruleset 7, 13, 32, 78, 89, 109, 114, 157f., 161, 180, 186, 188, 202, 211

sandbox 14, 51, 57, 70, 110, 129, 133, 157, 159, 188, 194
scope 10, 12, 15, 19, 24, 29, 41, 43, 90, 95, 98f., 114, 116, 118, 122, 128, 130, 142, 153, 164, 181, 189, 192, 196, 210
Second World War 4, 6f., 12–15, 23, 42–46, 48, 51, 64f., 73, 83, 85, 87f., 92, 99, 110f., 114f., 118, 123, 126, 128, 142–144, 146f., 154–156, 161–164, 171, 173, 175, 181f., 187, 192, 196, 202, 204
simulation 7, 9, 13, 15, 18, 21f., 77, 80, 94, 108, 110, 127, 139, 166, 168, 173, 198
slavery 115f., 119, 144, 176–178, 202
South America 58, 138, 180
Southgate, Beverley 183

Soviet 42f., 48, 59, 151, 154, 161f., 171, 187
speculate 83
Steam 67, 79, 81, 105, 129
Stellaris 23f., 95, 210, 225
studio life 198
supplementary design 69, 82, 85f., 118, 120, 123, 140, 164f., 193f.
Sweden 61, 66, 136, 149, 171
symbol 13
synergy 11, 125, 127, 152, 204
systems of signification 140

taxation 40
technical parameters 8, 66, 78, 82, 169
technology 39f., 52–54, 67, 80f., 86, 89, 118, 138f., 167, 172, 195, 198
tension 8–10, 12, 33, 42, 50, 73, 79, 92, 159, 171, 175, 189f., 197, 199–201
testing 5, 20, 75, 81, 87, 98–103, 105f., 117, 164, 172, 191, 198
Teutonic Knights 33, 86
The War of Mine 175
Thirty Years War 33
timeliness 16, 90, 167
tools 11, 28, 70, 78f., 139, 157, 163, 211
trade 7, 12, 29, 38–40, 48, 50, 52f., 59f., 92, 115f., 143, 153, 169, 178–180, 182, 192, 195, 202, 204
– trade goods 40
– trade routes 40, 179f.
tragedy 4, 10
triple-A 89, 166
trivialisation 113–115, 114f., 202, 204
trope 137, 177
truth 8, 75, 127, 150, 158

unhistorical 128
uniform 86, 172
United States 42, 46, 48, 94, 102, 125, 143f., 148, 151, 154f., 176f., 196
units 13, 28, 36f., 40f., 49–52, 54, 60, 74, 143, 163, 212
unpaid work 106
unpredictability 45, 113, 127f.
user 31f., 69, 79f., 89, 105, 108, 115, 211
uses of history 1–3, 6–10, 12, 14, 17f., 22, 24f., 27f., 63, 66, 75, 112, 120–124,

126, 149, 151, 155 f., 158 f., 168 f., 176, 193, 197, 200 f., 203 f., 206

Valiant Hearts: The Great War 78, 225
values 3, 8, 14, 16, 25 f., 66, 70, 73, 75, 89, 107 f., 116–118, 121, 126, 140, 167, 181 f., 190, 197, 204 f., 213
verisimilitude 4, 6 f., 9, 12, 21, 32, 35, 75, 84, 92, 109, 119, 121, 127 f., 145, 159 f., 165 f., 168, 183, 191, 198, 201, 203
veto 104, 110
Victoria 23–25, 95, 132, 176 f., 225
– *Victoria: An Empire Under the Sun* 225
– *Victoria II: Heart of Darkness* 225
– *Victoria III* 177, 225
virtual history 10, 28, 83, 108, 122, 124–127, 150, 157 f., 163, 168 f., 184, 203
volunteer 5, 87, 106, 117, 193

war crimes 6, 113–115, 153, 175, 202
warfare 41, 52–54, 149, 164 f., 174, 203
weighted 24, 127, 129, 145, 148
wishful thinking 10 f., 120–122, 124–126, 132, 136 f., 143, 150–152, 155, 157, 169, 173, 195 f., 200
Wolfenstein 14 f.
– *Wolfenstein: The New Order* 15, 154, 225
– *Wolfenstein II* 15, 225
workflow 79 f., 101
World in Conflict 154
World of Darkness 67

Zerubavel, Eviatar 3, 134 f., 154 f., 182

www.ingramcontent.com/pod-product-compliance
Lightning Source LLC
Chambersburg PA
CBHW050523170426
43201CB00013B/2056